Statutory Interpretation

Statutory Interpretation

by the late

Sir Rupert Cross, DCL FBA
Solicitor, Vinerian Professor of English Law
in the University of Oxford

Second edition by

John Bell, MA, D Phil
Fellow and Tutor in Law,
Wadham College, Oxford

Sir George Engle, KCB, MA, QC
Formerly First Parliamentary Counsel

London · Butterworths · 1987

United Kingdom	Butterworth & Co (Publishers) Ltd, 88 Kingsway, LONDON WC2B 6AB and 61A North Castle Street, EDINBURGH EH2 3LJ
Australia	Butterworths Pty Ltd, SYDNEY, MELBOURNE, BRISBANE, ADELAIDE, PERTH, CANBERRA and HOBART
Canada	Butterworths, A division of Reed Inc., TORONTO and VANCOUVER
New Zealand	Butterworths of New Zealand Ltd, WELLINGTON and AUCKLAND
Singapore	Butterworth & Co (Asia) Pte Ltd, SINGAPORE
USA	Butterworths Legal Publishers, ST PAUL, Minnesota, SEATTLE, Washington, BOSTON, Massachusetts, AUSTIN, Texas and D & S Publishers, CLEARWATER, Florida

British Library Cataloguing in Publication Data
Cross, *Sir* Rupert
   Statutory interpretation.——2nd ed.
   1. Statutes——England   2. Law——
   Interpretation and construction
   I. Title   II. Bell, John, *1953*–
   III. Engle, *Sir* George
   344.208′22   KD691

ISBN 0 406 57017 5

Typeset by Phoenix Photosetting, Chatham, Kent
Printed in Great Britain by Billing & Sons Ltd Worcester.

Preface

'The subject of statutory interpretation does not lend itself to legislation, and the extraction from the cases of reasonable general principles of interpretation was a task for the academic lawyer, even though they [sic] had long neglected it. Cross's book is a major contribution, temperate, constructive, and scholarly, to the repair of that neglect.'[1]

This comment of Herbert Hart explains the special quality of Rupert Cross's *Statutory Interpretation* which justifies its appearance in a new edition. Although, since its first appearance in 1976, there have been published many articles and some books which have done much to repair the academic neglect of the subject, Cross's book remains unrivalled as a short, systematic introduction to the general principles of statutory interpretation, intended primarily for law students.

The aim of this new edition is to make available Cross's insights to a new generation of students by updating some of the examples and by applying Cross's approach to recent developments both in the case-law and in academic writings. The text shows significant changes from the first edition, but we have attempted to retain the basic ideas which Cross brought to the subject. Only at a very few points have we departed from the views expressed in the first edition. Indeed, many of Cross's opinions have been amply justified by subsequent events: notably the dominance of a single rule of (purposive) interpretation, the inappropriateness of legislation as a means of reforming the rules of statutory interpretation, the undesirability of excluding treaties and international conventions as aids to interpretation, as well as the justifiability of 'rectifying' statutory provisions in some circumstances. Chapters 2 and 8 have undergone the most substantial changes.

---

1. H L A Hart, 'A R N Cross', LXX *Proceedings of the British Academy* at 432 (1984).

Chapter 2 has been rewritten to reflect recent jurisprudential preoccupations, and this has involved a substantial recasting of the text without, we hope, abandoning Cross's own insights. Opinion having turned away from legislation as a way forward in this field, Chapter 8 no longer contains a section dealing with 'legislative proposals'. The section on legislative drafting has been revised and extended.

Cross's own background as an academic and as a practitioner has been reflected by the employment of two editors. John Bell has been primarily responsible for selecting new cases and for the discussions of academic writings. George Engle has brought to bear his experience as Parliamentary Counsel both in improving the discussions of legislative drafting and procedure, notably in Chapter 8, and in ensuring greater precision and uniformity in the text. We hope that our efforts may give a new lease of life to Cross on *Statutory Interpretation*.

June 1987   John Bell
                                                               George Engle

Preface to the first edition

When reading for a law degree at Oxford in the early 1930s, I studied jurisprudence, a subject which, then as now, was commonly assumed to include statutory interpretation. I was told to write an essay criticising the English rules and I dutifully said my piece about the literalism of the Courts, their failure to implement the purpose of the statutes with which they dealt and, worst of all, their intransigent refusal to consult *travaux préparatoires*. All the time I was experiencing a malaise which, I am bound to confess, was not wholly set at rest by my tutor, with regard to the nature of the English rules of interpretation. What were they? Where were they stated? I then practised the law for a decade and it was as much as I could do to make sense of the day-to-day operation of the legislation that came my way. The mystery of the precise nature of the general rules of statutory interpretation remained unsolved.

When teaching law at Oxford in the 1950s and 1960s I treated my pupils as I had been treated and told them to write essays criticising the English rules governing the subject. By that time Willis's landmark article mentioned on p 194 of this book had appeared in the Canadian Bar Review. Each and every pupil told me that there were three rules—the literal rule, the golden rule and the mischief rule, and that the Courts invoke whichever of them is believed to do justice in the particular case. I had, and still have, my doubts, but what was most disconcerting was the fact that whatever question I put to pupils or examinees elicited the same reply. Even if the question was What is meant by 'the intention of parliament'? or What are the principal extrinsic aids to interpretation? back came the answers as of yore: 'There are three rules of interpretation—the literal rule, the golden rule and the mischief rule.' I was as much in the dark as I had been in my student days about the way in which the English rules should be formulated.

This book, an enlargement on lectures given from time to time at

Oxford, has been composed in order to clarify my own mind as much as anyone else's. It is intended for law students, but I hope that it may be found to be sufficiently brief to constitute spare time reading for any practitioner who likes to devote part of his spare time to the contemplation of the law.

May 1976   Rupert Cross

Contents

List of cases

Introduction

This book is concerned with the major contemporary canons of statutory interpretation, but the subject is best approached through history and jurisprudence, matters which are dealt with in the first two chapters. The basic rules are set out and illustrated in Chapters 3 and 4 which enlarge on some points made in Chapters 1 and 2. The essential rule is that words should generally be given the meaning which the normal speaker of the English language would understand them to bear in the context in which they are used. It would be difficult to over-estimate the importance of this rule because the vast majority of statutes never come before the courts for interpretation. If it were not a known fact that, in the ordinary case in which the normal user of the English language would have no doubt about the meaning of the statutory words, the courts will give those words their ordinary meaning, it would be impossible for lawyers and other experts to act and advise on the statute in question with confidence. The reference to lawyers and other experts is made advisedly because we would be deceiving ourselves if we were to imagine that some form of expertise is not necessary for the comprehension of most statutes; indeed, the ordinary meaning rule is qualified so as to allow for the application of a technical meaning when the words in question are used in a statute dealing with a particular trade or business. The regulation of most of the affairs with which they deal is such a complex matter that it is unlikely that it will ever be possible to draft Acts of Parliament in such a way that a significant number of them will be comprehensible to the ordinary layman; but this unfortunate fact should not be allowed to depreciate the importance of the ordinary meaning rule. Some criticisms of the canons of statutory interpretation are couched in terms which suggest that their authors do not realise that it is only a very small proportion of the statute book that ever comes before the courts.

Even when full allowance has been made for the context, there will inevitably be a number of occasions on which doubt may legitimately be entertained on the question of the ordinary meaning of certain statutory provisions. Drafting is not always as clear as it might be and, owing to the lack of human prescience, there will always be cases for which inadequate provision is made by the statute. Valuable assistance may often be derived from various aids to interpretation which are discussed in Chapters 5 and 6. Over the years the courts have acted on certain presumptions which sometimes help in doubtful cases. For example, when it is unclear whether the conduct of the accused comes within a criminal statute, there is a presumption in favour of a narrow construction which would result in an acquittal; or, where one interpretation would produce an unjust or inconvenient result and another would not have these effects, there is a presumption in favour of the latter. These presumptions are only guides, and two of them may point in different directions in the same case, but they certainly have their uses; the more important of them are discussed in Chapter 7.

The emphasis which has been placed upon the merits of the plain meaning rule must not be taken to suggest that anything in the nature of an attitude of complacency with regard to the contemporary canons of statutory interpretation is justified. They have been the subject of much scrutiny and criticism in recent years, notably in the Law Commission paper of 1969, which was discussed ultimately in the House of Lords sitting in its legislative capacity.[1]

Legislative drafting is, and almost always has been, under attack (much of it unjustified). It was the principal subject of a report entitled *The Preparation of Legislation*, produced in 1975 by a committee chaired by Sir David (now Lord) Renton,[2] and of a study by Sir William Dale,[3] among many other recent commentaries. Some aspects of legislative drafting will be considered in Chapter 8. Over and above these specific points, a number of more general questions are raised in Chapter 8. Do the courts interpret statutes too narrowly without adequate regard to the social purpose of the legislation? Are they unduly timorous when confronted with an obvious mistake or omission in a particular statute? Is their approach to interpretation of statutes designed to effect social change too conservative? These questions lose none of their interest even if it is the case, as it probably is, that any deficiencies which their discussion may reveal can hardly be remedied

---

1. *The Interpretation of Statutes* (Law Com No 21; Scottish Law Com No 11; 1969). For Parliamentary debates see 405 HL Deb (5th series), cols 276–306 (13 February 1980), 418 HL Deb, cols 64–83 (9 March 1981) and cols 1341–7 (26 March 1981).
2. Cmnd 6053.
3. *Legislative Drafting: A New Approach* (London, 1977); also 'Statutory Reform—The Draftsman and the Judge' (1981) 30 ICLQ 141.

by legislation. One of the problems of the day is how to convey messages to judges otherwise than by statute. Lord Wilberforce may well have been right when he doubted whether law reform can really grapple with statutory interpretation. He said 'it is a matter of educating the judges and' practitioners and hoping that the work is better done'.[4] The author and the editors must at once disclaim any intention of attempting to do any such thing in this little book which is intended more for the student than for the practitioner.

Although this book is only seriously concerned with the major contemporary canons of statutory interpretation, it is important to bear in mind the context in which they are situated. There are three contexts to which the judicial canons studied here should be related. First, a statute is above all part of the political process. Most of government policy is established and implemented by means of ministerial decisions or directions, or by delegated legislation. It has been calculated that, in a typical session, an average of only 42 programme Bills are presented to Parliament by the government.[5] Most of them, however, are likely to be of considerable importance, both because of their political content and because of the authority they provide for subsequent ministerial actions or for delegated legislation. Judicial interpretations can affect the success of such political programmes. Second, the statute has to be implemented, most frequently by officials who will require guidance on the objectives to be pursued and workable procedures by which to achieve them. Statutory provisions rarely provide complete solutions, and an official will rely on guidance from his superiors. Judicial interpretation will define the scope for discretion exercised by officials in completing the details of a policy, and will affect their flexibility in responding to new situations. Third, the ultimate subjects of the law are human or legal persons who seek to organise their lives and activities in the light of their legal powers and duties. For this, they will often need the help of legal and other advisers. All the same, the freedom of the subject to choose what to do is enhanced by the predictability of judicial interpretation.

Viewed as a whole, the canons of interpretation represent a position taken by the judiciary on their constitutional role in relation to those

---

4. 277 HL Deb, col 1294 (16 November 1966); also 418 HL Deb, col 73 (9 March 1981). As the Law Commission has remarked more recently, the improvement of legal analysis is not normally an appropriate purpose for legislation: *The Parol Evidence Rule* (Law Com No 154; 1986) para 3.2.
5. G Engle, ' "Bills are made to pass as razors are made to sell": practical constraints in the preparation of legislation' [1983] Stat LR 7, 11. See generally D R Miers and A C Page, *Legislation* (London 1982) Chs 1–5, and M Zander, *The Law-Making Process* (2nd edn, London, 1985) pp 1–21.

who establish the political programme, those who have to carry it out, and those affected by it. The interests of these groups may well conflict, so that the canons adopted by the judges will effect a balance between them. As we shall see, the canons of statutory interpretation are frequently statements not so much of hard-and-fast rules of law, as of a general judicial approach to the task of interpreting statutes in particular contexts.[6]

It is also useful to say a few introductory words about the duration and varieties of statutes, though for more detailed discussion the reader is referred to Bennion's *Statutory Interpretation*.[7] Provided that an Act appears on the Parliament Roll, the courts will treat it as an Act of Parliament and will not accept any challenge to its validity.[8] Statutes come into force on the day on which they receive the royal assent in the absence of a provision to the contrary.[9] The endorsement by the Clerk of the Parliaments on the Act, immediately after its title, of the date of the royal assent forms part of the Act. Express provisions in the Act with regard to the date of coming into force of the whole or any part of it are very common. Where the two differ, references to 'the passing of this Act' are references to the first moment of the day of royal assent and not to the date on which the Act comes into force.[10] There is no doctrine of desuetude in English law, so a statute never ceases to be in force merely because it is obsolete. Normally there must be an express repeal, but the whole or part of an enactment may be impliedly repealed by a later statute.

> 'The test of whether there has been a repeal by implication by subsequent legislation is this: are the provisions of a later Act so inconsistent with, or repugnant to, the provisions of an earlier Act that the two cannot stand together.'[11]

The fact that two provisions overlap is therefore not enough, and general words in a later enactment do not repeal earlier statutes dealing with a special subject. Accordingly it was held in *R v Horsham JJ, ex p Farquarson*[12] that s 4(2) of the Contempt of Court Act 1981, which empowered a court 'in any legal proceedings' to postpone the

---

6. Infra, pp 36–7.
7. London, 1984, sections 47, 164–9, 173–88, 195–228.
8. *British Railways Board v Pickin* [1974] AC 765, [1974] 1 All ER 609; *Bennion*, pp 119–21.
9. Acts of Parliament (Commencement) Act 1793.
10. *Coleridge-Taylor v Novello & Co Ltd* [1938] Ch 608, [1938] 2 All ER 318.
11. *West Ham Church Wardens and Overseers v Fourth City Mutual Building Society* [1892] 1 QB 654 at 658 per A L Smith J.
12. [1982] QB 762; [1982] 2 All ER 269.

publication of a report of those proceedings, did not prevail over the special provision about the reporting of committal proceedings contained in s 8 of the Magistrates' Court Act 1980. Contrary to what was the common law rule, where an Act passed after 1850 repeals a repealing enactment, 'the repeal does not revive any enactment previously repealed, unless words are added reviving it'.[13]

The general rule with regard to territorial extent is that 'every parliamentary draftsman writes on paper which bears the legend, albeit in invisible ink, "this Act shall not have an extra-territorial effect, save to the extent that it expressly so provides"'.[14] Notable instances of statutes with an extra-territorial effect are the Royal Marriages Act 1772,[15] the Hijacking Act 1971, and the Suppression of Terrorism Act 1978. In general the jurisdiction of the English criminal courts is confined to crimes committed in this country, but there are exceptions applicable to British subjects, for example, murder and bigamy.[16] It is now usual for statutes to provide expressly that they shall not extend to Scotland or Northern Ireland, where this is the intention.

A distinction is drawn between public general Acts and private Acts. A public general Act relates to some matter of public policy, while a private Act relates to the affairs of some individual or body in a matter which is not of public concern. The only clear practical importance of the distinction relates to the law of evidence, and even that is minimal nowadays. Someone who wishes to rely on the provisions of a public general Act does not have to produce any special kind of copy whereas private Acts must be proved by production of a Queen's Printer's copy or, if they have not been printed, by an examination or certified copy of the original. Section 3 of the Interpretation Act 1978 provides that every Act passed after 1850 shall be a public general Act and judicially noticed as such unless the contrary is expressly provided by the Act. Some of the older cases show a tendency to construe private Acts more strictly than public general Acts,[17] but the distinction is of no importance in relation to the general law of interpretation.

Another distinction of limited importance in this field is that between consolidating and codifying statutes. A consolidating statute is one which collects the statutory provisions relating to a particular topic, and embodies them in a single Act of Parliament, making as a

---

13. Interpretation Act 1978, s 15 and Sch 2, para 2.
14. *R v West Yorkshire Coroner, ex p Smith* [1983] QB 335 at 358 per Donaldson LJ; also *Clark (Inspector of Taxes) v Oceanic Contractors Inc* [1983] 2 AC 130 at 152.
15. *Sussex Peerage* claim (1844) 11 Cl & Fin 85.
16. Offences Against the Person Act 1861, ss 9 and 57.
17. *Bennion*, p 369.

rule only minor amendments and improvements, if any. A codifying statute is one which purports to state exhaustively the whole of the law on a particular subject (the common law as well as previous statutory provisions).[18] An example of a consolidating statute is the Companies Act 1985, while the Bills of Exchange Act 1882 is one of the comparatively few instances of a codifying statute. The importance of the distinction is now confined to the existence of a special procedure with regard to consolidating statutes.

The Consolidation of Enactments (Procedure) Act 1949 lays down a special procedure, allowing for minor amendments in the consolidated provisions of the relevant statutes. Since 1965 there has existed a procedure whereby consolidation effected by the Law Commissions, which may contain amendments that are not merely minor, can be placed before the relevant joint committee of both Houses of Parliament with a view to prompt enactment. Changes in wording under these procedures may produce a different result from the earlier legislation,[19] and the presumption against a change of law on consolidation does not extend to provisions amended in the course of consolidation.[20]

Consolidating and codifying statutes are interpreted fundamentally like any other statute, namely by giving primacy to the ordinary meaning of their provisions read in context. Superseded statutes or the previous common law can be consulted only where the consolidating or codifying statute is ambiguous or, exceptionally, where a word or phrase can be understood only by examining its original social context. As Lord Wilberforce said,[1]

> 'I would agree and endorse the principle that it is quite wrong that, in every case where a consolidation Act is under consideration, one should automatically look back through the history of its various provisions, and the cases decided upon them, and minutely trace the language from Act to Act . . . Self-contained statutes, whether consolidating the previous law, or doing so with amendments, should be interpreted, if reasonably possible, without recourse to antecedents, and . . . the recourse should only be had when there is a real and substantial difficulty or

---

18. For a full discussion see ibid, ss 232–3.
19. Eg *Champion v Maughan* [1984] 1 All ER 680; *Pocock v Steel* [1985] 1 All ER 434, CA.
20. See *Farrell v Alexander* [1977] AC 59 at 82–3.
1. *Farrell v Alexander* [1977] AC at 72–3. See also Lord Simon of Glaisdale, ibid at 87–8, and *Maunsell v Olins* [1975] AC 373 at 392; *R v West Yorkshire Coroner, ex p Smith* [1983] QB 335, infra, p 171.

ambiguity which classical methods of construction cannot resolve.'

Where a consolidated statute may be consulted, so may judicial decisions interpreting it; and where the new Act is identical with the previous Act, those decisions will retain their value as precedents.[2] From these developments it follows that the presumption that consolidating statutes do not change the law has lost much of its force. Where it is clear from the Lord Chancellor's Memorandum which accompanies a consolidation Bill under the 1949 procedure, that no amendment of the previous law was intended, then the presumption retains its force.[3] It is submitted that a similar approach should be adopted in the case of a consolidation with amendments proposed by the Law Commission.[4]

In a sense the distinction between remedial and other statutes is of greater importance from the point of view of the law of interpretation than either of the distinctions previously mentioned; but it is not one which it is possible to draw with precision. The essence of a remedial statute is that it was passed to remedy some defect in the common law or, more usually today, in statute law. The cases suggest that such a statute should be broadly construed. A good example is the Water Charges Act 1976 which enabled water charges to be levied on the occupier of a 'hereditament' if he had the 'use' of facilities draining to a sewer or drain provided by a water authority. The House of Lords held that this applied to the rateable occupier of a ground floor shop which had no water supply or drainage into the sewer, but which formed part of a structure whose roof drained into the sewer. Lord Scarman said that the English language was flexible and that the words used should not be narrowly construed:[5]

'I have no doubt that it would be contrary to the legislative purpose of the enactment to restrict or refine their breadth and flexibility in the context of this legislation, which has to cover a wide range of circumstances and situations present and future. A restrictive interpretation of the legislature's language would defeat the broad purpose of this innovative and reforming statute.'

Finally it is necessary to mention Interpretation Acts. Many statutes contain interpretation sections relating to some of their key words, but

---

2. The re-enactment of a statutory provision does not imply Parliamentary approval of judicial interpretations made of it: see infra, pp 171–2.
3. Lord Upjohn, *Atkinson v United States* [1971] AC 197 at 249.
4. Cf Lord Simon of Glaisdale, *Maunsell v Olins* [1975] AC 373 at 392.
5. *South West Water Authority v Rumble's* [1985] AC 609 at 619, [1985] 1 All ER 513 at 517.

an Interpretation Act provides that, unless the contrary intention appears, all statutes shall be construed as indicated; for example, so that the singular includes the plural, the masculine the feminine, and vice versa. The current English Interpretation Act is that of 1978. There were earlier ones in 1850 and 1889, hence the reference to the former year in the citation from the 1978 Act above.[6] Some countries have more ambitious Interpretation Acts. For instance s 5(j) of the Acts Interpretation Act 1924 of New Zealand reads as follows:

'Every Act, and every provision or enactment thereof, shall be deemed remedial, whether its immediate purport is to direct the doing of anything Parliament deems to be for the public good, or to prevent or punish the doing of anything it deems contrary to the public good, and shall accordingly receive such fair, large and liberal construction and interpretation as will best ensure the attainment of the object of the Act and of such provision or enactment according to its true intent, meaning and spirit.'

It only remains to add that what is said about interpretation in the following chapters applies, where relevant, to subordinate legislation. Its construction is sometimes particularly affected by that of the parent statute and, in the case of subordinate legislation, there is the general question of *ultra vires* with which we shall have no concern.

---

6. Some provisions of the Interpretation Act 1978 apply only to statutes passed after 1850, and yet others only to statutes passed after 1889: Sch 2, paras 2 and 3.

Chapter 1
Historical[1]

.*

The most frequent complaint concerning the contemporary approach of the courts to statutory interpretation is that it is excessively literal. All too frequently, it is urged, is the purpose of the legislature frustrated by an undue insistence on the part of the courts on applying the statutory words to the particular case in a strictly literal sense. The merits of such complaints are considered in Chapter 8, but it is important to realise at the outset that the approach of the courts varies according to the judges' perception of their constitutional role at any given period.

In the 16th century, Plowden reports *Stradling v Morgan*,[2] a case in which a statute of Edward VI's reign referring to receivers and treasurers without any qualifying words was held to be confined to such officials appointed by the King and not to extend to receivers and treasurers acting on behalf of private persons. Various authorities were cited—

'from which cases it appears that the sages of the law heretofore have construed statutes quite contrary to the letter in some appearance, and those statutes which comprehend all things in the letter they have expounded to extend but to some things, and those which generally prohibit all people from doing such an act they have interpreted to permit some people to do it, and those which include every person in the letter they have adjudged to

---

1. This chapter owes a great deal to the article by J A Corry entitled 'Administrative Law and the Interpretation of Statutes', 1 Toronto LJ 286 (1936). It is reprinted with new introductory paragraphs in Appendix 1 of E A Driedger's *The Construction of Statutes* (2nd edn, Toronto, 1983), a work to which this book owes a very great deal. On the history of statutory interpretation, see also S E Thorne's introduction to T Egerton, *A Discourse upon the Esposicion and Understandinge of Statutes* (1570, San Marino, Ca 1942).
2. (1560) 1 Plowd 199 at 205.

reach some persons only, which expositions have always been founded on the intent of the legislature which they have collected sometimes by considering the cause and necessity of making the Act, sometimes by comparing one part of the Act with another, and sometimes by foreign circumstances. So that they have ever been guided by the intent of the legislature, which they have always taken according to the necessity of the matter, and according to that which is consonant to reason and good discretion.'

In modern terms *Stradling v Morgan* was an example of restrictive interpretation; the broad effect of general words was held to be limited by the context which was mainly concerned with royal revenue. *Heydon's* case,[3] on the other hand, could be said to have been an instance of extensive interpretation because a grant of copyholds for life at the will of the lord was held to create 'an estate and interest for lives' within the meaning of the statute of Henry VIII in spite of decisions to the effect that the words in question were, when used in other statutes, confined to freeholds; but its real importance lies in the resolutions of the Barons of the Exchequer which contain the classic statement of the 'mischief rule' upon which reliance is often placed by the courts of today.

'And it was resolved by them that for the sure and true interpretation of all statutes in general (be they penal or beneficial, restrictive or enlarging of the common law), four things are to be discerned and considered:

1st. What was the common law before the making of the Act,
2nd. What was the mischief and defect for which the common law did not provide,
3rd. What remedy the Parliament hath resolved and appointed to cure the disease of the Commonwealth, and
4th. The true reason of the remedy;

and then the office of all the judges is always to make such construction as shall suppress the mischief, and advance the remedy, and to suppress subtle inventions and evasions for continuance of the mischief, and *pro privato commodo*, and to add force and life to the cure and remedy, according to the true intent of the makers of the Act, *pro bono publico*.'

Heydon's case was decided in 1584 and the spirit which animated the Barons of the Exchequer tended in the main to animate the judges of the 17th century. In fact it has never been extinguished, for no modern lawyer would deny the relevance of the purpose of a statute to its

---

3. (1584) 3 Co Rep 7a at 7b; cf Egerton, pp 146–7.

interpretation; but the resolutions of 1584 were, like Plowden's observations in *Stradling v Morgan*, the typical product of the period preceding the complete establishment of the sovereignty of Parliament. As late as 1701 Holt CJ felt able to say 'Let an Act of Parliament be ever so charitable, yet if it give away the property of a subject it ought not to be countenanced'.[4]

A more literal approach is to be discerned in the decisions of the 18th and 19th centuries. This was the outcome of the attitude towards government engendered by Locke and the revolution of 1688. No doubt the words of Holt CJ were an exaggeration, but any Parliamentary change in the existing state of affairs must, if it were to be enforced by the courts, be cast in the clearest possible terms. Examples of this approach are provided by decisions placing a strikingly strict interpretation on criminal statutes, and by the courts' complacent attitude towards the *casus omissus*—the inexplicable and probably inadvertent failure of the draftsman to use words entirely apt to cover the instant case.

It is open to question whether the Barons of the Exchequer had criminal statutes in mind when, in *Heydon's* case, they declared their resolutions to be applicable to all statutes in general 'be they penal or beneficial'.[5] Other legal writing of that period suggests that, whereas statutes remedying the common law would receive a wide interpretation, those encroaching on the liberty of the subject or on common law rights would not.[6] It is certain, however, that the 18th century witnessed the growth of a presumption in favour of a strict construction of criminal statutes which persists to this day. In *R v Harris*[7] it was held that an accused who bit off a joint of her victim's finger was not guilty of wounding within the meaning of a statute of George IV which punished anyone who 'shall unlawfully and maliciously stab, cut, or wound any person'. The court took the view that the intention of Parliament was, according to the words of the statute, that an instrument should have been used, a conclusion strengthened by an earlier reference to shooting. The decision is rendered nugatory so far as the construction of the contemporary statutory equivalent is concerned by the inclusion in the prohibition of wounding or inflicting grievous bodily harm by s 20 of the Offences Against the Person Act 1861 of the words 'either with or without any weapon or instrument'.

. *Jones v Smart*[8] may be taken as an illustration of the attitude of an

---

4. *Callady v Pilkington* (1694) 12 Mod 513.
5. See *A-G v Sillem* (1864) 2 H & C 431 at 509.
6. See Egerton, Ch 9.
7. (1836) 7 C & P 446.
8. (1784) 1 Term Rep 44.

18th-century court to the *casus omissus*. The question was whether a doctor of physic was qualified to kill game under a statute of Charles II which disqualified those who lacked various property qualifications 'other than the son and heir apparent of an esquire, or other person of higher degree'. It was not disputed that he was of higher degree than an esquire or the son and heir apparent of an esquire, but the majority of the court held that the words 'son and heir apparent' governed 'other persons of higher degree', although the *casus omissus* could easily have been provided for by confining them to esquires.

As we shall see, strict construction of penal statutes and timidity in the face of a *casus omissus* are not simply things of the past. Indeed there is something to be said on both sides with regard to the merits of such an approach. The important point for present purposes is that they are apt to produce a Parliamentary reaction. This has been the baneful effect of the literal approach to statutory interpretation as contrasted with the approaches canvassed in *Stradling v Morgan* and *Heydon's* case.[9] At times a state of war appears to exist between the courts and the Parliamentary draftsman. The courts decline to come to the rescue when a *casus omissus* is revealed, so words appropriate to cover the *casus omissus* are added to the statute. More frequently the draftsman gets in first and, anticipating a strict construction by the courts coupled with a total lack of sympathy if there should happen to be a *casus omissus*, he produces a statute which is nothing less than horrific in its detail. One of the most notorious examples was, until 1983, provided by s 1 of the Wills Act Amendment Act 1852.[10] It was passed in order to resolve doubts concerning the requirement of the Wills Act 1837 that the will must be signed 'at the foot or end thereof' and it reads:

> 'Where by an Act passed in the First Year of the Reign of Her Majesty Queen Victoria, intituled An Act for the Amendment of the Laws with respect to Wills, it is enacted, that no Will shall be valid unless it shall be signed at the Foot or End thereof by the Testator, or by some other Person in his Presence, and by his Direction: Every Will shall, so far only as regards the Position of the Signature of the Testator, or of the Person signing for him as aforesaid, be deemed to be valid within the said Enactment, as explained by this Act, if the Signature shall be so placed at or after, or following, or under, or beside, or opposite to the End of the Will, that it shall be apparent on the Face of the Will that the

---

9. *Supra*, pp 9–10.
10. The Act was repealed by the Administration of Justice Act 1982 (s 17 of which simplified the formal requirements for making wills).

Testator intended to give Effect by such his Signature to the Writing signed as his Will, and that no such Will shall be affected by the Circumstance that the Signature shall not follow or be immediately after the Foot or End of the Will, or by the Circumstance that a blank Space shall intervene between the concluding Word of the Will and the Signature, or by the Circumstance that the Signature shall be placed among the Words of the Testimonium Clause or of the Clause of Attestation, or shall follow or be after or under the Clause of Attestation, either with or without a blank Space intervening, or shall follow or be after, or under, or beside the Names or One of the Names of the subscribing Witnesses, or by the Circumstance that the Signature shall be on a Side or Page or other Portion of the Paper or Papers containing the Will whereon no Clause or Paragraph or disposing Part of the Will shall be written above the Signature, or by the Circumstance that there shall appear to be sufficient Space on or at the Bottom of the preceding Side or Page or other Portion of the same Paper on which the Will is written to contain the Signature; and the Enumeration of the above Circumstances shall not restrict the Generality of the above Enactment; but no Signature under the said Act or this Act shall be operative to give Effect to any Disposition or Direction which is underneath or which follows it, nor shall it give Effect to any Disposition or Direction inserted after the Signature shall be made.'

This is not a book on legislative drafting, an insufficiently appreciated art,[11] but it is important to appreciate the mutual dependence of the draftsman and the courts when the latter are engaged in statutory interpretation. It is the courts' duty to give effect to the intention of Parliament[12] but their main source of information on this matter is the wording of the statute; if this is not clear there is obviously a risk that the courts will be unable to do their work properly. On the other hand the draftsman will find it difficult to convey the Parliamentary intent to the courts unless he knows that they will attach the same meaning to his words as that in which he employs them. Hence the need for a common standard of interpretation, and there can hardly be a better standard than the ordinary, or, in appropriate cases, the technical, meaning of English words.

As legislation increased in quantity and as it came to deal more and

---

11. Useful books are E A Driedger, *The Composition of Legislation* (2nd edn, Ottawa, 1976), Reed Dickerson, *The Fundamentals of Legal Drafting* (Boston, 1965), and G C Thornton, *Legislative Drafting* (3rd edn, London, 1987).
12. Infra, pp 22–30.

more with matters unknown to the common law, the resolutions of *Heydon's* case became less and less satisfactory as the sole guide to interpretation. Primacy, though not total supremacy, had to be given to the words of the statute. The mischief rule came to be largely, though not entirely, superseded by the 'literal' or, as it came to be called in America, the 'plain meaning' rule. One of the most frequently quoted of the numerous statements of this latter rule is that of Tindal CJ when advising the House of Lords on the *Sussex Peerage* claim:[13]

'The only rule for the construction of Acts of Parliament is that they should be construed according to the intent of the Parliament which passed the Act. If the words of the statute are in themselves precise and unambiguous, then no more can be necessary than to expound those words in that natural and ordinary sense. The words themselves alone do, in such case, best declare the intention of the lawgiver. But if any doubt arises from the terms employed by the legislature, it has always been held a safe means of collecting the intention, to call in aid the ground and cause of making the statute, and to have recourse to the preamble, which, according to Chief Justice Dyer,[14] is "a key to open the minds of the makers of the Act, and the mischiefs which they intend to redress".'

This passage is of especial interest because it states the commonly accepted view concerning the relationship of the literal and mischief rules. *Heydon's* case is only applicable when the court finds that the statutory words are obscure or ambiguous. Whether the purpose of the statute is not something which may be taken into account at an earlier stage even though it may suggest that an otherwise clear and unambiguous meaning is not the right one is a point to be considered in Chapter 3.

The principal question at the hearing of the *Sussex Peerage* case was whether the claimant's father had been validly married. He was a descendant of George II and his marriage was void for want of the requisite consent if the Royal Marriages Act 1772 applies to marriage ceremonies celebrated abroad. Section 1 reads as follows:

'No descendant of the body of His Late Majesty King George II, male or female, (other than the issue of princesses who have married or may hereafter marry into foreign families) shall be capable of contracting matrimony, without the previous consent of His Majesty, his heirs or successors, signified under the great

---

13. (1844) 11 Cl & Fin 85 at 143.
14. *Stowell v Lord Zouch* (1569) 1 Plowd 353 at 369.

seal, and declared in council (which consent, to preserve the memory thereof, is hereby directed to be set out in the licence and register of marriage, and to be entered in the books of the Privy Council); and every marriage or matrimonial contract of any such descendant, without such consent first had and obtained, shall be null and void to all intents and purposes whatsoever.'

It was held that the claimant's marriage was void because the words of the Act applied in their ordinary sense to any marriage of a descendant of George II wherever it might be celebrated, subject of course to the exception mentioned in the first set of brackets. This exception was thought to strengthen the case against the validity of the claimant's father's marriage for it would have been of dubious necessity if the Act were confined to marriages celebrated within the realm. Tindal CJ also found support for the conclusion that the marriage was invalid from the second section of the Act of 1772 which validates marriages of descendants of the body of George II above the age of 25, even though the consent required by s 1 was not obtained, provided a year's notice is given and no objection is raised by Parliament. These points are worth mentioning because it seems that Tindal CJ recognised that, before deciding whether the words are 'in themselves precise and unambiguous', the court must have regard to the whole of the enacting part of the statute. The proper application of the literal rules does not mean that the effect of a particular word, phrase or section is to be determined in isolation from the rest of the statute in which it is contained.

This had been recognised by Parker CB in the middle of the 18th century; but his words may be thought to have contained the germs of a third rule which, in order that it may be distinguished from the mischief and literal rules, is commonly called the 'golden' rule.[15] It allows for a departure from the literal rule when the application of the statutory words in the ordinary sense would be repugnant to or inconsistent with some other provision in the statute or even when it would lead to what the court considers to be an absurdity. The usual consequence of applying the golden rule is that words which are in the statute are ignored or words which are not there are read in. The scope of the golden rule is debatable, particularly so far as the meaning of an 'absurdity' is concerned. This word was not used by Parker CB who said:[16]

15. The 'literal' rule, with or without the qualification mentioned in the text, is also often spoken of as the 'golden' rule.
16. *Mitchell v Torup* (1766) Park 227 at 233.

'In expounding Acts of Parliament, where words are express, plain and clear, the words ought to be understood according to their genuine and natural signification and import, unless by such exposition a contradiction or inconsistency would arise in the Act by reason of some subsequent clause, from whence it might be inferred that the intent of the Parliament was otherwise.'

In *Becke v Smith*[17] Parke B (as he then was) said:

'It is a very useful rule, in the construction of a statute, to adhere to the ordinary meaning of the words used, and to the grammatical construction, unless that is at variance with the intention of the legislature, to be collected from the statute itself, or leads to any manifest absurdity or repugnance, in which case the language may be varied or modified, so as to avoid such inconvenience, but no further.'

Neither Parker CB nor Parke B found it necessary to modify the application of the literal rule in the judgments from which the above passages are taken. In *Becke v Smith*, Parke B may have used the word 'absurdity' to mean no more than repugnant to other provisions in the statute;[18] but the same judge's statement of the golden rule in *Grey v Pearson*,[19] a case concerned with the construction of a will, is less easily susceptible of that interpretation and this statement of the rule (made after Parke B had become Lord Wensleydale) is probably the one which is most commonly cited today:

'I have been long and deeply impressed with the wisdom of the rule now, I believe, universally adopted, at least in the courts of law in Westminster Hall, that in construing wills and indeed statutes, and all written instruments, the grammatical and ordinary sense of the words is to be adhered to, unless that would lead to some absurdity, or some repugnance or inconsistency with the rest of the instrument, in which case the grammatical and ordinary sense of the words may be modified, so as to avoid the absurdity and inconsistency, but no farther.'

On occasions the golden rule simply serves as a guide to the court where there is doubt as to the true import of the statutory words in their ordinary sense. When there is a choice of meanings there is a

---

17. (1836) 2 M & W 191 at 195.
18. 'I subscribe to every word of that [the statement of Parke B in *Becke v Smith*], assuming the word "absurdity" to mean no more than "repugnance".' (Willes J, *Christopherson v Lotinga* (1864) 15 CBNS 809 at 813).
19. (1857) 6 HL Cas 61 at 106.

presumption that one which produces an absurd, unjust or inconvenient result was not intended; but it should be emphasised that when the rule is used as a justification for ignoring or reading in words resort may only be made to it in the most unusual cases. This is borne out by two dicta in the same volume of Appeal Cases which also reveal the difference of opinion about the scope of the rule discernible in a number of judgments.

'It is a strong thing to read into an Act of Parliament words which are not there, and in the absence of clear necessity it is a wrong thing to do.'[20]

'We are not entitled to read words into an Act of Parliament unless clear reason for it is to be found *within the four corners of the Act* itself.'[1]

In their review of statutory interpretation in 1969, the Law Commissions concluded that there was a tendency among some judges to over-emphasise a narrow version of the literal rule and to refuse to go beyond the meaning of a statutory provision in the light of its immediate and obvious context.[2] They proposed that judges should adopt a 'purposive' approach to the construction of statutes, namely 'that a construction which would promote the general legislative purpose underlying the provision in question is to be preferred to a construction which would not'.[3] Although this has much in common with the 'mischief' rule, the Law Commissions disapproved of that term. First, the rule in *Heydon's* case related to a different constitutional context and stressed the curing of a defect in the law without adequate emphasis on the extent to which the judge should adhere to the actual wording of the statute. Second, the rule is archaic and misleading:[4]

'In a modern statement of the law we prefer to avoid words which, at least for the layman, have an archaic ring. Even for the lawyer the expression is unsatisfactory. It tends to suggest that legislation is only designed to deal with an evil and not to further a positive social purpose. Furthermore, it seems too narrow to speak of the "mischief of the statute". The general legislative purpose underlying a provision may emerge from a series of

---

20. Lord Mersey in *Thompson v Gould & Co* [1910] AC 409 at 420.
1. Lord Loreburn in *Vickers, Sons and Maxim Ltd v Evans* [1910] AC 444 at 445.
2. *The Interpretation of Statutes* (Law Com No 21; Scottish Law Com No 11) para 80(c), infra p 189.
3. Ibid, Appendix A, Draft Bill, clause 2(a).
4. Note 177; see also para 33.

statutes dealing with the same subject matter . . . or from other indications of that purpose [afforded by information relating to legal, social, economic and other aspects of society of which a judge is able to take judicial notice].'

Since the Law Commissions' report, the judges have embraced a 'purposive' approach to the construction of statutes. They have rejected the narrow literalism which the Law Commissions criticised, but this does not mark a radical departure from the approach suggested in *Grey v Pearson*.[5] Two cases drawn from the same volume of the Appeal Cases illustrate the way 'purposive' construction differs from earlier approaches to the interpretation of statutes.

Johnson v Moreton[6] concerned the interpretation of s 24 of the Agricultural Holdings Act 1948, which, unlike other sections in the Act, did not provide that 'this section shall have effect notwithstanding any agreement to the contrary'. Nevertheless, the House of Lords held that a tenant could exercise his right under the section to apply to the Agricultural Land Tribunal, despite his agreement with his landlord to the contrary. Their Lordships based their interpretation on the policy which the Act was designed to serve, namely the protection of tenants in the interests of promoting agricultural efficiency. Unlike the approach of the golden rule, there was no reliance on an absurdity manifest from the statute read as a whole, but rather the policy was derived from the legislative history and from the social background against which the Act was passed. Under the purposive approach, the judge may look beyond the four corners of the statute to find a reason for giving a wider or narrower interpretation to its words, and his role is one of active co-operation with the policy of the statute.

All the same, this purposive approach is more limited than the appeal to the 'equity of the statute' found among 16th-century mischievists. This can be illustrated by *Jones v Wrotham Park Estates Ltd*.[7]

The Leasehold Reform Act 1967 gave the tenant of a long lease the right to purchase the freehold from his landlord at the equivalent of the going market rate when occupied by the tenant. Two days before Jones gave notice of his intention to exercise this right, his landlord entered into a 300-year lease of the reversion with an associated property company at a highly favourable rent. The effect of this transaction was to raise the value of the freehold from £300 to £4,000 at the going

5. For an example of a recent judgment expressing essentially the 'golden' rule with modified wording see Donaldson MR, *Re British Concrete Pipe Association* [1983] 1 All ER 203 at 205.
6. [1980] AC 37, [1978] 3 All ER 37.
7. [1980] AC 74, [1979] 1 All ER 286.

market rate. The House of Lords thought that, had such a device been considered by Parliament, it would have been proscribed, since it made the purchase of the freehold by tenants more difficult. However, their Lordships applied the clear wording of the statute in favour of the landlord, requiring the tenant to pay the £4,000 if he wished to purchase the reversion and holding the lease of the reversion valid. Lord Diplock noted that there were limits to the purposive approach:[8]

> 'First, it [must be] possible to determine from a consideration of the provisions of the Act read as a whole what the mischief was that it was the purpose of the Act to remedy; secondly, it [must be] apparent that the draftsman and Parliament had by inadvertence overlooked, and so omitted to deal with, an eventuality that required to be dealt with if the purpose of the Act was to be achieved; and thirdly, it [must be] possible to state with certainty what were the additional words that would have been inserted by the draftsman and approved by Parliament had their attention been drawn to the omission before the Bill passed into law. Unless this third condition is fulfilled any attempt by a court of justice to repair the omission in the Act cannot be justified as an exercise of its jurisdiction to determine what is the meaning of a written law which Parliament has passed. Such an attempt crosses the boundary between construction and legislation. It becomes a usurpation of the function which under the constitution of this country is vested in the legislature to the exclusion of the courts.'

Thus the purposive approach is more limited than one which tries to 'suppress the mischief, and advance the remedy, and to suppress subtle inventions and evasions for continuance of the mischief'.[9]

Though the precise contours of the purposive approach will be considered later, what is clear is that it retains elements of what Bennion has aptly called 'literal' and 'strained' interpretations[10] of an Act, so that there is no radical discontinuity with the past.

---

8. Ibid, at pp 105–6.
9. *Heydon's* case, supra, p 10.
10. Sections 314–5.

Chapter 2
Jurisprudential

There is a great deal of juristic writing on the subject of statutory interpretation, and no attempt will be made here to summarise it all. This chapter will content itself with presenting a number of key jurisprudential issues raised in connection with the subject. The issues involve an analysis both of the basic approach of the judges in the interpretation of statutes and of the character of the canons and methods adopted in their performance of this task. With regard to the former, it is necessary to ask what the judges are seeking to interpret, and especially what is the relationship they conceive between the text of a statute and the intention of Parliament. Equally, one must be concerned with what 'interpretation' involves and how it differs from the application of a statutory provision or from its amendment. With regard to the canons and methods, it is necessary to ask what is the status of the 'rules' and 'principles' which are often invoked by the judges in explaining their decisions, and whether the normal common law methods for the judicial elaboration of legal rules can be applied to the task of interpreting statutes. Although the presentation will be essentially analytical, the constitutional questions which the subject necessarily raises will require some consideration of its political aspects.

A. THE SUBJECT MATTER OF STATUTORY INTERPRETATION

As Bennion points out, the 'unit of enquiry' in statutory interpretation is 'an enactment whose legal meaning in relation to a particular factual situation falls to be determined'.[1] The text of the relevant enactment

---

1. *Bennion*, section 72.

20

may be determined by looking at a single Act of Parliament, or even a single provision within it, or by combining elements from several Acts. Having thus established the wording of the statutory text, the lawyer can then proceed to determine its meaning in the light of the principles of interpretation or construction.[2]

Seen in this light, statutory interpretation involves determining the meaning of a text contained in one or more documents. Yet judges and writers frequently talk about interpreting 'the will of the legislator' or giving effect to 'the intention of Parliament'. Indeed, judges are often criticised for being tied too closely to the statutory words and for failing to give effect to the intentions of Parliament. Such language may appear to suggest that there are two units of enquiry in statutory interpretation—the statutory text and the intention of Parliament— and that the judge must seek to harmonise the two. However, this appearance is deceptive. English law takes the view that the two are closely connected, but that primacy is to be given to the text in which the intention of Parliament has been expressed. Blackstone tells us that:[3]

> 'The fairest and most rational method to interpret the will of the legislator is by exploring his intentions at the time when the law was made, by *signs* the most natural and probable. And these signs are either the words, the context, the subject matter, the effects and consequence, or the spirit and reason of the law.'

For him, words are generally to be understood 'in their usual and most known signification', although terms of art 'must be taken according to the acceptation of the learning in each art, trade and science'. 'If words happen still to be dubious', we may establish their meaning from the context, which includes the preamble to the statute and laws made by the same legislator on the same subject.

Words are always to be understood as having regard to the subject-matter of the legislation. 'But lastly, the most universal and effectual way of discovering the true meaning of a law, when the words are dubious, is by considering the reason and spirit of it; or the cause which moved the legislator to enact it.' This brief account of the rules of statutory interpretation approximates closely to the present law. All these precepts are typical rules of language applicable to understand-

---

2. A distinction is drawn in some works between interpretation and construction, but it is not employed in this book because it lacks an agreed basis.
3. *Commentaries on the Laws of England* (facsimile of 1st edition of 1765, University of Chicago Press, 1979) vol 1, p 59.

ing any text, whether legal or other.[4] As with literature, the role of the judge is to seek the intention of the legislative author from what is written in the text, and not to seek to construct a text on the basis of the subjective intentions of the author (assuming that they could be discovered).

Blackstone's approach would be adopted today with few modifications. As Lord Scarman stated:[5]

'If Parliament . . . says one thing but means another, it is not, under the historic principles of the common law, for the courts to correct it. That general principle must surely be acceptable in our society. We are to be governed not by Parliament's intentions but by Parliament's enactments.'

The criticism that judges are too tied to the wording of the statutory text is thus not a suggestion that the judges are looking at the wrong subject-matter when interpreting statutes. Rather, the criticism merely suggests that the judges are adopting too narrow a view of the context in which the statutory text is to be read.

B.   THE INTENTION OF PARLIAMENT

In the light of what has been said, it is necessary to ask what sense can be given to the notion of 'the intention of Parliament'.[6] The phrase is frequently used by the judges although it is meaningless unless it is recognised for what it is, an expression used by analogy, but in no way synonymously, with the intention of an individual concerning the general and particular effects of a document he prepares and signs. A testator may, with perfect propriety, be said to have intended to dispose of all of his property, to have intended to do so in accordance with a particular scheme (equality among his children, or with a preference for sons, for example) and to have intended that his will

---

4. See, for example, K S Abraham, 'Statutory Interpretation and Literary Theory: Some Common Concerns of an Unlikely Pair' 32 Rutgers L Rev 676 (1979), and the 'Interpretation Symposium' 58 Southern California L Rev, issue No 1 (1985), especially articles by R R Garet, D C Hoy and M J Perry.
5. 418 HL Deb, col 65 (9 March 1981).
6. There is an abundant literature on this subject which cannot be listed here. But, for example, see R Dickerson, *The Interpretation and Application of Statutes* (Boston, 1975) Ch 7; G C MacCallum, 'Legislative Intent' 75 Yale LJ 754 (1966) (reprinted in R S Summers (ed), *Essays in Legal Philosophy* (Oxford, 1970), 237), which contain references to many of the principal articles on the subject.

should have a certain effect in the situation before the court (eg that X should or should not benefit under one of its provisions); but the word 'intention' is used in a very different sense when it is said that, in passing the Race Relations Act 1968, Parliament did or did not intend the Act to apply to all racial discrimination, did or did not intend to distinguish between discrimination in the private and public sectors, and did or did not intend the Act to apply to clubs. Each of these statements can be used meaningfully although it is quite impossible to point to specific individuals, like the testator in the previous example, who did or did not entertain the intention in question.

The 'intention of Parliament' with regard to a particular statute cannot mean the intention of all those who were members of either House when the royal assent was given, for many of them might have been out of the country at all material times and never have heard of the statute. Equally plainly the phrase cannot mean the intention of the majority who voted for the statute as this will almost certainly have been constituted by different persons at the different stages of the passage of the Bill and, in any event, it would be rash to assume that all those who vote for it have the same intentions with regard to a particular piece of legislation. For example, it has been pointed out that, in a debate on what became the Statute of Westminster 1931, Mr Winston Churchill and the Solicitor-General agreed that there was no obscurity in the provisions concerning the Irish Free State, although they took diametrically opposite views concerning their effect.[7]

Someone bent on identifying the intention of specific human beings as that to which reference is made when people speak of the intention of Parliament might resort to the notion of agency. It could be said that the promoters of a Bill must have some consequences in mind as its general and particular effects, but promoters, whoever they may be, are initiators who place proposals before Parliament rather than act as its agents; and many Bills contain amendments which are not the work of the promoters. Nonetheless, if it were thought essential to regard the intention of Parliament as the same sort of thing as the intention of an individual legislator, or the intention of a number of individual legislators all of whom had in mind identical objects and effects of the statutes they jointly draft, the intention of the members of Parliament who promote Parliamentary legislation would be the closest approximation. In modern times they give instructions to the draftsman and he can be regarded as their agent. To quote Lord Simon of Glaisdale:[8]

---

7. G Marshall, *Constitutional Theory* (Oxford, 1971) p 76.
8. *Ealing London Borough Council v Race Relations Board* [1972] AC 342 at 360.

'It is the duty of a court so to interpret an Act of Parliament as to give effect to its intention. The court sometimes asks itself what the draftsman must have intended. This is reasonable enough: the draftsman knows what is the intention of the legislative initiator (nowadays almost always an organ of the executive); he knows what canons of construction the courts will apply; and he will express himself in such a way as accordingly to give effect to the legislative intention. Parliament, of course, in enacting legislation assumes responsibility for the language of the draftsman. But the reality is that only a minority of legislators will attend the debates on the legislation.'

An analogy could be drawn with cases in which the intention of its officers is imputed to a corporation, but it would be a false analogy. Parliament is not a corporation and those who speak of the intention of Parliament do so in spite of the fact that they know that proof that members of Parliament, even those who were the legislative initiators, believed that a statute would produce certain results is not a condition precedent to the proper use of the phrase. That use is the outcome of linguistic convention having nothing to do with such conclusions of law as the imputation of the intention of a particular individual to a corporation.

The meaning the court ultimately attaches to the statutory words will frequently be that which it believes members of the legislature attached to them, or the meaning which they would have attached to the words had the situation before the court been present to their minds. The object of the statute, or of a particular section of it, may be treated as part of its context, and, to the very limited extent discussed in Chapter 6, English courts may travel outside the four corners of the Act with which they are concerned in order to ascertain its object; but they may not go outside the statute in order to ascertain the meaning which members of the legislature attached, or would have attached, to a particular provision in its application to a particular situation. The following words of a South African judge surely hold good for English law:[9]

'Evidence that every member who voted for a measure put a certain construction upon it cannot affect the meaning which the court must place upon the statute, for it is the product, not of a number of individuals, but of an impersonal Parliament.'

This last quotation helps to make clear, as R M Dworkin has

---

9. *Swart & Nicol v De Kock* 1951 3 SA 589.

pointed out,[10] that the question of legislative intention is not about the historical or hypothetical views of legislators, but rather concerns the meaning of words used in a particular context. The objective is not to reconstruct a psychological model of Parliament or the promoters of a Bill, or even of the draftsman, and then to use it to determine what was meant by them when they used certain words, or what would have been provided had a particular eventuality been envisaged at the time of drafting or enactment. Although judicial language, like that of Lord Simon of Glaisdale, may sometimes give this impression, it is clear that judges do not act in this way and that they make little effort to discover what the legislator or draftsman thought that the words meant. Judges are concerned instead with using the conventions of ordinary language and of statutory interpretation to determine the meaning of words in their context.

In *Black-Clawson International Ltd v Papierwerke Waldhof-Aschaffenburg AG*[11] Lord Reid said: 'We often say that we are looking for the intention of Parliament, but that is not quite accurate. We are seeking the meaning of the words which Parliament used. We are seeking not what Parliament meant but the true meaning of what they said.' The remark is somewhat cryptic, but it does point to the fact that the intention to be attributed to the legislator is to be determined from the objective words used, rather than from any subjective intentions which were not expressed in the text. All the same, the remark suggests a distinction which is in reality less clear cut, because in ordinary language, when in doubt, we must do our best to make sense of what the author said in the context appropriate to his speaking, which requires some knowledge of the author and what he was trying to say.

In the context of the interpretation of statutes there are three principal situations in which people in general and judges in particular speak of the intention of Parliament. In the first place, whenever the meaning of specific words is under consideration, the idea that a particular meaning is that which would or would not have been attached to a word or phrase by the average member of Parliament, sitting at the time when the statute was passed, may be expressed or refuted by some such statement as 'that is (or is not) what Parliament intended by those words'. Second, when the consequences of a particular construction are under consideration, the idea that a particular consequence might well have been in the mind of the average member

---

10. 'Political Judges and the Rule of Law' (1978) 64 *Proceedings of the British Academy* 259, 270–4 (reprinted in R M Dworkin, *A Matter of Principle* (Cambridge, Mass. 1985) 9, 18–23), and *Law's Empire* (London, 1986) pp 317–27, 337–41.
11. [1975] AC 591, 613.

of Parliament is often expressed by some such statement as 'that was likely (or unlikely) to have been the intention of Parliament'. Finally, although it is impossible to identify the individual members whose purpose it was, it is common to speak of the purpose, aim or object of a statute as the intention of Parliament. The third situation is the most important if only because reflection upon it shows that those who feel uncomfortable about the use of the expression 'the intention of Parliament' ought not to feel any more at ease if they abandon the phrase for some other one such as 'the intention of the statute', 'legislative purpose' or 'the object of the statute'. Only human beings can really have intentions, purposes or objects, but, in the situation under consideration, the intentions, purposes or objects are not those of identifiable human beings. The words are used by close analogy to the intentions of a single legislator. The analogy is more remote when the 'intention of Parliament' is used as a synonym for what the average member of Parliament of a particular epoch would have meant by certain words or expected as the consequences of a statutory provision. All the same, the notion of 'the intention of Parliament' has an advantage over the phrase 'legislative purpose' in that a single statute, like the Companies Act 1985, may have several purposes which may have to be reconciled. The analogy with the human mind emphasises a certain coherence and consistency both within an enactment and between enactments which judges expect to find. Consistency and coherence are values which guide judicial interpretation of the law,[12] and the metaphor of a single legislative will or intention gives expression to this ideal. The expression is thus not so much a description as a linguistic convenience.

The major judicial statements with regard to the intention of Parliament have been made in cases in which the issue has been whether statutory wording could be ignored or the meaning of statutory language strained in order to prevent an injustice, or supposed injustice, which, it was thought, could not have been contemplated by Parliament. The answer has almost always been in the negative, and the preponderant view seems to be that, when the question is whether Parliament did or did not intend a particular result, the 'intention of Parliament' is what the statutory words mean to the normal speaker of English. The fact that a judge feels confident that, had the situation before him been put to them, the members of the Parliament in which the statute was passed would have voted for a different meaning or for additional words is immaterial.

---

12. See D N MacCormick, *Legal Reasoning and Legal Theory* (Oxford, 1978) pp 203–13; R M Dworkin, *A Matter of Principle* pp 327–8.

In *Saloman v Saloman & Co Ltd*[13] Lord Watson said:

'"Intention of the Legislature" is a common but very slippery phrase, which, popularly understood, may signify anything from intention embodied in positive enactment to speculative opinion as to what the legislature probably would have meant, although there has been an omission to enact it. In a Court of Law or Equity, what the legislature intended to be done or not to be done can only be legitimately ascertained from that which it has chosen to enact, either in express words or by reasonable and necessary implication.'

The case, decided in days when the one-man company was a novelty, raised the question whether a debenture, issued by such a company to its one-man as part payment for the business he transferred to it, entitled him to priority over unsecured creditors in the winding-up. The argument which found favour with the Court of Appeal was that an affirmative answer would have been contrary to the intention of the Companies Act 1862, but it could not be supported by reference to any provision in the Act. This was the background of Lord Watson's allusion to speculative opinion about what the legislature probably would have meant. The House of Lords unanimously decided that Saloman was, as a debenture holder, entitled to priority over the unsecured creditors of his company, and it is a reasonable inference from their speeches that the decision would have been the same even if every member of Parliament who participated in the debates preceding the 1862 Act had expressly stated that it did not permit the formation of such a company or the issue of such a debenture. The statutory words which clearly did permit these things were paramount.

Such an approach reflects a conception of the judicial role which is fundamentally linked to the constitutional principle of the rule of law. As Lord Simon of Glaisdale expressed the connection,[14]

'in a society living under the rule of law citizens are entitled to regulate their conduct according to what a statute has said, rather than by what it was meant to say or by what it would otherwise have said if a newly considered situation had been envisaged.'

By giving effect to the meaning which the normal speaker of English would attribute to the words in their context, the judges are giving effect to the normal expectations of citizens and are upholding this conception of the rule of law.

---

13. [1897] AC 22 at 38.
14. *Stock v Frank Jones (Tipton) Ltd* [1978] ICR 347 at 354; also idem, 418 HL Deb, col 76 (9 March 1981).

Despite its difficulty, there are three constitutional reasons for retaining the notion of 'the intention of Parliament'. The first is that it expresses the subordination of the judiciary to Parliament. As J W Hurst put it:[15]

'Of course we use a fiction if we speak of the legislature as if it were a being of one mind. But so durable a fiction endures because it has a use validated by experience. This formula reminds all who deal with a statute that they are operating in a field of law in which they are not free to define public policy simply according to their own judgment.'

The courts try to give effect to the instructions they have received from Parliament and do not simply decide as they think best. All the same, this dichotomy can be overstated. Subordinates do receive instructions, but they are usually left with a degree of latitude about how to execute them. At best, the notion of 'the intention of Parliament' identifies a perspective or orientation within which judicial decision-making takes place, rather than a rigid set of instructions whose execution requires little originality or discretion.

The second reason for appealing to 'the intention of Parliament' is the desire of the judiciary to disavow a large creative role in the interpretation of statutes. Denning LJ may have said in *Magor and St Mellons RDC v Newport Corpn*:[16]

'We do not sit here to pull the language of Parliament and of Ministers to pieces and make nonsense of it. That is an easy thing to do, and it is a thing to which lawyers are too often prone. We sit here to find out the intention of Parliament and of Ministers and carry it out, and we do this better by filling in the gaps and making sense of the enactment than by opening it up to destructive analysis.'

But this approach was rejected by the House of Lords at the time,[17] and in later cases Lord Denning MR's approach to statutes came under similar criticism for being unduly creative. For example, in *Duport Steels Ltd v Sirs*,[18] s 13(1) of the Trade Union and Labour Relations

---

15. *Dealing with Statutes* (New York 1982) p 33.
16. [1950] 2 All ER 1226 at p 1236; also *Nothman v Barnet London Borough Council* [1978] ICR 336 at 344; *R v Sheffield Crown Court, ex p Brownlow* [1980] QB 530 at 538–9. At one point Lord Denning accepted that judges cannot fill in gaps: see *London Transport Executive v Betts* [1959] AC 231 at 247.
17. See *Magor and St Mellons RDC v Newport Corporation* [1952] AC 189.
18. [1980] 1 All ER 529, [1980] 1 WLR 142; also *Nothman v Barnet London Borough Council* [1979] ICR 111.

Act 1974 (as amended) gave an immunity from suit for 'an act done by a person in contemplation or furtherance of a trade dispute'. There was no specific provision which prevented this immunity extending to actions directed against employers other than the one with whom the employees were in dispute. Nevertheless, the Court of Appeal, presided over by Lord Denning MR, granted an injunction against union officials who were seeking to induce their members working for private steel companies to come out on strike in order to make more effective their strike action against the nationalised British Steel Corporation. It restricted the wording of the Act by requiring that the actions protected by the immunity should not be too remote from the dispute, and Lord Denning MR justified this by pointing to the serious and deleterious consequences for the country of such secondary action. The House of Lords unanimously reversed the decision, and categorically denounced the approach of the Court of Appeal. While having sympathy with the view that secondary action ought not to be lawful, their Lordships were of the opinion that it was not the role of the courts to outlaw such action by means of statutory interpretation. As Lord Diplock put it:

> 'My Lords, at a time when more and more cases involve the application of legislation which gives effect to policies that are the subject of bitter public and parliamentary controversy, it cannot be too strongly emphasised that the British Constitution, though largely unwritten, is firmly based upon the separation of powers: Parliament makes the laws, the judiciary interprets them. When Parliament legislates to remedy what the majority of its members at the time perceive to be a defect or lacuna in the existing law . . ., the role of the judiciary is confined to ascertaining from the words that Parliament has approved as expressing its intention what that intention was, and giving effect to it. Where the meaning of the statutory words is plain and unambiguous it is not for the judges to invent fancied ambiguities as an excuse for failing to give effect to its plain meaning because they themselves consider that the consequences of doing so would be inexpedient, or even unjust or immoral. In controversial matters such as are involved in industrial relations there is room for differences of opinion as to what is expedient, what is just and what is morally justifiable. Under our Constitution it is Parliament's opinion on these matters that is paramount.'[19]

The third reason is that of legal certainty, which was invoked by Lord

---

19. [1980] 1 All ER at 541.

Diplock and other members of the House of Lords in the *Duport Steels* case, as well as in other cases.[20] The certain injustice of a legislative text may be preferable for the citizen in the long run than the uncertainty caused by judicial interventions to correct perceived 'injustices'. Even if an appeal to 'the intention of Parliament' is justified, the use made of it differs from judge to judge. It is used as a statement of attitude or approach, not an element of social fact to be researched. Such statements are expressions of a constitutional role adopted by judges, and the quotations given here and elsewhere in this book illustrate that the judges are not unanimous in their perception of what is the correct constitutional role for them to adopt.

C. THE MEANING OF INTERPRETATION

If the intention of Parliament is not to be a dominant ingredient in the formulation of our basic rules of interpretation, we cannot accept the definition of interpretation given by the American jurist J C Gray as—

> 'the process by which a judge (or indeed any person, lawyer or layman, who has occasion to search for the meaning of a statute) constructs from the words of a statute-book a meaning which he either believes to be that of the legislature, or which he proposes to attribute to it.'[1]

It would be better to say that interpretation is the process by which the courts determine the meaning of a statutory provision for the purpose of applying it to the situation before them.

It is hardly necessary to state that the meaning which persons other than a judge trying a case would attach to a statutory provision for the purpose of applying it to a given situation is dependent on their views of what the courts have done in similar situations, or would do in the situation were it to come before them. Throughout the rest of this book it is assumed that the word 'interpretation' is only apt in its application to statutes when there is a dispute about the meaning of words. This excludes the discussion of two procedures which certainly have claims to be described as 'interpretation', the process of determining how words of undisputed meaning apply to an undisputed situation of fact and the process of applying words of undisputed meaning after a conclusion has been reached with regard to disputed facts. These

---

20. See especially Lord Scarman, ibid at p 551; Lord Simon of Glaisdale, *Stock v Frank Jones (Tipton) Ltd* [1978] ICR at 354.
1. *The Nature and Sources of Law* (2nd edn, New Haven, 1921) p 176.

processes are best referred to as 'application' of the statute. The first of these processes takes place out of court. It is the process followed by legal advisers and any number of other kinds of adviser. Someone consults a solicitor about his rights under the intestacy of a parent or brother. The solicitor gives his advice with confidence on the assumption that the facts are as stated by his client. There is a sense in which the solicitor is interpreting the relevant statutory provisions for his client who may even have read the provisions without understanding them. If it be thought that, in the case of intestacy, these provisions are simple enough for anyone to understand, let the case be one in which a solicitor or accountant is consulted on a simple question of tax liability when the relevant statutory provisions are almost certain to be double Dutch to the layman even though they are clear beyond the possibility of dispute to the expert adviser. Equally, state officials, such as tax inspectors assessing a tax return or civil servants at a local office of the Department of Health and Social Security processing a claim for unemployment benefit, are most typically involved in the application of rules to the facts of individual situations. Whether it be right or wrong to call this process 'interpretation' it is the process to which statutes are most commonly subjected and one which renders it essential that the first rule of statutory interpretation should be that the courts must give effect to the ordinary, or, where appropriate, the technical meaning of statutory words. The fact that most statutes are 'interpreted' in the sense mentioned in this paragraph out of court is one of the justifications of the restrictions on admissible evidence of the purpose of a statute mentioned in Chapter 6.

Courts spend more of their time applying words of undisputed meaning to facts which have been disputed than in interpreting statutory words of disputed meaning. To appreciate the truth of this assertion it is only necessary to think of the imposition of prison sentences within the maxima allowed by the various statutes, or the apportionment of damages in the ordinary case of contributory negligence. Likewise the decisions of officials may involve disputed questions of fact, such as whether a person is 'living with' another person in a permanent and stable relationship so as to affect her eligibility for supplementary benefit. The point does not call for comment.

The process of interpretation has also to be contrasted with that of alteration. At first sight, the process of making sense of the wording of a statutory text would appear clearly distinct from that of amending its wording. In *Of Laws in General*, Bentham distinguished the two processes under the headings of 'strict' and 'liberal' interpretation:[2]

---

2. *Of Laws in General* (edited by H L A Hart, London, 1970) p 162. This book was substantially completed in 1782 but not published in Bentham's lifetime.

'It may be styled strict where you attribute to the legislator the will which at the time of making the law, as you suppose, he really entertained. It may be styled liberal where the will you attribute to him is not that which you suppose he really entertained, but a will which as you suppose he failed of entertaining only through inadvertency: insomuch that had the individual case which calls for interpretation been present to his view, he would have entertained that will, which by the interpretation put upon his law you act up to, as though it had been his in reality.'[3]

Liberal interpretation is subdivided into extensive and restrictive. An extensive interpretation applies a statutory provision to a case which does not fall within its words when literally construed; restrictive interpretation fails to apply a statutory provision to a case which does fall within its words when literally construed.

'In either case thus to interpret a law is to alter it: *interpretation* being put by a sort of euphemism for *alteration*. Now to extend an old law is in fact to establish a new law: as on the other hand to qualify the old law is *pro tanto* to destroy it. The only circumstance that can serve to distinguish the alteration itself, when made in this way, from alteration at large is, that the alteration goes no farther from what it appears was the legislator's will to what, it is supposed, would have been his will had the case in question been present to his view: from his actual to his hypothetical will. If then there is a new law made, it is made however upon the pattern, and with some of the materials of the old: if there is part of the old law destroyed, it is such part only as he himself it is supposed would have destroyed, had the particular case in question come before him.'[4]

Bentham was not opposed to liberal interpretation. He spoke of it as 'that delicate and important branch of judiciary power, the concession of which is dangerous, the denial ruinous'.[5] He suggested that, whenever a statute was interpreted liberally, the judge should draw up a statement to be placed before the legislature indicating how the statute should be amended, the proposed amendment to have the force of law if not vetoed within a specified time.[6] No doubt the implementation of such a proposal would give rise to many difficulties.

---

3. Ibid, p 162. Words such as 'strict', 'liberal', 'restrictive' and 'extensive' are frequently used with less precision, roughly as synonyms for narrow and broad.
4. Ibid, pp 163–4.
5. Ibid, p 239.
6. Ibid, p 241.

In reality, it is not easy to distinguish between cases in which an interpretation is 'liberal' in Bentham's sense of attributing to the legislator an intention with regard to a particular situation which he plainly did not entertain, and cases where an interpretation attributes to the legislator's words a restricted or extended meaning on account of an intention which he was believed to entertain. It is said that the courts have no power to amend the statute, although they may read in words which it can be inferred that the legislature meant to insert.

'It is one thing to put in or take out words to express more clearly what the legislature did say, or must from its own words be presumed to have said by implication, it is quite another matter to amend a statute to make it say something it does not say, or to make it say what it is conjectured that the legislature could have said or would have said if a particular situation had been before it.'[7]

But do the courts really confine their activities to putting in words which were already in the statute by implication? Section 3 of the Official Secrets Act 1920 provides that 'no person shall *in the vicinity of* any prohibited place obstruct any member of Her Majesty's Forces . . .' In *Adler v George*[8] the defendant, a member of the Committee of 100, was actually on a Norfolk airfield (a prohibited place) when he obstructed a member of the Forces; nonetheless he was convicted because 'in the vicinity of' could be taken to mean 'in' as well as 'near'. Lord Parker CJ said:[9]

'I am quite satisfied that this is a case where no violence is done to the language by reading the words "in the vicinity of " as meaning "in or in the vicinity of ". Here is a section in an Act of Parliament designed to prevent interference with members of Her Majesty's Forces, among others, who are engaged on guard, sentry, patrol or other similar duty in relation to a prohibited place such as this station. It would be extraordinary, I venture to think it would be absurd, if an indictable offence was thereby created when the obstruction took place outside the precincts of the station, albeit in the vicinity, and no offence at all was created if the obstruction occurred on the station itself . . . There may, of course, be many contexts in which "vicinity" must be confined to its literal meaning of "being near in space", but under this section, I am

---

7. E A Driedger, *Construction of Statutes* (2nd edn, Toronto, 1983) p 101.
8. [1964] 2 QB 7, [1964] 1 All ER 628.
9. Ibid, at pp 9–10.

quite clear that the context demands that the words should be construed in the way I have said.'

Was this a case in which the ordinary meaning of the words was rejected in favour of an implied extended meaning which they were just capable of bearing, or was it a case of rectification by the insertion of the intended, though inadvertently omitted, words 'in or'? The point is a nice one and Lord Parker evidently took the former view. A clear case of rectification is *Deria v General Council of British Shipping*.[10] Section 4(1) of the Race Relations Act 1976 made it unlawful to discriminate, among other things, by refusing a person employment 'in relation to employment by him at an establishment in Great Britain', and s 8(1) provided further that, for this purpose, 'employment is to be regarded as being at an establishment in Great Britain unless the employee does his work wholly outside Great Britain'. An employment agency refused to recruit three Somali sailors in Cardiff for service on a requisitioned ship due to sail from Gibraltar to the Falkland Islands and back during a military campaign. The alleged ground of refusal was the policy of the agency to recruit crews on the basis that cabins would not be shared by seamen of mixed races. The agency contended that the alleged discrimination fell outside the scope of s 4(1) (and of s 14 which related specifically to employment agencies) because the voyage for which the sailors had sought employment was to be performed wholly outside Great Britain. Now, contrary to the original plans, the ship had docked at Southampton on its return voyage some four months after setting sail, and the crew had been paid off there. The sailors argued that, since the crew had actually done work in British territorial waters, the work which they had sought was not work that 'the employee does . . . wholly outside Great Britain', and that the discrimination thus fell within s 4(1). The Court of Appeal rejected this argument, considering that the words 'the employee does his work wholly outside Great Britain' in s 8(1) must refer to the intention of the employer at the time when the crew was to be engaged, and not to what actually happened. Accordingly, s 8(1) had to be read as providing that 'employment is to be regarded as being at an establishment in Great Britain unless the employee does *or is to do* his work wholly outside Great Britain'. The italicised words added to the subsection would make sense in the case of a person refused employment, who would necessarily never 'do' any work for the prospective employer. Furthermore, they would enable the employer to be certain of his position at the time of the act in

---

10. [1986] 1 WLR 1207.

question, rather than permit this position to be altered by subsequent events.

'Rectification' is the right word for this procedure because it is a word which at least implies some sort of intention on the part of Parliament with regard to the added words whereas an amendment could result in words the presence of which in the statute was neither intended nor ever would have been intended by the Parliament which passed it.

The foregoing points demonstrate clearly that, if the word is construed broadly, 'interpretation' is a many-sided process.

D. THE CANONS OF INTERPRETATION

Ever since R M Dworkin published a seminal article in 1967,[11] it has become fashionable to divide the contents of a legal system into rules and principles. One of the examples of a rule given by him is 'the maximum legal speed on the turnpike is 60 miles per hour'.

> 'Rules are applicable in an all-or-nothing fashion. If the facts a rule stipulates are given, then either the rule is valid, in which case the answer it supplies must be accepted, or it is not, in which case it contributes nothing to the decision.'[12]

One of Dworkin's examples of a principle is 'no man may profit from his own wrong'. This is recognised by English law and has formed the basis of a number of decisions, but judges are not obliged to apply it in the sense in which they are obliged to apply a rule after making certain findings of fact. Our law sometimes permits a man to profit from his own wrong as when it protects the adverse possessor of property even against the owner. Once a principle has been applied in a case it frequently creates a rule to which effect must be given in similar situations in the future. A principle may rationalise a number of specific legal rules or set out a goal of the law in a generalised way, but there is no requirement that a principle be applied in the same way or to the same extent in relation to different statutes.

> 'All that is meant, when we say that a particular principle is a principle of our law, is that the principle is one which officials

---

11. 35 University of Chicago L Rev 14 (reprinted under the title 'Model of Rules I' in R M Dworkin, *Taking Rights Seriously* (revised edn, London, 1978) 14). See also D N MacCormick, *Legal Reasoning and Legal Theory* pp 152–3.
12. *Taking Rights Seriously* p 24.

must take into account, if it is relevant, as a consideration inclining in one direction or another.'[13]

Principles, unlike rules, may conflict without detriment to the operation of the legal system as a whole, and, again unlike rules, they may vary in the degree of their persuasiveness. Of course rules can and do have exceptions, but if two rules are contradictory of each other there is something seriously wrong with the law. No one has suggested that there is something seriously wrong with the canons of statutory interpretation because of the frequent conflict between the principles that statutes should be construed so as to alter the common law as little as possible, and that they should be construed so as to conform to international law.

If we apply Dworkin's terminology to the canons of statutory interpretation, there are two rules, one so general as to approximate to a principle, and the other subject to an ill-defined limitation. For the rest there is a congeries of principles capable of pointing in different directions and incapable of arrangement in any kind of systematic hierarchy according to their differing degrees of persuasiveness. This paucity of rules and confusion of principles amply justifies Lord Wilberforce's description of statutory interpretation as 'what is nowadays popularly called a non-subject.'[14] He has since amplified this remark by stating:

'I still think that the interpretation of legislation is just part of the process of being a good lawyer; a multi-faceted thing, calling for many varied talents; not a subject which can be confined in rules.'[15]

Lord Wilberforce was expressing doubts about the subject's suitability for law reform, but the matters which have just been mentioned also render it extremely difficult to give a coherent account of the subject or to assess the merits of criticisms.

The following three passages from speeches of Lord Reid in the House of Lords may be cited in support of the remarks made at the beginning of the last paragraph:

(i) 'In determining the meaning of any word or phrase in a statute the first question to ask always is what is the natural or ordinary meaning of that word or phrase in its context in the statute? It is only when that meaning leads to some result which cannot reasonably be supposed to have been

---

13. Ibid, p 26.
14. 274 HL Deb, col 1294 (16 November 1966).
15. 418 HL Deb, col 73 (9 March 1981).

the intention of the legislature that it is proper to look for some other possible meaning of the word or phrase.'[16]
(ii) 'Then [in case of doubt] rules of construction are relied on. They are not rules in the ordinary sense of having some binding force. They are our servants, not our masters. They are aids to construction, presumptions or pointers. Not infrequently one "rule" points in one direction, another in a different direction. In each case we must look at all relevant circumstances and decide as a matter of judgment what weight to attach to any particular "rule".'[17]
(iii) 'It is a cardinal principle applicable to all kinds of statutes that you may not for any reason attach to a statutory provision a meaning which the words of that provision cannot reasonably bear. If they are capable of more than one meaning, then you can choose between those meanings, but beyond that you must not go.'[18]

The inverted commas round the word *rule* in the second quotation show that Lord Reid was fully aware of the distinction between rules and principles taken by Dworkin; but consistency with the terminology used by the latter requires the substitution of 'principle' for 'rule' in that quotation.

The first quotation sets out a rule combining the literal and golden rules mentioned in Chapter 10. It is plainly a rule in Dworkin's sense of the word—the judge *must* ask himself what is the natural or ordinary meaning of the word or phrase in question and apply it to the facts of the case unless the result is something which cannot reasonably be supposed to have been intended by the legislature; but the rule is one which leaves a lot to the choice of the particular judge. In a great many cases it can plausibly be contended that there is more than one ordinary meaning in the context. In that event the judge may consider that there is sufficient doubt to bring the principles mentioned in the second quotation into play; but he may also conclude that there is no doubt that one of the meanings is the ordinary one. In cases which come before appellate tribunals it is by no means uncommon for different judges to express diametrically opposite views with regard to the ordinary meaning of a word or phrase,[19] and the same is true when

---

16. *Pinner v Everett* [1969] 3 All ER 257 at 258–9.
17. *Maunsell v Olins* [1975] AC 373 at 382.
18. *Jones v Director of Public Prosecutions* [1962] AC 635 at 662.
19. Eg *Newbury DC v Secretary of State for the Environment* [1981] AC 578, [1980] 1 All ER 731 where the House of Lords adopted an interpretation of the word 'repository' which Lawton LJ in the Court of Appeal had described as one which 'no literate person' would adopt: see [1979] 1 All ER 243 at 252, [1978] 1 WLR 1241 at 1253.

the question is whether the result of applying the ordinary meaning to the facts can or cannot reasonably be supposed to have been intended by the legislature. A decision on the interpretation of one statute generally cannot constitute a binding precedent with regard to the interpretation of another statute. The consequence is that a rule of interpretation, unlike most other common law rules, can never be rendered more specific by decisions on points of detail; it can only create other rules applicable to particular statutes. Rule (i) is liable to be stated in a variety of ways. The reference to context is comparatively new. That word does not occur in any of the statements of the literal and golden rules in the previous chapter; nor does it occur in the statement of Alderson B in *A-G v Lockwood*[20] which is frequently cited today:

> 'The rule of law I take it upon the construction of all statutes is, whether they be penal or remedial, to construe them according to the plain literal and grammatical meaning of the words in which they are expressed unless that construction leads to a plain and clear contradiction of the apparent purpose of the Act or to some palpable and evident absurdity.'

What is far more disconcerting is the fact that there are dicta flatly denying that the courts have any power to reject the natural or ordinary meaning of a word or phrase on the ground that it leads to some result which cannot reasonably be supposed to have been intended by the legislature. For example, in *R v City of London Court Judge* Lord Esher MR said:[1]

> 'If the words of an Act are clear, you must follow them, even though they lead to a manifest absurdity. The court has nothing to do with the question whether the legislature has committed an absurdity. In my opinion the rule has always been this—if the words of an Act admit of two interpretations, then they are not clear; and if one interpretation leads to an absurdity and the other does not, the court will conclude that the legislature did not intend to lead to an absurdity, and will adopt the other interpretation.'

The contrast between this passage and the concluding portion of Lord Reid's first quotation is striking enough, but its contrast with the following observation in another of Lord Reid's speeches is even more striking:

---

20. (1842) 9 M & W 378 at 398.
1. [1892] 1 QB 273 at 290.

'It is only where the words are absolutely incapable of a construction which will accord with the apparent intention of the provision and will avoid a wholly unreasonable result, that the words of the enactment must prevail.'[2]

This remark was part of the *ratio decidendi* of a tax case in which a majority of the House of Lords rejected the natural and ordinary meaning of statutory words in favour of a decidedly strained construction in order to avoid what was considered to be an absurd result which could not have been intended by the legislature. Remarks such as those of Lord Esher and Lord Reid cannot both be taken to represent the law and the preponderance of authority certainly favours Lord Reid. The precise nature of the absurdity required to bring the golden rule into play will be considered in Chapter 4.

The second of the three quotations from Lord Reid's speeches set out on page 37 comes from a case in which he entertained doubts about the meaning of the word 'premises' in s 18(5) of the Rent Act 1968. Was the word in the particular context limited to premises which were dwelling houses? There was a wide choice of meanings and no question of avoiding an absurdity produced by the application of the literal meaning. Accordingly, when answering the question raised in the affirmative, Lord Reid considered it was right to review the legislative history of the provision and to lean in favour of the construction involving the least interference with the common law. Although there is no fixed hierarchy of the rules of construction (or presumptions) to which Lord Reid was referring, we shall see in Chapter 7 that some are, in general, less compelling than others.

The third of the numbered quotations from Lord Reid's speeches refers to a rule rather than a principle in the sense in which those terms are used by Dworkin. It is an absolute prohibition on going beyond certain limits; the words must not be given a meaning they cannot, by any stretch of imagination, bear. This point was neatly put by Eyre CB in a case concerned with the construction of private documents.

'All latitude of construction must submit to this restriction: namely that the words may bear the sense which, by construction, is put upon them. If we step beyond this line, we no longer construe men's deeds, but make deeds for them.'[3]

The restriction marks the boundary between interpretation and alteration which has already been discussed.

It is not simply the paucity and generality of the legal rules which

---

2. *Luke v Inland Revenue Commrs* [1963] AC 557 at 577.
3. *Gibson and Johnson v Minet and Fector* (1791) H Bl 569 at 615.

distinguish statutory interpretation from other legal subjects such as criminal law, evidence or contract. The rules are of a different kind from those requiring that property must belong to another before there can be theft, or that there must be consideration or a seal to create a valid contract. The rules of statutory interpretation provide criteria for identifying legal rules, and belong to the category of 'secondary rules' of the legal system, to which H L A Hart assigns what he terms 'rules of recognition'.[4] A rule of this kind has a double aspect in that it is both a legal rule and a social practice. Seen from the perspective of the ordinary judge, the rules and principles of statutory interpretation are legally binding statements of the approach he should adopt, even if their content is more general and vaguer than other rules and principles of the legal system. The rules and principles for identifying the rules contained in a statutory enactment also form a social practice as to how lawyers should set about this task. The judiciary (and sometimes the legislator) establishes them according to the needs of the particular epoch and its view of the judiciary's proper constitutional role. They thus establish the respective competences of the courts and Parliament in the overall context of developing and changing the law. But, as in other constitutional contexts, the rules are not always stated with great precision and are often susceptible of diverging interpretations. It is the social practice aspect which explains the vagueness and the changing content of the rules and principles of statutory interpretation.

Judicial statements on statutory interpretation are thus not authoritative in quite the same way as in ordinary branches of substantive law. They may well be more like statements of attitude or approach, at best expressing principles rather than legal rules. The currently accepted practice is likely to change to a greater or lesser extent from epoch to epoch as the judges adapt to different constitutional climates. Even within a particular epoch there are, as has been seen, conflicts of opinion about the proper judicial role, and consequently about the rules and principles of statutory interpretation to be adopted. These features inevitably weaken the authority of particular statements about the rules and principles of statutory interpretation and indicate that they are frequently to be considered more as illustrations of current practice than as binding rules and principles of law. Thus the canons presented in this book should be viewed as expressing the current approach of the English judiciary to the interpretation of statutes. To this extent, Lord Wilberforce was right about the difference between statutory interpretation and other legal subjects.

---

4. *The Concept of Law* (Oxford, 1961) pp 92–3, 97–107; D N MacCormick, *H L A Hart* (London, 1981) pp 111–5.

E. COMMON LAW METHODS IN STATUTORY INTERPRETATION

Since statute and case-law are distinct sources of English law, it might be asked whether the ordinary common law methods of reasoning and of elaborating rules can be applied to statutes in the same way as to common law rules and principles. While statute and case-law are thus distinct, they interact in significant ways. Writing in 1908, Roscoe Pound suggested that there were four different ways in which the courts might deal with legislative innovation.[5] First, they might incorporate it fully into the body of the law and treat it as a source of principle higher than the common law. This approach would justify reasoning by analogy from statutes. Second, they might receive it fully into the law to be reasoned from by analogy as of equal status to common law rules and principles. Third, they might both refuse to accept it fully into the body of the law and refuse to reason by analogy, but might give it a liberal interpretation. Fourth, they might give statutes a strict construction and refuse to reason by analogy from them. Pound thought that the fourth hypothesis represented the common law of his day. Rupert Cross in *Precedent in English Law*[6] suggested that the second hypothesis applied to English law in 1977 in that 'a legislative innovation is received fully into the body of the law to be reasoned from by analogy in the same way as any other rule of law'.[7] However, this view has recently been doubted by P S Atiyah.[8] The question is whether statute law and the common law are to be conceived as separate divisions of English law to be handled distinctly. There is a significant amount of support in recent judicial statements for this view, at least in relation to some specific areas of the law. In *Shiloh Spinners Ltd v Harding*[9] Lord Wilberforce said:

> 'In my opinion where the courts have established a general principle of law or equity, and the legislature steps in with particular legislation in a particular area, it must, unless showing a contrary intention, be taken to have left the cases outside that area where they were under the influence of the general law.'

The presumption is for a minimum change to be effected by legislation in a common law area, in this case mortgages.

By contrast, where an area is substantially one of legislative cre-

---

5. 'Common Law and Legislation' 21 Harv L Rev 383 at 385 (1908).
6. (3rd edn, Oxford, 1977) pp 166–71.
7. Ibid, p 170.
8. 'Common Law and Statute Law' (1985) 48 MLR 1.
9. [1973] AC 691 at 725.

ation, the judges are reluctant to admit the use of common law principles to interpret or to supplement the legislative 'code'. In *Pioneer Aggregates (UK) Ltd v Secretary of State for the Environment*, Lord Scarman remarked:[10]

> 'Planning control is a creature of statute. It is an imposition in the public interest of restrictions on private rights of ownership of land . . . It is a field of law in which the courts should not introduce principles or rules derived from private law unless it be expressly authorised by Parliament or necessary in order to give effect to the purpose of the legislation. Planning law, though a comprehensive code imposed in the public interest, is, of course, based on land law. Where the code is silent or ambiguous, resort to the principles of private law (especially property and contract law) may be necessary so that the courts may resolve difficulties by application of common law or equitable principles. But such cases will be exceptional.'

Similarly, the care of children is governed by a large body of statute law and the courts have treated this as a 'code', so that it limits the scope of the equitable jurisdiction of wardship which can now be invoked only in rare cases not covered by the 'code'.[11] In such rare cases a common law power may be admitted to supplement the legislation, such as the power to exclude members of the public from a meeting where they were causing disorder, even though the statute required that the meeting be open to the public and had not provided for disruption caused by the public.[12] In a statutory area, reasoning by analogy within the statutory 'code' is perfectly acceptable by application of the general rule permitting the use of other statutes on the same subject as a guide to interpretation.[13]

While the approach expressed by Lord Wilberforce seems to suggest that a statute creates only rules and not principles in a common law area, the approach of Lord Scarman suggests that a statute may give rise to principles capable of justifying reasoning by analogy within a statutory 'code', but that the application of these principles is confined to statutes dealing with the same subject. Furthermore, legislative innovations can certainly be seen to give rise to rules which are

---

10. [1985] AC 132 at 140–1, [1984] 2 All ER 358 at 363.
11. *A v Liverpool City Council* [1982] AC 363 at 373 per Lord Wilberforce; *Re W (A Minor) (Wardship: Jurisdiction)* [1985] AC 791 at 796–7 per Lord Scarman and 807 per Lord Brightman.
12. *R v Brent HA, ex p Francis* [1985] QB 869, [1985] 1 All ER 74, infra, pp 121–2.
13. See *Pioneer Aggregates* and the discussion on the use of statutes on the same subject, infra, pp 148–50.

liberally interpreted if their purpose so requires and their wording permits it. As will be seen in Chapter 4, the courts do not necessarily permit the extension of a statute by interpretation to cover a case not provided for. As the *Jones* case showed,[14] even where a case is clearly within the mischief of the legislation, the courts may refuse to interpret the statute by analogy to cover it. All the same, they may be willing to bring new developments within the ambit of a provision, provided this does not do too much violence to the statutory words used.[15] But there are clearly limits to the possibilities of an expansive interpretation of a statutory rule.

Reasoning by analogy goes further than expansive interpretation by treating the statutory provision as an illustration of a principle which can be applied generally to other areas outside the scope of the statutory rule. It is clear that this does happen in some areas of the law. A statute which imposes a duty or prohibits certain actions may, in some cases, be treated as giving rise to civil liability on the part of the wrongdoer for breach of a statutory duty or to the unenforceability of a contract by reason of illegality, even where the statute contains no provisions to this effect and merely specifies a criminal penalty or no sanction at all. In other areas, as Atiyah has shown, such reasoning by analogy from a statute is harder to find, and not all judges use this method. All the same, he does note[16] that there are cases where a legislative intervention to abolish a common law rule has been treated by the courts as also abolishing the principle on which the rule rested, so that the use of the principle to justify reasoning by analogy is no longer possible, or so that a re-adjustment of other common law rules is required. Thus the Law Reform (Contributory Negligence) Act 1945 did not merely abolish the common law rule that the defendant needed to be solely to blame for a tortious loss, but also encouraged some judges to treat as abrogated the rule that a person was solely to blame if he had the last opportunity for avoiding the loss, since this latter rule had merely been a device for circumventing the harshness of the old common law rule.[17] Judges may see a trend in legislation which encourages them to perceive a change in common law principles and hence to develop common law rules in a new direction. Thus in *Erven Warnink BV v John Townsend & Sons (Hull) Ltd*,[18] Lord Diplock saw in recent legislation a trend towards demands for a higher standard of commercial probity which justified an expansion of the common law rules on

---

14. Supra, pp 18–19.
15. Infra, pp 50–2.
16. Op cit, pp 21–3.
17. *Davies v Swan Motor Co* [1949] 2 KB 291.
18. [1979] AC 731 at 743, [1979] 2 All ER 927 at 933.

the tort of passing off to include the use of misleading brand names. Similarly in *Universe Tankships Inc of Monrovia v International Transport Workers Federation*,[19] the provisions of the Trade Union and Labour Relations Act 1974 (as amended) conferred an immunity *in tort* for actions during a trade dispute. In a *restitution* action for money obtained by duress, the House of Lords accepted that those provisions, though not directly applicable, could provide guidance as to what constituted legitimate pressure by a union on an employer.[20]

Legislative innovation frequently acts, however, as a disincentive to judicial development of the law. Recent decisions have shown that the courts treat legislative activity in the field of consumer protection as a reason for not expanding the common law on exclusion clauses or unconscionability.[1]

Overall, judges are wary of treating statutes as generating principles which can be applied generally within the law. In some circumstances, this process is undoubtedly accepted as legitimate. But the mere fact that a rule is expressed in a statute does not, of itself, make reasoning by analogy appropriate. Appropriateness depends on the character of the statutory provision and of the common law which it is claimed to affect, as well as of the proper judicial role in the branch of law in question. All the same, it is hard to see how a radical distinction in legal reasoning can be maintained when common law and statute law interact. Where common law principles, such as those of natural justice, are used to help interpret a statute, it is difficult to imagine how one could have one method for treating statutory rules and another for the common law rules used to supplement them. The proper approach for both is simply that analogies are drawn where, in all the circumstances, they are appropriate.

F. CONCLUSION

The last section merely serves to emphasise the point that the rules and principles of interpretation and reasoning from statutes represent positions adopted by the judiciary concerning its constitutional role

19. [1983] 1 AC 366, [1982] 2 All ER 67.
20. See Lord Diplock, [1983] 1 AC at 385, Lord Cross at 391, and Lord Scarman at 401.
1. See especially *Photo Production Ltd v Securicor Transport Ltd* [1980] AC 827, [1980] 1 All ER 556; *National Westminster Bank plc v Morgan* [1985] AC 686, [1985] 1 All ER 821; cf *Levison v Patent Steam Co Ltd* [1978] QB 69 at 79 per Lord Denning MR. Legislative inaction may equally dissuade judicial action: eg *President of India v La Pintada Cia Navigacion SA* [1985] AC 104, [1984] 2 All ER 773.

vis-à-vis Parliament in the development of the law. Reasoning by analogy, even more than liberal interpretation, envisages the roles of the judge and the legislator as partners in the cooperative venture of reforming the law, much in the spirit of what Denning LJ advocated in *Magor and St Mellons RDC*. A more restrictive approach to analogy and to interpretation reflects the concern for the rule of law and the separation of powers mentioned by other judges.[2] In this view, the rule of law requires Parliament to state clearly what it intends, and the separation of powers requires the judge not to presume that he knows how best to complete the legislative scheme. In between these positions, a whole range of different views is possible. Nevertheless, the current tendencies among English judges would appear to incline away from the role proposed by Denning LJ and more towards the rule of law approach.

---

2. Notably Lord Simon of Glaisdale, supra, p 27 and Lord Diplock, supra, p 29.

Chapter 3
The basic rules stated

This chapter begins with a statement of the basic rules of English law concerning statutory interpretation. The statement is made with all the diffidence, hesitancy and reservation that the subject demands. No guidance is to be derived from a statute, for the Interpretation Act 1978, like its predecessor, contains no general principles, and various attempts to enact such principles have come to nothing. There are no binding judicial decisions on the subject of statutory interpretation generally as opposed to the interpretation of particular statutes; all that there is is a welter of judicial dicta which vary considerably in weight, age and uniformity. Naturally it is the last of these variables which confronts anyone attempting a coherent account of the subject with most difficulty. To quote from the first paragraph of the preface to the 12th edition of Maxwell *On the Interpretation of Statutes:*

> '*Maxwell* might well be sub-titled "The practitioners' armoury": it is, I trust, not taking too cynical a view of statutory interpretation in general, and this work in particular, to express the hope that counsel putting forward diverse interpretations of some statutory provision will each be able to find in *Maxwell* dicta and illustrations in support of his case.'

The practitioner's boon is the academic's bugbear. It shows no disrespect to the author and editor of that admirable work to say that Maxwell is useless for anyone hoping for a general view of the subject which has the remotest claim to coherence.[1] Invaluable as those dicta and illustrations must be to a protagonist in search of authority, they cannot all be right for the simple reason that a large proportion of them are mutually contradictory. The academic must chance his arm at least

---

1. A more systematic treatment is now to be found in Bennion's *Statutory Interpretation* (London, 1984).

to the extent of preferring some dicta to their opposites; but he owes it to his readers to make it clear when this has been done. He must also be on his guard against reading too much into the comparatively few dicta and illustrations which he selects.

It is submitted that the following is a reasonably brief and accurate statement of the rules of English statutory interpretation:

1. The judge must give effect to the grammatical and ordinary or, where appropriate, the technical meaning of words in the general context of the statute; he must also determine the extent of general words with reference to that context.
2. If the judge considers that the application of the words in their grammatical and ordinary sense would produce a result which is contrary to the purpose of the statute, he may apply them in any secondary meaning which they are capable of bearing.
3. The judge may read in words which he considers to be necessarily implied by words which are already in the statute and he has a limited power to add to, alter or ignore statutory words in order to prevent a provision from being unintelligible, absurd or totally unreasonable, unworkable, or totally irreconcilable with the rest of the statute.[2]
4. In applying the above rules the judge may resort to the aids to construction and presumptions mentioned in Chapters 5–7 of this book.

A very full statement of rules 1 and 2 is that of Lord Simon of Glaisdale in *Maunsell v Olins:*[3]

'. . . in statutes dealing with ordinary people in their everyday lives, the language is presumed to be used in its primary ordinary sense, unless this stultifies the purpose of the statute, or otherwise produces some injustice, absurdity, anomaly or contradiction, in which case some secondary ordinary sense may be preferred, so as to obviate the injustice, absurdity, anomaly or contradiction or fulfil the purpose of the statute: while, in statutes dealing with technical matters, words which are capable of both bearing an ordinary meaning and being terms of art in the technical matter of the legislation will presumptively bear their primary meaning as such terms of art (or, if they must necessarily be modified, some secondary meaning as terms of art).'

2. Per Lord Reid in *Federal Steam Navigation Co Ltd v Department of Trade and Industry* [1974] 2 All ER 97 at 100.
3. [1975] AC 373 at 391. The fact that it occurs in a dissenting speech in no way detracts from the authoritative nature of this statement which was made with the concurrence of Lord Diplock, the other dissentient in the case.

The first three rules are fully illustrated in the next chapter. In this chapter something will be said about the context of a statute, the admissibility of evidence concerning the meaning of statutory words and different kinds of meaning between which the courts must choose in interpreting those words.

A. CONTEXT

As we saw in discussing the intention of the legislature, the meaning of statutory words is determined not by reference to any subjective intentions of the legislators, but by reference to the sense which an informed legal interpreter would give to them in the context in which they are used. The context of statutory words is both internal and external. The internal context requires the interpreter to situate the disputed words within the section of which they are part and in relation to the rest of the Act. The external context involves determining the meaning from ordinary linguistic usage (including any special technical meanings), from the purpose for which the provision was passed, and from the place of the provision within the general scheme of statutory and common law rules and principles.

For some time the law relating to statutory interpretation was bedevilled by the notion that it was wrong for a court to look beyond the words with which it was immediately concerned if their meaning was clear when they were considered in isolation. Blackstone had said that recourse should only be had to the context if the words 'happen to be still dubious'[4] and the notion derived support from Tindal CJ's advice to the House of Lords in the *Sussex Peerage* case:

> 'if the words of the statute are in themselves precise and unambiguous, then no more can be necessary than to expound those words in that natural and ordinary sense . . . But if any doubt arises from the terms employed by the legislature, it has always been held a safe means of collecting that intention to call in aid the ground and cause of the making of the statute. . . .'[5]

It is difficult to believe that the notion of construction in complete isolation was ever taken wholly seriously, and we saw that Tindal CJ was not above relying on the second section of the Royal Marriages Act 1772 as support for his construction of the first. Nonetheless, even in

---

4. *Commentaries on the Laws of England* 1st edn, 1765, p 60.
5. Supra, p 14.

the 20th century, it has proved necessary for appellate courts to administer mild rebukes to judges for their isolationist approach to statutory construction.[6] However, today it is clear that the internal context includes all elements of the Act—other subsections, sections and schedules, as well as the long title and preamble (if any).[7]

In determining the external context, it has never been doubted that the date of a statute may be very relevant to its construction simply because the meaning of a word may change with the passage of time and the material time is generally said to be that at which the word was used. One of the stock examples is *The Longford*,[8] a case concerned with a private Act of William IV's reign which provided that 'no *action* in any of His Majesty's courts of law' should be brought against certain shipowners without a month's notice. The question was whether the word 'action' was apt to cover an Admiralty action *in rem* and Lord Esher gave the answer of the Court of Appeal in the following telling words:[9]

'The first point to be borne in mind is that the Act must be construed as if one were interpreting it the day after it was passed. . . . The word "action" mentioned in the section was not applicable, when the Act was passed, to the procedure of the Admiralty Court. Admiralty actions were then called "suits" or "causes"; moreover, the Admiralty Court was not called and was not one of His Majesty's Courts of Law.'

It is open to doubt whether this constitutes a rule of general application, or whether it is confined to the interpretation of Acts intended to apply only to a particular grievance current at the time of enactment. In the first edition of this book Cross took the former view,[10] whereas the present editors share the views of Bennion, Burrows, and Hurst that there is a general rule in favour of an 'updating' or 'ambulatory' approach, rather than an 'historical' one.[11]

The somewhat quaint statement that a statute is 'always speaking' appears to have originated in Lord Thring's exhortations to draftsmen concerning the use of the word 'shall': 'An Act of Parliament should be

---

6. See eg *Re Bidie* [1948] 2 All ER 995, CA.
7. See infra, pp 122–3.
8. (1889) 14 PD 34.
9. Ibid, at pp 36–7.
10. 1st edn, p 45. Both *The Longford* and the *Hanover* case fall into this category.
11. *Bennion*, s 146; J F Burrows, 'The Problem of Time in Statutory Interpretation' [1978] *New Zealand Law Journal* 253; D J Hurst, 'The Problem of the Elderly Statute' (1983) 3 *Legal Studies* 21; id, 'Palm Trees in the House of Lords—Some Further Thoughts on *Boland*'s case' [1983] Stat LR 142.

deemed to be always speaking and therefore the present or past tense should be adopted, and "shall" should be used as an imperative only, not as a future'.[12] But the proposition that an Act is always speaking is often taken to mean that a statutory provision has to be considered first and foremost as a norm of the current legal system, whence it takes its force, rather than just as a product of an historically defined Parliamentary assembly. It has a legal existence independently of the historical contingencies of its promulgation, and accordingly should be interpreted in the light of its place within the system of legal norms currently in force. Such an approach takes account of the viewpoint of the ordinary legal interpreter of today, who expects to apply ordinary current meanings to legal texts, rather than to embark on research into linguistic, cultural and political history, unless he is specifically put on notice that the latter approach is required.

At the very least, Lord Esher's words require serious qualification. First, the courts regularly apply a statutory provision to new developments in technology or society which come within its original purpose and wording. The former situation can be illustrated by *Royal College of Nursing of the United Kingdom v Department of Health and Social Security*.[13] The Abortion Act 1967 permitted the termination of a pregnancy 'by a registered medical practitioner' in certain circumstances. At the time, only surgical and intra-amniotic methods existed for terminating a pregnancy, and both required the continuous presence of a doctor. However, since 1971 a new, extra-amniotic method had become current, which involved inducing the abortion over a long period of up to 30 hours by the administration of a drug, prostaglandin. The Department of Health and Social Security advised that, as long as a doctor approved and started the process, a nurse could lawfully continue it, starting and regulating the supply of the drug. The Royal College of Nursing sought a declaration that this advice was incorrect, and that the Act did not protect the nurse in the application of extra-amniotic methods. By a majority, the House of Lords upheld the view of the Department. The majority of their Lordships reasoned that the new method came within the purpose of the Act, designed to liberalise legal abortions. The inclusion of a telephone within the notion of 'telegraph' in the Telegraph Act 1869,[14] or a microfilm within that of 'bankers books' in the Bankers Books Evidence Act 1879[15] are further examples of this process.

No one would suggest that a written constitution should be con-

---

12. *Practical Legislation*, p 82. See also *Ex p Pratt* (1884) 12 QBD 334 at 340.
13. [1981] AC 800, [1981] 1 All ER 545.
14. *Att-Gen v Edison Telephone Co* (1880) 6 QBD 244, CA.
15. *Barker v Wilson* [1980] 2 All ER 81, DC.

strued for all time as if the court were sitting the day after it was enacted, and, when considering the question whether the British North America Act 1869 empowered the Canadian legislature to abolish the right of appeal from Canadian courts to the Privy Council, Lord Jowett said:[16]

> 'It is, as their Lordships think, irrelevant that the question is one which might have seemed unreal at the date of the British North America Act. To such an organic statute the flexible interpretation must be given that changing circumstances require.'

Again, the use of general words such as 'reasonably practicable', as in Part I of the Health and Safety at Work etc Act 1974, necessarily implies that the courts have a power to adjust the application of an expression according to contemporary standards.

In the case of changes in society, the courts may go further. For example, section 12(1)(g) of the Rent and Mortgage Interest Restriction Act 1920[17] provided that:

> 'The expression "tenant" includes the widow of a tenant . . . who was residing with him at the time of his death, or where a tenant . . . leaves no widow, or is a woman, such member *of the tenant's family* so residing as aforesaid as may be decided in default of agreement by the county court.'

In 1950 the Court of Appeal decided, in *Gammans v Ekins*,[18] that the tenant's 'common law husband' who had had no children by her was not a member of her family within the meaning of the subsection in spite of a prolonged residence with her. In *Dyson Holdings Ltd v Fox*,[19] the same court held 25 years later that a tenant's childless 'common law wife' who had been residing with him for a long time when he died in 1961 was a member of his family. Bridge LJ said:

> 'If the language can change its meaning to accord with changing social attitudes, then a decision on the meaning of a word in a statute before such a change should not continue to bind thereafter, at all events in a case where the courts have constantly affirmed that the word is to be understood in its ordinary accepted meaning.'[20]

---

16. *Att-Gen for Ontario v Att-Gen for Canada* [1947] AC 127 at 154.
17. Now Rent Act 1977, Sch 1, para 3.
18. [1950] 2 KB 328, [1950] 2 All ER 140.
19. [1976] QB 503, [1975] 3 All ER 1030.
20. [1976] QB at 513.

A further example is *Williams & Glyn's Bank v Boland*[1] where it was held that a wife was a person 'in actual occupation' of a house where she lived with her husband, within s 70(1)(g) of the Land Registration Act 1925, even if she would not have been so considered in 1925. According to Lord Wilberforce, the interpretation had to be made 'in the light of current social conditions'.

An updating of more doubtful validity occurs when the purpose of the Act is reformulated in the light of the current state of the law. *R v Brittain*[2] concerned the Forcible Entry Act 1381 (now repealed), which provided that 'none may henceforth make entry into any lands or tenements, but in case where entry is given by the law; and in such case not with strong hand nor with multitude of people'. It was part of a series of measures in the 14th and 15th centuries designed to ensure that people did not settle land disputes by force, and to punish those who took the law into their own hands. For 590 years, the statute had never been applied to a situation where there was no intention to occupy the premises or to assert a legal right to the land. Yet in 1971 the Court of Appeal treated the statute as a measure designed to prevent public disorder and applied it to convict a number of people who had gatecrashed a party without any intention of occupying the premises or claiming title to them. Other attempts to redefine the purpose of a statutory provision in the light of current legal policies have been less well received,[3] and this approach must be considered as still controversial.

The adoption of either an historical or an updating approach not only affects the meaning given to statutory words, but may also have an important bearing on the question whether the court should depart from their ordinary meaning on the ground that adherence to it would lead to results contrary to the purpose of the enactment. This was made very clear by the decision of the House of Lords (affirming the decision of the Court of Appeal) in *A-G v Prince Ernest Augustus of Hanover*.[4] In 1955 the Prince sought a declaration that he was a British subject by virtue of his lineal descent from the Electoress Sophia of Hanover. The validity of his claim depended on the construction of a statute of Queen Anne's reign which provided that the Electoress and

---

1. [1981] AC 487, [1980] 2 All ER 408; D J Hurst, supra note 12.
2. [1972] 1 QB 357.
3. See especially *Ahmad v ILEA* [1978] QB 31, where Scarman LJ proposed to interpret s 30 of the Education Act 1944 in the light of current race relations legislation and of the European Convention on Human Rights of 1950, whereas Orr LJ kept to the original meaning of the section in 1944. See also *R v Barnet London Borough Council, ex p Nilish Shah*, infra pp 93–4.
4. [1957] AC 436, [1957] 1 All ER 49.

the issue of her body 'and all persons lineally descended from her *born or hereafter to be born* be, and shall be deemed to be, natural born subjects of this kingdom'. The preamble stated that: 'to the end that the said princess and the heirs of her body and all persons lineally descended from her may be encouraged to become acquainted with the laws and constitutions of this realm it is just and highly reasonable that they *in your Majesty's lifetime* should be naturalised'. The preamble could be invoked in support of an argument that the words 'in your Majesty's lifetime' should be read into the enacting part of the statute after the words 'hereafter to be born.' This argument was accepted by the trial judge, Vaisey J, who refused to make the declaration sought by the Prince. Vaisey J took the view that it is not permissible to take account of the preamble when the enacting words are clear but, in this instance, he thought them unclear because they led to absurd results:[5]

> 'To suppose that Parliament thought that every descendant, however remote in time or distant in kinship of the Electoress, ought to study English law is really rather absurd, however salutary the topic would have been to the immediate successors of Queen Anne.'

The Court of Appeal also commented on the absurd effects of the statute in the 20th century:[6]

> 'If the construction of the Act for which the plaintiff contends is the right one, it would follow that the German Kaiser Wilhelm II was a British subject and that there are some four hundred persons scattered about Europe who are entitled to British nationality by virtue of this statute . . .'

But the Court of Appeal held that Prince Ernest was a British subject because the question whether the enacting words led to an absurdity was to be determined by the conditions prevailing when the statute was passed. The House of Lords affirmed the decision of the Court of Appeal in favour of the Prince:[7]

> 'The question is one of interpretation, and it is not in doubt that the Act must be construed as it would have been construed immediately after it became law.'

Like *The Longford*,[8] this case was concerned with a statute remedying

---

5. [1955] Ch 440 at 449.
6. [1956] Ch 188 at 216 per Romer LJ. It seems to follow that the Kaiser could have been prosecuted for treason after the 1914 war.
7. [1957] AC at 465 per Lord Normand.
8. Supra, p 49.

a problem specific to a particular time, and it is doubtful whether this affirmation of the historical approach can be taken as applying to the interpretation of all statutes.

The Hanover case is of special importance on account of the views expressed in the House of Lords concerning the use that may be made of a preamble when there is one, and further reference is made to this aspect of the decision in Chapter 5. The case is also important because of the broad views taken in the House of Lords, notably by Viscount Simonds and Lord Somervell concerning the context of a statute. They suggest that account may be taken of the general context, including the purpose of the statute, in determining the meaning of the statutory provision before the court in the first instance, and not merely at a later stage, should it become necessary to do so on account of the ambiguity of the provision. The remarks are to some extent revolutionary and no apology is made for quoting them at length. Viscount Simonds said:[9]

'. . . words, and particularly general words, cannot be read in isolation, their colour and content are derived from their context. So it is that I conceive it to be my right and duty to examine every word of a statute in its context, and I use "context" in its widest sense, which I have already indicated as including not only other enacting provisions of the same statute, but its preamble, the existing state of the law, other statutes *in pari materia*, and the mischief which I can, by those and other legitimate means, discern the statute was intended to remedy.'

Lord Somervell said:[10]

'It is unreal to proceed as if the court looked first at the provision in dispute without knowing whether it was contained in a Finance Act or a Public Health Act. The title and the general scope of the Act constitute the background of the contest. When a court comes to the Act itself, bearing in mind any relevant extraneous matters, there is, in my opinion, one compelling rule. The whole or any part of the Act may be referred to and relied on. It is, I hope, not disrespectful to regret that the subject was not left where Sir John Nicholl left it in 1826.

"The key to the opening of every law is the reason and spirit of the law—it is the '*animus imponentis*', the intention of the lawmaker, expressed in the law itself, taken as a whole. Hence, to arrive at the true meaning of any particular phrase

---

9. [1957] AC at 461.
10. Ibid at 473. The citation from Sir John Nicholl is from *Brett v Brett* (1826) 3 Add 210 at 216. 'Purview' is an old word meaning the enacting provisions of an Act.

in a statute, that particular phrase is not to be viewed, detached from its context in the statute: it is to be viewed in connection with its whole context—meaning by this as well the title and preamble as the purview, or enacting part, of the statute."'

Viscount Simonds's words were cited by Lord Upjohn in his speech in favour of the majority decision of the House of Lords in *Director of Public Prosecutions v Schildcamp*,[11] a case which shows that the place in a statute occupied by a particular provision may be decisive with regard to its construction. Section 332 of the Companies' Act 1948 appeared among a group of sections under the cross-heading 'Offences antecedent to or in course of Winding-Up'. Section 332(1) provided that 'If *in the course of the winding-up* of a company it appears that any business has been carried on with intent to defraud creditors . . . or for a fraudulent purpose' the court might declare that some of its officers were personally responsible for its debts. Section 332(3) read: 'Where any business of a company is carried on with such intent or for such purpose as is mentioned in subsection (1) of this section, every person who is knowingly a party to the carrying on of the business in manner aforesaid, shall be liable on conviction on indictment to imprisonment . . .' Was it an essential prerequisite of a conviction under subsection (3) that a winding-up order should have been made? The answer of the majority was in the affirmative.

The above discussion justifies us in regarding the context of a statutory provision as including the whole of the statute in which it is contained, title and preamble, if any, as well as the enacting parts; the place occupied by the provision within the statute; other statutes on the same subject; the circumstances in which the statute was passed, and its purpose. A few words may be added about this last.

The significance of the purpose of the statute in the sense of the mischief to be remedied and the remedy provided has of course been appreciated since the days of *Stradling v Morgan* and *Heydon's* case.[12] It will have been observed, however, that Viscount Simonds spoke of ascertaining the mischief which the statute was intended to remedy from the whole enactment (including the preamble), the existing state of the law, other statutes and 'other legitimate means'. This was a reference to the restrictions to be discussed in Chapter 6 on the use which the courts may make of such extrinsic materials as reports of committees and Parliamentary debates. These restrictions, coupled with the almost total absence of preambles in modern statutes, mean that the courts' opportunities of appreciating to the full the purpose of

---

11. [1971] AC 1 at 23.
12. Supra, pp 9–10.

complicated legislation is limited. At the other extreme, there is a danger that references to the purpose of a statute will become trivial simply because they are so obvious. There is not much point in exhorting a judge to keep in mind the purpose of the generality of the provisions in such statutes as the Offences Against the Person Act 1861, the Theft Acts 1968 and 1978, and the Criminal Damage Act 1971. They are all aimed at the suppression of various types of crime. A further difficulty arises from the multifarious nature of many statutes. One Act often deals with a multitude of subjects and, even when it is confined to a single subject, it may deal with many aspects of it. It is inept to speak of 'the purpose' of Acts such as the Companies Act 1985 or most Local Government or Finance Acts. It is only possible to seek out the purpose of particular provisions and, even when this has been done, it may be necessary to recognise that a single provision has more than one purpose.

Subject to reservations such as those which have just been expressed, it would be difficult to exaggerate the importance of the bearing which the purpose of statutes or statutory provisions has upon their interpretation. The significance of the speeches in the *Hanover* case lies in their recognition of the fact that the purpose is something to be taken into account in arriving at the ordinary meaning of a provision and not, as the words of Tindal CJ in the *Sussex Peerage* case suggest, merely something to be considered 'if any doubt arises from the terms employed by the legislature'.[13] The notion that the ordinary meaning of statutory words is something to be arrived at by a purely semantic process or, at most, with the aid of the other enacting parts of the statute in which they occur, has been finally exorcised. This does not mean that the purpose of the statute has no bearing on the resolution of doubt in cases in which the courts are confronted with a choice of ordinary meanings, or a choice between the primary and secondary meaning of a word. The purpose is material at two stages of the judge's deliberations, that at which he enquires whether the words are 'in themselves precise and unambiguous', and that at which, having answered this question in the negative, he is seeking to resolve doubts arising from the terms employed by the legislature. To put the same point in a different way, the mischief rule is both a primary and a secondary canon of interpretation.[14]

This distinction is subtle but not, it is believed, over-subtle. It is also difficult to illustrate from the *ipsissima verba* of judges for, on the whole, judges are not accustomed to give details of every stage of their

---

13. Supra, p 14.
14. See per Lord Simon of Glaisdale in *Maunsell v Olins* [1975] AC 373 at 385.

reasoning when deciding a point of interpretation, and the attempt to subdivide their reasoning into stages would often be unreal. It is frequently perfectly right and proper for a judge to begin by saying that he has had doubts concerning which of two meanings is the correct one for the purpose in hand, and then to express a preference for one of them on a variety of grounds including, in some cases, the purpose of the particular provision. This can be illustrated by *Bank of Scotland v Grimes*,[15] where the defendant and her husband took out a loan for 25 years secured by an endowment mortgage. They failed to keep up the interest payments and the bank sought possession of the house. Section 8(1) of the Administration of Justice Act 1973 empowered the court to grant relief to a mortgagor who 'is entitled or is to be permitted to pay the principal sum secured by instalments or otherwise to defer payment of it in whole or in part'. Since, under an endowment mortgage, there is no obligation to repay the principal until the end of the loan period, the county court judge held that the mortgage agreement could not be said to contain an entitlement to defer payment of the whole or part of the principal within the meaning of s 8(1).

In the Court of Appeal, Sir John Arnold P confessed that he was unable to make sense of part of the subsection. Nevertheless, the purpose of the legislation was clearly to provide a measure of relief to those persons who found themselves in temporary financial difficulties and thus unable to meet their commitments under a mortgage. This purpose applied as much to an endowment mortgage as to an instalment mortgage. Accordingly both he and Griffiths LJ concluded that, however obscure its wording, s 8(1) applied to enable the court to grant relief in the case of an endowment mortgage.

On other occasions, it will be equally right and proper simply to say that such and such a meaning is the natural one in the context and to refer to the purpose as one of the reasons for the conclusion. For example, *Mandla v Dowell Lee*[16] concerned the interpretation of the word 'ethnic' in the definition of a racial group against whom discrimination was not lawful under s 1(1)(b) of the Race Relations Act 1976. The headmaster of a private school had refused to admit a boy who was an orthodox Sikh and so wore long hair under a turban, unless he removed the turban and had short hair like the rest of the boys in the school. Since the Sikhs were not a race separate from other Punjabis, it was argued that no discrimination was being made by reference to 'colour, race, nationality or ethnic or national origins'. Lord Fraser of Tullybelton giving the judgment of the House of Lords held that

15. [1985] 2 All ER 254.
16. [1983] 2 AC 548, [1983] 1 All ER 1062.

'ethnic' was not limited to strictly racial or biological characteristics in current ordinary language. It had a racial flavour, but was used to include other characteristics commonly thought of as being associated with a common racial origin and making a group distinct. The Sikh community had such a distinctive identity. He then went on to show how this interpretation fitted the purpose of the Act and the International Convention on the Elimination of All Forms of Racial Discrimination to which the United Kingdom was a signatory.

When the purpose of the statute is called in aid to resolve an ambiguity, it has the force of a mere presumption that a construction which tends to suppress the mischief and advance the remedy is to be preferred to one that does not have these effects. This is a presumption which is liable to be defeated by other presumptions, and, in criminal cases, it frequently is defeated by the presumption in favour of a strict construction of penal statutes.[17]

B. EVIDENCE

The ordinary meaning of words, a matter of obvious concern to the law of interpretation, is a question of fact. Thus, in *Brutus v Cozens*,[18] the defendant was charged with an offence under s 5 of the Public Order Act 1936 on the ground that he had used 'insulting behaviour' whereby a breach of the peace was likely to be occasioned in a public place. To the annoyance of the spectators, he had interrupted play in a match at the Wimbledon Tennis Championships by going onto the court. His action was a protest against the participation of a South African player in the tournament, but the prosecution's case was that it was the spectators who had been insulted. The magistrates dismissed the case on the ground that the defendant's behaviour had not been 'insulting'. The Divisional Court reversed their decision because what the defendant had done evinced disrespect or contempt for the rights of others which reasonable people would foresee was likely to cause a protest. The House of Lords restored the decision of the magistrates on the ground that it is incorrect to say that conduct evincing a disrespect or contempt for the rights of others is always insulting and, the question being one of fact, the magistrates were entitled to decide the case as they did. Like many of the cases concerned with error of law in

---

17. See infra, Chapter 7.
18. [1973] AC 854, [1972] 2 All ER 1297. See A Briggs, 'Judges, juries and the meaning of words' (1985) 5 *Legal Studies* 314.

administrative law, this case shows the way in which the characteri-sation of a question of interpretation as one of fact rather than law is used to delimit the reviewing powers of a superior court.[19]

But, although the meaning of ordinary words is a question of fact, it is very far from being an ordinary fact for legal purposes. In the first place one is apt to think of questions of fact as something upon which evidence can be called on each side. This is certainly not the law of statutory interpretation so far as the ordinary meaning of words is concerned. In *Marquis Camden v Inland Revenue Commrs*[20] the evi-dence of a valuer with regard to the meaning of 'a nominal rent' was held to have been inadmissible, Phillimore LJ disposing of the matter with the remark that 'it is enough to say that in construing a modern statute, not dealing with the particular customs of a particular locality, or with the practice of a particular trade, but of general application, evidence such as is sought to be adduced in this case is inadmissible'.[1] Lord Esher stated the theoretical position with regard to the admissibi-lity of evidence concerning the meaning of words on questions of interpretation when he said:[2]

'If the Act is directed to dealing with matters affecting everybody generally, the words used have the meaning attached to them in the common and ordinary use of language. If the Act is one passed with reference to a particular trade, business, or trans-action, and words are used as everybody conversant with that trade, business or transaction knows and understands to have a particular meaning in it, then the words are to be construed as having that particular meaning, though it may differ from the common or ordinary meaning of the words.'

These remarks come from a case in which the question was whether the power conferred upon justices by s 65 of the Highway Act 1835 to direct trees near the highway to be 'pruned or lopped' was confined to directions to cut off lateral branches or whether it extended to 'topping'. It was held that the justices' powers did not extend that far. Evidence had been called on the difference between lopping and topping, but it was said to be unnecessary because every countryman is familiar with the distinction. It may therefore be assumed that evi-dence of the ordinary meaning of statutory words is theoretically

---

19. See generally J Beatson, 'Judicial Review for Error of Law' (1984) 4 Oxford JLS 22; *Edwards v Bairstow* [1956] AC 14 at 33–6; *R v Hillingdon LBC, ex p Puhlhofer* [1986] AC 484, infra, pp 79–81.
20. [1914] 1 KB 641.
1. Ibid, at 650.
2. *Unwin v Hanson* [1891] 2 QB 115 at 119.

inadmissible,[3] although it may be received in practice comparatively frequently. When it is agreed or contended that statutory words have a technical meaning, evidence with regard to that meaning is unquestionably admissible, and it should generally be preferred to information gleaned from other sources such as dictionaries.[4] Expert evidence may well be admissible to determine the meaning of a statute giving the force of law to the provisions of a treaty originally written in another language.[5] Where words have changed their meaning, their original sense will be determined principally from dictionaries based on historical principles.

The second reason why the meaning of ordinary words is no ordinary question of fact is that it is the subject of judicial notice. This has at least two highly significant consequences. The first is that, although the direct evidence of witnesses concerning the ordinary meaning of statutory words is inadmissible, recourse may be had to all the other sources of information which a judge may tap when considering whether a fact is one of which judicial notice should be taken. These include dictionaries. To return to *Mandla v Dowell Lee*,[6] the Court of Appeal had held that 'ethnic' required a common racial characteristic, and both Lord Denning MR and Kerr LJ referred to numerous dictionaries to justify their interpretation. In the House of Lords, Lord Fraser of Tullybelton also referred to a wide range of dictionaries, particularly the 1972 Supplement to the Oxford English Dictionary, in support of a wider meaning. However, the dictionaries were not treated as authoritative, and Lord Fraser found the definition in the 1972 Supplement, which defined 'ethnic' as pertaining to 'common racial, cultural, religious or linguistic characteristics', as too loose. Oliver LJ remarked in the Court of Appeal that, 'I doubt whether one can obtain anything but the most general assistance from dictionaries'.[7]

Textbooks and the practice of the business community or conveyancers may be called in aid on similar principles. Where they are relevant assistance may also be gained from historical works and purely literary sources. In *London and North Eastern Rail Co v Berriman*,[8] for instance, a will of 1587 and Milton's *Paradise Lost* were cited

---

3. Eg *R v Staniforth, R v Jordan* [1977] AC 699. The difficulty is that the distinction between an ordinary and a technical meaning is not all that easy to draw.

4. *Prophet v Platt Brothers & Co Ltd* [1961] 2 All ER 644; *Central Press Photos Ltd v Department of Employment and Productivity* [1970] 3 All ER 775.

5. See eg *Fothergill v Monarch Airlines Ltd*, infra pp 163–4.

6. Supra, pp 57–8. For the Court of Appeal decision see [1983] QB 1.

7. [1983] QB 1 at 15.

8. [1946] AC 278, [1946] 1 All ER 255.

to the House of Lords to help them decide the question whether a railway worker was engaged in 'repairing' within the meaning of rules made under the Railway Employment Prevention of Accidents Act 1900 when engaged on the routine oiling and maintenance of the apparatus in a signal box.

The other highly significant consequence of the ordinary meanings of statutory words being the subject of judicial notice is that decisions with regard to them, unlike other decisions on questions of fact, become binding precedents so far as the construction of the statute in question is concerned. As Kerr LJ remarked in *R v London Transport Executive, ex p Greater London Council*,[9]

'The interpretation of the intention of Parliament as expressed in our statutes is a matter for the courts. Once the meaning of an Act of Parliament has been authoritatively interpreted, at any rate by the Judicial Committee of the House of Lords as our highest tribunal, that interpretation is the law, unless and until it is thereafter changed by Parliament.'

In that case, the Divisional Court simply applied to a different package of measures designed to secure a similar object, namely lower fares on public transport in London, the interpretation given to the Transport (London) Act 1969 by the House of Lords in the previous year.[10] However, while a judicial decision may count as a precedent on the interpretation of the statute in question, it will not necessarily be authoritative for the interpretation of a consolidating statute which subsequently re-enacts the provision, unless the wording is unaltered.[11]

There is a further reason, not directly connected with the meaning of words, why the practice of taking judicial notice is of great importance in relation to statutory interpretation. The courts' powers of investigating the purpose of a statute are restricted by the fact that there are certain types of evidence, such as Parliamentary debates, which may not be considered.

'In this country we do not refer to the legislative history of an enactment as they do in the United States of America. We do not look at the explanatory memoranda which preface the Bills

---

9. [1983] QB 484 at 490. Even if the House of Lords has laid down an authoritative interpretation, it may sometimes overrule its previous decision: see, eg *R v Shivpuri* [1986] 2 All ER 334, *infra*, p 176.
10. *Bromley London Borough Council v Greater London Council* [1983] 1 AC 768; [1982] 1 All ER 129.
11. See *supra*, pp 6–7.

before Parliament. We do not have recourse to the pages of Hansard. All that the courts can do is to take judicial notice of the previous state of the law and of other matters generally known to well-informed people.'[12]

C. THE DIFFERENT KINDS OF MEANING

In the last chapter interpretation was spoken of as the process by which the courts determine the meaning of a statutory provision for the purpose of applying it to the situation before them.[13] Something must now be said about the different kinds of meaning with which this process is concerned.[14] Distinctions are often drawn between ordinary and fringe meanings, primary and secondary meanings, and 'literal' and 'strained' meanings. It is useful to clarify these terms.

It is assumed that when judges speak, as they frequently do, about the 'ordinary' or 'natural' meaning of words and phrases they have in mind the meaning which would be attached to those words and phrases by the normal speaker of English. This is taken to have been the meaning intended by the draftsman or, after due allowance has been made for the metaphor, by Parliament. It is not uncommon for a judge to ask himself the direct question what the ordinary man would understand by the words; but there are limits to the utility of this process in the case of disputed interpretation because everything depends on the context and there is often a choice of ordinary meanings. For example, s 3(1) of the Extradition Act 1870 provides that 'a fugitive criminal shall not be surrendered if the offence in respect of which his surrender is demanded is one *of a political character*'. If the ordinary man were asked the meaning of the words 'an offence of a political character', he might, after a good deal of prompting, finish up by saying 'an offence committed as part of a plan to overthrow a government': but what if the offence were attempted murder of an official of the regime to be overthrown committed while he was on a visit to the country requesting extradition? Having been told that attempted murder is an offence for which extradition can be sought and, if the offence is of a political

---

12. *Escoigne Properties Ltd v Inland Revenue Commrs* [1958] AC 549 at 566 per Lord Denning.
13. Supra, p 30.
14. The best introduction to this subject for lawyers is provided by the articles on 'Language and the Law' by Professor Glanville Williams in 61 LQR 71, 179, 293, 384 and 62 LQR 387 (1945–6), and his 'The Meaning of Literal Interpretation' (1981) 131 NLJ 1128, 1149. See also *Bennion*, Part XXI.

character, refused, would the ordinary man say 'for the purposes of the Extradition Act the offence must have been part of a plan to overthrow the government of the state requesting extradition in order that it should be an offence of a political character?' In *R v Governor of Pentonville Prison, ex p Cheng*,[15] Lord Simon of Glaisdale answered this question in the negative. He was confident that the most harassed commuter from Clapham would say 'of course the offence was of a political character'. But Lord Simon's was a dissenting speech and the effect of the majority decision is that, for the purposes of s 3(1) of the 1870 Act 'offence of a political character' means an offence designed to overthrow the government of the requesting state.

The ordinary meaning of a term may be a question of fact, albeit a somewhat special one, but the construction of a statute is a question of law and an issue with regard to the choice of ordinary meanings in a particular context is concerned with statutory construction. The judge takes judicial notice of ordinary meanings and chooses the one which he considers to be the most appropriate in the context.The normal speaker of English is not often of much assistance with regard to the choice, although he may have rendered yeoman service in indicating what were possible and impossible ordinary meanings just as he renders yeoman service as the yardstick of statutory interpretation, if that be the right word, where there is no problem simply because there is no possibility of a choice of meanings.[16]

Nothing need be said at this stage about the distinction between ordinary and technical meanings, but something must be said about the problem of 'fringe meaning' and the cognate problem of the restrictions to be placed on the interpretation of general words. Both are problems in defining the scope of any ordinary or specialised meaning. Problems of fringe meaning are sometimes spoken of as 'problems of the penumbra', the point being that, in the case of a great many words, there is no doubt about the hard core of their meanings, but different views may well be taken on the question whether the word is applicable to things or situations outside that hard core. No one doubts that a chair is furniture, but what about linoleum? A fully equipped motor-car is certainly a vehicle, but what if the engine and wheels are removed? Is a bicycle a carriage? Different minds may take different views concerning the answer to these and countless similar

---

15. [1973] AC 931 at 951.
16. In 'The Theory of Legal Interpretation' 12 *Harvard LR* 417, 418 (1899), Holmes says: 'But the normal speaker of English is merely a special variety, a literary form, so to speak, of our old friend the prudent man'. In the case of statutory interpretation, the existence of a legal context which can sometimes be very complicated makes the analogy somewhat questionable.

questions. In a great many cases the answer will of course vary according to the context in which the problem arises and the courts will be
guided by the object of the legislation they are considering, but very
frequently the judge can do little more than say that a line has to be
drawn somewhere and that he has decided to draw it beyond or short of
the facts of the case before him.

Fringe meaning raises the question how far words extend in ordinary
language as well as in law. There is the converse question, usually,
though by no means always, an exclusively legal one, of whether any
limit should be placed upon the generality of statutory words. We have
already had an example of this kind of question in *R v Horsham JJ, ex p
Farquarson*,[17] where the general power to postpone the publication of
a report of proceedings in court under the Contempt of Court Act 1981
had to be restricted. The problem is, however, frequently solved by
recourse to very strong presumptions, such as the presumption that
statutes do not, in the absence of express provision, deprive an accused
of the general defences to a criminal charge, or to less strong presumptions such as the presumption that *mens rea* is required as part of the
definition of every crime. No statutory crime is defined in such a way as
to admit in ordinary language of such defences as insanity, duress and
necessity, but it has never been contended that these defences are not
available. Quite a lot of statutory crimes are defined in absolute terms,
but it is by no means uncommon for the courts to imply a requirement
of guilty knowledge. The problem of the limitations, if any, to be
placed upon general words is not exclusively a legal one for we shall see
in Chapter 5 that there is an important rule of language, the *ejusdem
generis* rule (or *of the same kind* rule), which restricts the apparently
general effect of words such as 'or other' where these follow words of
limited meaning.

The distinction between primary and secondary meaning turns on
that between usual and less usual meanings. Many words and phrases
have more than one usual meaning since allowance has to be made for
a lot of different contexts. But a time comes when it is permissible to
say that, though a word is capable of bearing such and such meaning,
that meaning is unusual, ie secondary. As Professor Glanville Williams
has put it, whereas the primary meaning is the most obvious or central
meaning of the words, a secondary meaning is 'a meaning that can be
coaxed out of the words by argument'.[18] For example, the statement 'it
happened by accident' has a number of usual meanings. In criminal law
it may mean either that the accused did not intend the harm or else that

---

17. Supra, pp 4–5.
18. 131 NLJ at 1129.

he neither intended nor was guilty of negligence with regard to it. In industrial law an employee's injury may be said to have been an 'accident arising out of and in the course of his employment' even though it was deliberately inflicted, as when thugs murder a cashier while robbing him,[19] or pupils murder their schoolmaster.[20] But, if someone says 'X inherited a fortune by accident', meaning 'so many contingencies in the way of sudden deaths of relations had to occur that the settlor cannot be said to have intended X to inherit anything', the reply might well be, 'I see what you mean but your use of the word "accident" is rather odd.' 'He acquired a fortune by the accident of his birth' is a statement involving the use of the word accident in what must now be regarded as its secondary meaning of 'chance', although etymologically the word means 'anything that happens'; but, if someone were to say 'X's winning the race was more of an accident than Y's coming second', the reply would have to be 'you are giving the word accident a meaning it will not bear. You should say "the odds against X coming first were higher than those against Y coming second."'

The distinction between the different usual meanings of words and phrases is important for interpreters of statutes because they have to decide which sense is most appropriate in the particular context. The distinction between usual or ordinary meaning on the one hand, and secondary meaning on the other hand, is important for interpreters of statutes because, from time to time, they have to opt for a secondary meaning on account of the inconvenience, injustice or absurdity of applying any of the primary meanings to the situation before them. The question whether a particular 'interpretation' gives the words a meaning they will not bear is crucial because to do that is not interpretation; but there is a no-man's land between interpretation and making statutory provisions not made by the legislature where words are 'read in' to a section of a statute.

'Ordinary' and 'primary' meaning are often used as synonyms for the 'literal' or 'grammatical' meaning of words, as in the phrase 'literal rule' which figured in Chapter 1. But, when applied to the construction of statutes, 'literal' is often used pejoratively. Then it is the meaning which results from giving to each word an ordinary meaning without much reference to the context and applying the provision to a particular situation without any regard to its purpose. Take, for example, s 8 of the Road Traffic Act 1972. It read in part as follows:

---

19. *Nisbet v Rayne and Burn* [1910] 2 KB 689; cf *West Bromwich Building Society Ltd v Townsend* [1983] ICR 257 for a similar approach to the Health and Safety at Work etc Act 1974.

20. *Trim Joint District School Board of Management v Kelly* [1914] AC 667, HL.

'A constable in uniform may require any person *driving or attempting to drive* a motor vehicle on a road or other public place to provide a specimen of breath for a breath test there or nearby if the constable has reasonable cause (*a*) to suspect him of having alcohol in his body. . . .'

The literal meaning of this provision is that, if cases of attempted driving are excluded, a constable can only make the request for a breath test while the driver is driving. It would therefore have been open to a motorist stopped by a constable who had every reason to suspect him of having alcohol in his body to retort with the subsequent blessing of the court, 'Too late, I am stinking drunk but I am not, by any stretch of the imagination, "driving".'[1]

Section 38(1) of the Children and Young Persons Act 1933 enables a child of tender years to give unsworn evidence in criminal cases. The following is the proviso:

'Provided that where evidence admitted by virtue of this section is given on behalf of the prosecution the accused shall not be liable to be convicted of the offence unless that evidence is corroborated by some other material evidence in support thereof implicating him.'

Unquestionably the effect of this proviso, 'literally construed', is that a conviction for burglary would have to be quashed notwithstanding the fact that three adult witnesses gave overwhelming evidence against the accused, if the prosecution had called a child to give uncorroborated unsworn evidence on some minor point. Few people, whether or not they happen to be lawyers, would dissent from Lord Diplock's statement that 'so preposterous an intention cannot reasonably be ascribed to Parliament'.[2] Some such words as 'in consequence of such evidence' must be read in after the word 'offence'. The House of Lords has held that the object of the proviso is to prevent a conviction based on nothing but the unsworn evidence of children, accordingly the words 'other evidence' must be given the slightly restricted meaning of 'evidence admissible otherwise than by virtue of this section.'[3]

So far as appears from reported cases no one has tried to argue that a conviction is unlawful if it resulted from a trial at which any uncorroborated evidence had been given by an unsworn child of tender years however peripheral that evidence may have been; but when a wholly

---

1. Cf W Twining & D Miers, *How to do Things with Rules* (2nd edn, London, 1982) p 7: 'The Case of the Legalistic Child'.

2. *Director of Public Prosecutions v Hester* [1973] AC 296 at 323.

3. *Director of Public Prosecutions v Hester*, supra; *Cross on Evidence*, 6th edn, p 211.

different provision was under consideration, the Appellate Division of the Supreme Court of Alberta was once confronted with an argument in favour of a construction no less literal. The case concerned the construction of a bye-law directing that 'all drug shops shall be closed at 10 pm on each and every day of the week'. It was contended for the defendants that there was no infringement if a drug shop were closed at 10 pm and opened a few minutes later on the same day. This contention was dismissed with the contempt it deserved and with the observation that no-one but a lawyer would ever have thought of imputing such a meaning to the bye-law.[4] Presumably this is the kind of thing which Stephen J had in mind when he said that it is not enough for the drafting of Acts of Parliament to attain to a degree of precision which a person reading them in good faith can understand, 'but it is necessary to attain if possible to a degree of precision which a person reading in bad faith cannot misunderstand'.[5] The words 'if possible' were well chosen. Relatively little of what has to be said in a statute can be said in such a way that it may not be reduced to utter nonsense by a strictly literal and wholly unimaginative construction.

---

4. *R v Liggetts-Finlay Drug Stores Ltd* [1919] 3 WLR 1025.
5. *Re Castioni* [1891] 1 QB 149 at 167.

Chapter 4

The basic rules illustrated

It is now proposed to illustrate the basic rules set out on page 47 by treating some of the more important or more instructive cases on statutory interpretation as involving choices of the different kinds of meaning mentioned in the last section of the previous chapter. The first three sections of this chapter illustrate the first of our basic rules: 'The judge must give effect to the grammatical and ordinary or, where appropriate, the technical meaning of words in the general context of the statute; he must also determine the extent of general words with reference to that context'. The remaining two sections of the chapter illustrate the second and third of the basic rules.

A. CHOICE BETWEEN ORDINARY MEANINGS IN THE CONTEXT

In a number of cases the choice between ordinary meanings in the context is not a very difficult one. These are often criminal appeals in which the point of statutory construction causing the case to be reported was the last resort or forlorn hope of the appellant. In *Abrahams v Cavey*,[1] for example, the Ecclesiastical Courts Jurisdiction Act 1860 was under consideration in a case in which the defendant had caused a disturbance at a Sunday morning church service at which some leading politicians were present by shouting out criticisms of their policy. The relevant provision penalises 'any person who shall be guilty of riotous, violent, or *indecent* behaviour at divine service.' No doubt 'indecent' often means 'obscene', but it can also be used by ordinary people in the sense of 'unbecoming' and it is difficult to

---

1. [1968] 1 QB 479, [1967] 3 All ER 179.

believe that it took the Divisional Court much time to reach the conclusion that, in the particular context, the word bore the latter meaning. The court treated the word as falling within the general category of creating a disturbance in a sacred place. In *Mills v Cooper*[2] the defendant was charged with a contravention of s 127 of the Highways Act 1959 under which it was an offence 'if without lawful authority or excuse, . . . a *gypsy* . . . encamps on a highway'. Some four months earlier the defendant had been acquitted on a similar charge. If 'gypsy' in this context meant a member of the Romany race a plea of issue estoppel might well have succeeded, but not if it meant a person leading a nomadic life of no fixed employment or abode, because the defendant might have taken to that mode of life between the two charges. The court adopted the second meaning on account of the other provisions of the section which were solely concerned with interferences with the amenities of the highway. There was a choice between the dictionary and colloquial meanings of the word 'gypsy' and 'it is difficult to think that Parliament intended to subject a man to a penalty in the context of causing litter and obstruction on the highway merely by reason of his race'.[3]

The decision on the appropriate ordinary meaning depends on consideration of the language used within the context of the provision, taking account particularly of the purpose of the enactment. We have already observed in *Mandla v Dowell Lee*[4] the difficulty of determining the ordinary meaning of the word 'ethnic'. Was it necessary that Sikhs be a biologically separate race or would a distinct social and cultural identity suffice? The differences of view between the Court of Appeal and the House of Lords related essentially to the limits of the purpose of the Race Relations Act 1976—how was racial discrimination to be distinguished from discrimination on religious or other grounds? A similar problem arose in *Ealing London Borough Council v Race Relations Board*[5] over the meaning of 'national origins' in an earlier version of the same provision contained in s 1 of the Race Relations Act 1968. The Act prohibited discrimination in relation to housing. Ealing London Borough Council gave priority to British subjects when allocating housing accommodation at their disposal. The test case was that of a Polish national resident in Ealing whose name was not placed on the council's housing list. Stated concisely the issue was whether 'national origins' included nationality or meant only something akin to

---

2. [1967] 2 QB 459, [1967] 2 All ER 100.
3. Per Lord Parker CJ, [1967] 2 QB at 467. The reference to a 'gypsy' was repealed in 1980.
4. Supra, pp 57–8.
5. [1972] AC 342, [1972] 1 All ER 105.

race. Swanwick J held that the phrase referred to citizenship and accordingly made no declaration, but the House of Lords held by a majority of 4 to 1 that the phrase meant something akin to race and accordingly made the declaration sought by the council. 'The ground for the discrimination was that he [the Polish national] was not a British subject. It was his nationality at the time when he applied, not his national origins, which led to the refusal to put his name on the waiting list.'⁶ Discrimination against a naturalised British subject on the ground of his nationality at birth would no doubt have constituted an infringement of the Act, and the same might well have been true of discrimination against a British subject one of whose parents was a foreigner. The context of the Act suggested a concentration on racial rather than national discrimination, but there is plainly force in the argument which commended itself to Swanwick J that present nationality and national origins are usually the same with the result that the practical effect of the council's rule was that the vast majority of people of other national origins were treated less favourably than people of British or Commonwealth origins.

A word may be capable of more than one ordinary meaning. In such a case, the court will have to decide whether they are all admissible, or whether one particular interpretation is to be preferred. A good example is *Bromley London Borough Council v Greater London Council*.⁷ The Transport (London) Act 1969 imposed a duty on the Greater London Council to develop policies and to encourage measures promoting the provision of 'integrated, efficient and *economic* transport facilities and services' for Greater London. Similarly the operator, the London Transport Executive, had to perform its functions with due regard to 'efficiency, *economy* and safety of operation'. The Greater London Council instructed the London Transport Executive to reduce fares by an average of 25% and decided to make up the deficit by levying a supplementary precept on the London boroughs. The instruction and the supplementary precept were challenged by Bromley London Borough Council on the ground that the statutory words 'economic' and 'economy' were confined to acting on business principles, and could not cover the running of the transport services at a large operating loss and balancing the books by means of a subsidy from the rates. The Greater London Council argued that 'economic' and 'economy' meant simply 'not wasteful of resources', and in no way precluded the decision taken. The Divisional Court⁸ held that both interpretations were admissible and that the choice

---

6. Per Viscount Dilhorne at 359.
7. [1983] 1 AC 768, [1982] 1 All ER 129 (CA & HL).
8. (1981) Times, 4 November.

between them should be left to politicians. The Court of Appeal and the majority of the House of Lords disagreed, and held that Bromley's interpretation was the only one permissible, and that the decision of the Greater London Council was illegal. The House of Lords based its interpretation on a review of the history of legislation dealing with London transport.

In other cases, the courts have been unwilling to determine the meaning to be ascribed to ordinary words in such circumstances, preferring to leave the choice of the appropriate interpretation to politicians, administrators or tribunals, subject to judicial control only where the interpretation given to the words is unreasonable.[9]

The judicial choice of a meaning may simply be defended on grounds of the ordinary usage of the English language, though the results may be less satisfactory than where reference is made to the purpose of the legislation. *Bourne v Norwich Crematorium Ltd*[10] is an example. The issue was whether a crematorium was an 'industrial building or structure' within the meaning of s 271(1)(*c*) of the Income Tax Act 1952. If it was, the company by which it was managed was entitled to a tax allowance. The subsection defined 'an industrial building or structure' as one in use 'for the purposes of a trade which consists in the manufacture of goods or materials or *the subjection of goods or materials to any process.*' Stamp J emphatically rejected the claim to tax relief in the following words:[11]

'What has to be decided here is whether what is done by the taxpayer viz. the consumption or destruction by fire of the dead body of a human being is within the phrase "the subjection of goods or materials to any process". I can only say that, giving the matter the best attention that I can, I conclude that the consumption by fire of the mortal remains of homo sapiens is not the subjection of goods or materials to a process within the definition of "industrial building or structure" contained in s 271(1)(*c*) of the Income Tax Act 1952.'

Perhaps it is unrealistic to talk about the ordinary meaning of 'the subjection of goods or materials to any process', but it does seem that there was more to be said in favour of the claim to relief than Stamp J allowed. It is arguable that there were two linguistic issues: (i) is a dead body 'goods or materials'? and (ii) is destruction by fire a 'process'? If

9. See *R v Hillingdon London Borough Council, ex p Puhlhofer* [1986] AC 484, infra, pp 80–1. Also *R v Preston Supplementary Benefits Appeal Tribunal, ex p Moore* [1975] 1 WLR 624, [1975] 2 All ER 807, CA; *R v Boundary Commission for England, ex p Foot* [1983] QB 600, [1983] 1 All ER 1099, CA.
10. [1967] 1 All ER 576.
11. Ibid, at 578.

the answer given to (i) were that a dead body may properly be described as 'materials' and to (ii) that destruction by fire can properly be described as a process, it is difficult to see how language would have been distorted in the context of taxation. Stamp J protested against 'subjecting the English language, and more particularly a simple English phrase to this kind of process of philology and semasiology'. He did not appear to consider the context and this may be an instance in which the letter was unnecessarily allowed to prevail over the spirit in the court's answer to a question of statutory interpretation.

B.   CHOICE BETWEEN AN ORDINARY AND A TECHNICAL MEANING

Many cases bear out the distinction taken by Lord Esher in the following passage which has already been quoted:

'If the Act is directed to dealing with matters affecting everybody generally, the words used have the meaning attached to them in the common and ordinary use of language. If the Act is one passed with reference to a particular trade, business, or transaction, and words are used which everybody conversant with that trade, business or transaction knows and understands to have a particular meaning in it then the words are to be construed as having that particular meaning, though it may differ from the common or ordinary meaning of the words.'[12]

To take the second half of the passage first, in *Jenner v Allen West & Co Ltd*[13] the Court of Appeal held that 'crawling boards' within the meaning of the Building (Safety, Health and Welfare) Regulations 1948 meant boards with battens on them to prevent workmen who used such boards when placed over portions of a building from which the roof had been removed from slipping. The trial judge heard evidence on the point and the ordinary meaning of plain boards on which workmen could crawl was rejected. Similarly in *Prophet v Platt Brothers & Co Ltd*[14] Harman LJ made the point that the meaning of the word 'fettling' as used in the schedule to the Protection of Eyes Regulations 1938 was not to be gathered from looking at a dictionary (from which it might have appeared that the word referred to the lining of a furnace). The 'fettling of metal castings' appeared from the

---

12. *Unwin v Hanson* [1891] 2 QB 115 at 119; supra, p 59.
13. [1959] 2 All ER 115.
14. [1961] 2 All ER 644.

evidence to be 'a kind of trimming up of the castings as they come from the foundry'.[15] A more controversial case is *Fisher v Bell*[16] in which a shopkeeper was charged with offering a flick-knife for sale contrary to s 1(1) of the Restriction of Offensive Weapons Act 1959 under which 'any person who manufactures, sells or hires or *offers for sale* or hire, or lends or gives to any other person' any knife of the kind sometimes known as a flick-knife was guilty of an offence. The defendant had placed a flick-knife in his shop window, but the Divisional Court held that he had not offered it for sale because Parliament must be taken to have legislated with reference to the general law of contract according to which the placing of goods in a shop window constitutes an invitation to treat and not an offer. The court had a choice between the technical meaning of the term 'offer' as used in the law of contract and a popular meaning according to which goods placed in shop windows are offered for sale. It could perhaps be said without undue exaggeration that the Act being to a large extent addressed to shopkeepers it was passed with reference to a particular trade within the meaning of Lord Esher's dictum, but the decision is best regarded as one more example of the resolution of the conflict between the mischief rule and the presumption that penal statutes should be strictly construed in favour of the accused.

It will be recollected that Blackstone tells us that, although words are generally to be understood in their 'usual and most known signification', terms of art must be 'taken according to the acceptation of the learned in each art, trade and science'.[17] He illustrates this latter point by reference to the Act of Settlement limiting the Crown of England to the Princess Sofia and the heirs of her body, being Protestants. 'It becomes necessary to call in the assistance of lawyers to ascertain the precise idea of the words 'heirs of her body' which in a legal sense comprise only certain of her lineal descendants'.[18] In the case of quite a large number of statutes it is clear that words are used in their technical legal sense; but occasionally there are cases in which the point in issue is a choice between a legal and a popular meaning. Thus the strict legal meaning of 'hospital' is an eleemosynary institution in which persons benefited from a corporate body. Nonetheless it was held in *Lord Colchester v Kewney*[19] that the exemption of hospitals from land tax by statutes of 1797 and 1798 extended to all establishments popularly known as hospitals including an asylum for orphans. Similarly in *Re K*

---

15. Ibid, at 647–8.
16. [1961] 1 QB 394, [1960] 3 All ER 731.
17. Supra, p 21.
18. *Commentaries*, vol 1, p 59.
19. (1867) LR 1 Ex Ch 368.

deceased[20] the Court of Appeal held that the judge had power to award a widow who had killed her husband a share in his estate, then in the hands of his personal representatives, even though s 2(7) of the Forfeiture Act 1982 prevented orders affecting property 'acquired' by third persons. The word 'acquired' was to be interpreted in a non-technical sense. At first instance,[1] Vinelott J supported this interpretation by noting that the Act had resulted from a private Member's Bill. Furthermore, the wider interpretation best fitted the policy of the Act in permitting the distribution of property from the estate in deserving cases, even if the beneficiary had caused the death of the deceased.

Section 18(5) of the Rent Act 1968 (as originally enacted) accorded a measure of protection against eviction to a sublessee whose protected tenancy has been terminated by the death of his lessor. The subsection protected him against eviction by the head lessor 'where a dwelling house (a) forms part of *premises* which have been let as a whole on a superior letting but do not constitute a dwelling house let on a protected tenancy and (b) is itself let on a protected tenancy or statutory tenancy'. Did the word 'premises' bear its usual legal meaning in the common law context of landlord and tenant of that which constitutes the subject matter of a lease? The House of Lords answered this question in the negative in *Maunsell v Olins*[2] but only by a majority of 3 to 2. The plaintiff owned a farm comprising a hundred acres of land on which there was the farmhouse and two tied cottages. He let the farm to B who was allowed to sublet the cottages. B sublet one of the cottages to the first defendant, and it was not disputed that, as between B and the first defendant the latter's tenancy was protected by the Rent Act. B died and his tenancy of the farm terminated. The plaintiff claimed possession of the cottage from the first defendant. Obviously he failed if the word 'premises' was to be given its common law meaning in such a context and Lord Simon of Glaisdale supported this conclusion in a vigorous dissenting speech in which Lord Diplock concurred. From the sociological point of view the speech derived its strength from the fact that, when problems arise, persons affected by s 18(5) are likely to seek legal advice. The majority reached the conclusion that the subsection only applied to premises which, for the purposes of the 1968 Act, were to be treated as dwelling houses, giving more than one reason. The lease to B was governed by the Agricultural Holdings Act and it would be odd if the Rent Act had much to do with agricultural lettings; there is a presumption against any greater alter-

---

20. [1986] Ch 180, [1985] 2 All ER 833.
1. [1985] Ch 85 at 99.
2. [1975] AC 373.

ation of the common law than is required by the ordinary meaning of the words of the statute; and, if asked what he understood by the word 'premises', a farmer would probably not include farm land as distinct from farm buildings.

It should be noted that there may be a choice of technical meanings in relation to a particular word. Thus in *Re McC (A Minor)*,[3] a magistrate was held immune from a suit for damages in that he had not acted 'without jurisdiction or in excess of jurisdiction' within the meaning of s 15 of the Magistrates Courts Act (Northern Ireland) 1964, even though his decision against the plaintiff had been quashed for error of law and want of 'jurisdiction' in the sense given to the term by administrative law. The immunity was intended to protect magistrates in the exercise of their normal functions even where they made decisions wrong in law, and the decision the defendant had made against the plaintiff came within the normal scope of his functions.

C. FRINGE MEANING AND THE EXTENT OF GENERAL WORDS

Stock examples of the problem of fringe meaning are provided by *Newberry v Simmonds* and *Smart v Allan*. Each case turned on the construction of s 15(1) (as amended) of the Vehicles (Excise) Act 1949; 'if any person uses or keeps on a public road any *mechanically propelled vehicle* for which a licence under this Act is not in force he shall be liable . . .' In *Newberry v Simmonds*[4] a car which was kept standing on a road, and whose engine had been stolen, was held to be a mechanically propelled vehicle requiring a licence. In *Smart v Allan*[5] the defendant bought a car for £2 as scrap and left it on a road. The engine was rusted and did not work; three tyres were flat and one was missing; there was no gear box or electrical accessories and the car could not move under its own power. It was held not to be a mechanically propelled vehicle, Lord Parker CJ saying:[6]

> 'It seems to me as a matter of common sense that some limit must be put, and some stage must be reached, when one can say: "This is so immobile that it has ceased to be a mechanically propelled vehicle". Where, as in the present case, and unlike *Newberry v Simmonds*, there is no reasonable prospect of the vehicle ever

---

3. [1985] AC 528, [1984] 3 All ER 908.
4. [1961] 2 QB 345, [1961] 2 All ER 318.
5. [1963] 1 QB 291, [1962] 3 All ER 893.
6. Ibid, at 298.

being made mobile again, it seems to me that, at any rate at that stage, a vehicle has ceased to be a mechanically propelled vehicle.'

No useful purpose would be served by providing a multiplicity of illustrations of fringe meaning, but it must be emphasised that the solution of problems of this nature is one of the most common tasks of the courts in relation to statutory interpretation. Is a bicycle a 'carriage'?[7] Is a goldfish an 'article'?[8] Is orange juice pressed from fresh oranges a 'manufactured beverage'?[9] Is a newspaper competition card a 'literary work'?[10] Conundrums of this sort are part of the daily bread of judges and practitioners. In solving them the courts usually pay due regard to the context, but, in many instances, the answer must, in Lord Parker's words, be treated as a matter of common sense. The fact that a substantial proportion of the problems of statutory interpretation which confront them cannot be answered on principle is something to be borne in mind when the manner in which the courts perform their interpretative function is under discussion. The dictates of common sense are notoriously liable to produce different answers by different people to the same question, but this is not the kind of difficulty which can be overcome by law reform.

In the context of statutory interpretation the expression 'general words' is a broad one. It applies to any word, phrase or provision which refers to actions, persons or things as a class rather than individually. Plowden's report of *Stradling v Morgan* tells us that the sages of the law have construed statutes 'which comprehend all things in the letter . . . to extend but to some things, . . . and those which include every person in the letter they have adjudged to reach some persons only'.[11] A good modern example of this process is the construction of s 1 of the Sex Disqualification (Removal) Act 1919 adopted by the majority of the House of Lords' Committee of Privileges at the hearing of *Viscountess Rhondda's claim* to be entitled to be summoned to sit in the House as a peeress in her own right.[12] On the previous occasions when women had claimed that they were entitled to exercise such public functions as voting at Parliamentary elections they had been defeated by the express words of the statutes upon which they relied. General words like 'any person' were used, but persons subject to any legal

---

7. *Corkery v Carpenter* [1951] 1 KB 102, [1950] 2 All ER 745.
8. *Daly v Cannon* [1954] 1 All ER 315.
9. *Customs and Excise Comms v Savoy Hotel Ltd* [1966] 2 All ER 299.
10. *Express Newspapers plc v Liverpool Post & Echo plc* [1985] 3 All ER 680.
11. Supra, pp 9–10.
12. [1922] 2 AC 339.

incapacity were excepted, and women were held to be legally incapacitated from exercising public functions at common law.[13] The words of the 1919 Act are, however, perfectly general in their terms; 'a person shall not be disqualified by sex or marriage from the exercise of any public function.' The basis of the decision against the claim was that the creation of a new right must be distinguished from the removal of a disqualification and specific words, such as those used in earlier statutes conferring the right to exercise public functions on women, were necessary for the former purpose.

Another striking illustration of the manner in which the effect of broad general words may be limited by the courts is the interpretation of s 68 of the Education Act 1944 in *Secretary of State for Education and Science v Tameside MBC*.[14] This section empowered the Secretary of State to give directions to a local education authority if he was 'satisfied' that it was acting unreasonably in relation to any power conferred on it. A Conservative council elected in May 1976 sought to modify plans for the introduction of comprehensive education, due to start in September 1976, which had been adopted by its Labour predecessor, and to retain some grammar schools. The Secretary of State considered that the necessary selection process for admission to the grammar schools could not be completed in time for the September entry, and gave directions under s 68 that the council should retain the original plans for comprehensive schooling. The House of Lords quashed the direction on the ground that s 68 applied only where the local education authority was taking action which was so unreasonable that no reasonable authority would take it, and that the Secretary of State had failed to demonstrate that this was the case here. The general purpose of the Act in ensuring local autonomy in the structure and management of education was thus maintained by a limitation on the scope of ministerial supervisory powers, which appeared very general from the wording of the Act itself.

The maxim *'generalia specialibus non derogant'* (general words do not derogate from special words) expressing the rule, mentioned in the introduction, that general words in a later statute do not repeal an earlier statute dealing with a special subject, is a further illustration of the cautious approach adopted by the courts to the interpretation of broad provisions. The leading case is *The Vera Cruz* in which Lord Selborne said:

'Now if anything be certain it is this, that where there are general

---

13. *Chorlton v Lings* (1868) LR 4 CP 374; *Nairn v St Andrews University* [1909] AC 147.
14. [1977] AC 1014, [1976] 3 All ER 665.

words in a later Act capable of reasonable and sensible application without extending them to subjects specially dealt with by earlier legislation, you are not to hold that earlier and special legislation indirectly repealed, altered, or derogated from merely by force of such general words, without any indication of a particular intention to do so.'[15]

Of course general provisions are often given their full general effect for in this, as in most other cases, the courts pay due regard to the context. Section 1(1) of the Representation of the People Act 1983 entitles a person to vote in any constituency where he or she is 'resident' on the qualifying date. In *Hipperson v Electoral Registration Officer for the District of Newbury*[16] it was held that the Greenham Common women were entitled to be registered in the Newbury constituency even though they lived in tents forming a 'peace camp', inhabiting land on which they were not lawfully present. Their presence on the land was sufficiently permanent and its illegal character was not relevant for determining the place in which their fundamental right to vote was to be exercised.

In at least one instance the context and historical background has led to a vast extension of the meaning of general words. Section 1 of the Affiliation Proceedings Act 1957 provided that: 'a *single woman* who is with child, or has been delivered of an illegitimate child, may apply by complaint to a Justice of the Peace for a summons to be served on the man alleged by her to be the father of her child.' The effect of a series of cases going back for 150 years was that a married woman living apart from her husband,[17] even if they occupy the same house,[18] might apply for a summons and obtain an order against another man. The section derived from statutes of Elizabeth I, and the justification for the extended meaning of the phrase 'single woman' was 'public policy'. 'The law, differently interpreted, would fail to reach a very large proportion of illegitimate children'[19] The basic idea is that the child in respect of whom the order was sought should have been born outside matrimony and this was made clearer in the earlier statutes. It was even held that a woman living apart from her husband under a separation order could obtain an affiliation order against him in respect of a child born a few hours before her previous marriage had been finally dissolved by decree absolute and therefore not legitimated by her

---

15. (1884) 10 App Cas 59 at 68.
16. [1985] QB 1060, [1985] 2 All ER 456, CA.
17. *R v Luffe* (1807) 8 East 193.
18. *Whitton v Garner* [1965] 1 All ER 70.
19. Per Lord Denman CJ, *R v Collingwood and Tompkins* (1848) 12 QB 681 at 687.

subsequent marriage.[20] Devlin J said:[1]

> 'The artificiality of the construction which the courts have given to the expression "single woman" is brought into high relief when a wife asserts against her own husband that she is a single woman. Nevertheless once the point is reached when the fact of singleness is determined by looking at the actual state to which the woman has been reduced and not at her status in the eyes of the law, it seems to me that a woman whose husband has deserted her or cast her off can say to him, with as much force as she can say it to anyone else, that he has reduced her to living as a single woman.'

By the use of some kinds of general words Parliament deliberately confers considerable discretion on those who apply the statute, thus enabling the courts to lay down rules for the exercise of this discretion. Modern examples of general words include judicial powers to declare void exclusion clauses in contracts which are not 'reasonable', to undo consumer credit bargains which are 'unconscionable', or to wind up a company where it appears 'just and equitable' to do so.[2] The use of such phrases may result in a bulk of case-law enough to fill a book or make the least prescient reader realise that there is little hope of understanding the statutes in which they occur without a comprehensive reference to the law reports.

Occasionally the courts propose a test for determining on which side of a line a particular situation falls, but there is then always the danger that the test will become a substitute for the statutory words which it is the judges' duty to apply to the cases that come before them. This is illustrated by the way in which the courts have grappled with the Housing (Homeless Persons) Act 1977. Section 1(1) provides that for the purposes of the Act a person is homeless if he has no accommodation and

> 'a person is to be treated as having no accommodation for those purposes if there is no accommodation—(a) which he, together with any other person who normally resides with him as a member of his family or in circumstances in which the housing authority consider it reasonable for that person to reside with him—(i) is entitled to occupy by virtue of an interest in it or of any order of a court, or (ii) has, in England or Wales, an express or implied licence to occupy . . .'

---

20. *Kruhlak v Kruhlak* [1958] 2 QB 32. The rule on legitimation was altered by the Legitimacy Act 1959. Affiliation orders were abolished by s 17 of the Family Law Reform Act 1987.
1. Ibid, at 37.
2. See generally P S Atiyah, *From Principles to Pragmatism* (Oxford, 1978).

Nothing in the Act defined what was meant by 'accommodation' for this purpose. In *R v Wyre BC, ex p Parr*,[3] the Court of Appeal stated that it meant 'appropriate accommodation' and decided that this did not include accommodation found by the housing authority in the exercise of its duty to house homeless persons which was 150 miles away from where a person lived. Lord Denning MR explained what was meant by 'appropriate accommodation':[4]

'That means of course that the house—as a dwelling—must be appropriate for a family of this size. It must have enough rooms to house his wife and five children. If it is in an area with which he has a local connection, that is good enough. He cannot reasonably refuse suitable accommodation in his own area. But it is different when the offer is only accommodation in a far-off area with which he has no local connection.'

This definition was applied by subsequent judges. However, in *R v Hillingdon London Borough Council, ex p Puhlhofer*,[5] a different Court of Appeal and the House of Lords were forced to admit that this judicial definition was too rigid. Speaking for a unanimous House, Lord Brightman took the view that 'accommodation' meant simply any place which was capable of being described as accommodation within the ordinary use of that word in the English language and without a qualifying adjective. This left a greater discretion to the local authority in determining whether, given the conditions of their area and the nature of the accommodation occupied, a person was 'homeless' or not. Rather than requiring that the accommodation should be appropriate in all cases, the court would only intervene where the decision whether a person occupied 'accommodation' or not amounted to an abuse of power. For example, Diogenes in his tub could not be described as having occupied 'accommodation' within the meaning of the Act. Such an approach better fitted the policy of the Act, determined from the long title, which was that of providing the homeless with a lifeline of last resort, rather than providing homes to those who were inadequately housed and giving such people priority within the local authority's housing waiting list. On the facts, a local authority was entitled to find that a couple with two children living in a guest house where they had a bedroom but no cooking facilities were not without 'accommodation'' within the meaning of s 1(1). Overcrowding was a relevant factor to be considered, but here there was

---

3. (1982) 2 HLR 71.
4. Ibid, at 78.
5. [1986] AC 484, [1986] 1 All ER 467.

'accommodation' within the ordinary meaning of the word. By rejecting a judicial interpretation, the House of Lords was thus able to preserve the full scope of the local authority's discretion and evaluation of facts. This book is not concerned with the labyrinthine details of the Housing (Homeless Persons) Act 1977, but the cases point clearly to the priority of the statutory text over judicial elaboration. The danger that tests proposed by the courts for determining the meaning of general statutory words would be treated as a substitute for those words is further illustrated by cases turning on the construction of s 2(1) of the Race Relations Act 1968:

> 'It shall be unlawful for any person concerned with the provision to the public or a *section of the public* (whether on payment or otherwise) of any goods, facilities or services to discriminate against any person seeking to obtain or use those goods, facilities or services by refusing or deliberately omitting to provide him with any of them or to provide him with goods, services or facilities of the like quality in the like manner and on the like terms on which the former normally makes them available to other members of the public.'

In *Charter v Race Relations Board*[6] the East Ham Conservative Club rejected the application for membership of an Indian on the casting vote of the chairman of the club's Committee who indicated that he regarded the applicant's colour as a relevant consideration. Any man of 18 was eligible for membership if he was a Conservative and duly proposed and seconded. The County Court judge held that s 2(1) of the 1968 Act did not apply because members of the club were not a section of the public to whom the club provided facilities or services. The Court of Appeal reversed this decision, but it was reinstated by the House of Lords. In the Court of Appeal, Lord Denning MR said that the test for determining what was 'a section of the public' required the court to examine the quality which the group of persons concerned had in common and then 'ask whether the quality is essentially impersonal or essentially personal. If it is impersonal, the group will rank as a "section of the public". If it is personal, it will rank as a private group, and not a section of the public.'[7] But the House of Lords by a majority of 4 to 1 treated the words 'public or a section of the public' as words which limited what would otherwise have been the completely general terms of s 2(1). The provision of facilities and services to some people had to be outside the subsection and a club, being a private association

---

6. [1973] AC 868, [1973] 1 All ER 512.
7. [1972] 1 QB at 556.

of individuals, was outside the subsection if its election rules provided a genuine process of selection which was followed in practice. Lord Reid defended this position by noting the balance of the purposes in the Act:[8]

> 'I would infer from the Act that the legislature thought all discrimination on racial grounds to be deplorable but thought it unwise or impracticable to attempt to apply legal sanctions in situations of a purely private character.'

The dangers of the test propounded by Lord Denning are illustrated by *Applin v Race Relations Board*[9] which came before the county court judge while the appeal to the House of Lords in *Charter's* case was pending. The judge held that registered foster parents would not be infringing s 2(1) by discriminating against black children in care because children in care were not a 'section of the public' within Lord Denning's test. The Court of Appeal reversed this decision after the House of Lords had allowed the appeal in *Charter v Race Relations Board*, and the decision of the Court of Appeal in *Applin's* case was affirmed by a majority of 4 to 1 in the House of Lords.

A unanimous House of Lords was, unlike the Court of Appeal, unable to disinguish *Charter v Race Relations Board* in *Dockers' Labour Club and Institute Ltd v Race Relations Board*.[10] In that case a dockers' club which operated a colour bar was linked with 4,000 other working men's clubs in an association affording admission to a member of any associated club as an associate member of any other. A coloured member of one of the associated clubs was asked to leave the dockers' club. The Race Relations Board obtained a declaration from the county court judge that s 2(1) of the 1968 Act had been infringed and the judge's decision was upheld in the Court of Appeal where *Charter's* case was distinguished on the ground that, although club members elected by a *bona fide* process constituted a private group, something like a million members of other clubs had associate members' rights in the dockers' club without being personally approved by it. The House of Lords took the view that the policy of the Act was to separate the public from the private sphere, and numbers as such were therefore irrelevant. A notice on the door of the dockers' club reading 'Members of the public not admitted' would have been as appropriate as such a notice would be in the case of a much smaller club. The result of the construction adopted by the House of Lords was in many ways disas-

---

8. [1973] AC at 887.
9. [1975] AC 259, [1974] 2 All ER 73.
10. [1976] AC 285, [1974] 3 All ER 592.

trous, but the results of a test distinguishing between small clubs and big clubs and clubs which did or did not supply personal services would have been even more disastrous. The problem has now been abolished by ss 25 and 26 of the Race Relations Act 1976, but the cases demonstrate the way judicial interpretations can become treated as replacements for the text of the statutory provision. While, as we have seen, judicial decisions interpreting a statutory provision may bind later courts, judicial glosses on the text should not be treated as of equal weight to the words themselves.

For this reason, the courts have sometimes preferred to lay down 'guidelines' for the exercise of discretions granted by statute to the judges. In doing this, the courts have emphasised that these are not to be treated as hard and fast rules and that the flexibility of the discretion should be maintained. For instance, in *Wachtel v Wachtel*[11] the Court of Appeal stated that in determining the division of property on divorce under ss 2, 4 and 5 of the Matrimonial Property and Proceedings Act 1970 (now ss 23 to 25 of the Matrimonial Causes Act 1973) the judge should take as a guideline that one-third of the joint property should go to the wife. However, it was emphasised in this and subsequent cases that this was merely a guide and that the judge was free to depart from it in an appropriate case.[12]

D. CHOICE BETWEEN PRIMARY AND SECONDARY MEANING

The second of our basic rules set out on page 47 must now be illustrated: 'If the judge considers that the application of the words in their grammatical and ordinary sense would produce a result which is contrary to the purpose of the statute, he may apply them in any secondary meaning which they are capable of bearing.' To repeat a quotation from one of Lord Reid's speeches:[13]

> 'In determining the meaning of any word or phrase in a statute the first question to ask always is what is the natural or ordinary meaning of that word or phrase in its context in the statute. It is only when that meaning leads to some result which cannot reasonably be supposed to have been the intention of the legislature that it is proper to look for some other permissible meaning of the word or phrase.'

---

11. [1973] Fam 72.
12. Ibid, at 94 per Lord Denning MR; *S v S* [1977] Fam 127, CA.
13. *Pinner v Everett* [1969] 3 All ER 257 at 258.

This is of course substantially similar to Lord Wensleydale's golden rule as stated in *Grey v Pearson*:[14]

'. . . the grammatical and ordinary sense of the words is to be adhered to, unless that would lead to some absurdity, or some repugnance or inconsistency with the rest of the instrument, in which case the grammatical and ordinary sense of the words may be modified, so as to avoid the absurdity and inconsistency, but no further.'

More recently Lord Simon of Glaisdale in *Maunsell v Olins* said:[15]

'. . . the language is presumed to be used in its primary ordinary sense, unless this stultifies the purpose of the statute, or otherwise produces some injustice, absurdity, anomaly or contradiction, in which case some secondary ordinary sense may be preferred . . .'

The question whether words like 'repugnance', 'inconsistency', 'absurdity', 'anomaly' and 'contradiction' are helpful in this context is best considered after the propositions embodied in the above quotations have been illustrated. Certainly purposive construction most frequently requires giving effect to the ordinary and primary meaning of the words used, since the draftsman has chosen them with care to give effect to the purpose for which the legislation is passed. It is only in exceptional cases that a purposive construction requires the judge to seek out a secondary meaning.

There is much to be said for the view that there is no radical discontinuity between primary and secondary meanings. E A Driedger has suggested that:[16]

'the adoption of a secondary meaning is not a departure from the literal meaning; the secondary meaning is the literal meaning in the context in which the words are used. I have come to the conclusion that, except where a mistake is corrected or a meaning is given to senseless words, there is no such thing as a literal meaning as distinguished from some other meaning.'

He goes on to point out that the real distinction is between the 'first blush' or 'obvious' meaning of words and the less obvious. This has much in common with the views of Professor Glanville Williams noted in the last chapter.[17] The appropriate reading of words depends on the

---

14. (1857) 6 HL Cas 61, 106; supra, p 16.
15. [1975] AC 373 at 391.
16. 'Statutes: The Mischievous Literal Golden Rule' (1981) 59 Can Bar Rev 780.
17. Supra, p 64.

context, and in particular on the purpose of the statutory provision examined.

It must be emphasised at the outset that it is only when a secondary meaning is available that there can be any question of the courts' abandoning a primary meaning simply because it produces a result which they believe is contrary to the purpose of the Act. No judge can decline to apply a statutory provision because it seems to him to lead to absurd results nor can he, for this or any other reason, give words a meaning they will not bear. We have already seen this point, in connection with *Duport Steels Ltd v Sirs*.[18] It will be recalled that the Court of Appeal considered that the words 'any act done by a person in contemplation or furtherance of a trade dispute' had to be interpreted as qualified by the requirement that the acts should not be too remote from the dispute, because of the undesirable consequences which would flow from admitting as lawful all secondary action. Although expressing sympathy with this concern, the House of Lords considered that it could not but give effect to the plain words of the statute which covered *any act* done in contemplation or furtherance of a trade dispute. Lord Scarman said:[19]

'In this field Parliament makes, and un-makes, the law; the judge's duty is to interpret and to apply the law, not to change it to meet the judge's idea of what justice requires. Interpretation does, of course, imply in the interpreter a power of choice where differing constructions are possible. But our law requires the judge to choose the construction which in his judgment best meets the legislative purpose of the enactment. If the result be unjust but inevitable, the judge must say so and invite Parliament to reconsider its position. But he must not deny the statute. Unpalatable statute law may not be disregarded or rejected, merely because it is unpalatable. Only if a just result can be achieved without violating the legislative purpose of the statute may the judge select the construction which best suits his idea of what justice requires.'

The purpose of the Trade Union and Labour Relations Act was to grant a wide immunity to unions engaged in trade disputes and so the restrictive interpretation proposed by the Court of Appeal could not be acceptable.

In the context of statutory interpretation the word most frequently used to indicate the doubt which a judge must entertain before he can

---

18. Supra, pp 28–9.
19. [1980] 1 WLR at 168–9.

search for and, if possible, apply a secondary meaning is 'ambiguity'. In ordinary language this term is often confined to situations in which the same word is capable of meaning two different things; but in relation to statutory interpretation, judicial usage sanctions the application of the word 'ambiguity' to describe any kind of doubtful meaning of words, phrases or longer statutory provisions. It has been suggested that if, in a particular context, words convey to different judges a different range of meanings 'derived, not from fanciful speculations or mistakes about linguistic usage, but from true knowledge about the use of words, they are ambiguous'.[20] The author of the suggestion was not satisfied with the following answer which had already been provided by Viscount Simonds:[1]

'Each one of us has the task of deciding what the relevant words mean. In coming to that decision he will necessarily give great weight to the opinion of others, but if at the end of the day he forms his own clear judgment and does not think that the words are "fairly and equally open to divers meanings" he is not entitled to say that there is an ambiguity. For him at least there is no ambiguity and on that basis he must decide the case.'

It has since been said to be difficult to justify Viscount Simonds' answer on logical grounds,[2] but it is hard to see what logic has to do with the matter. There is a rule of law according to which the judge must apply the ordinary and natural meaning of statutory words in their context unless that would produce a result which cannot reasonably be supposed to have been intended by the legislature. There is of course general agreement about the ordinary and natural meaning of statutory words, but the agreement is not universal, a point which is borne out by the fact that a question of statutory interpretation is being litigated. In border-line cases judges are apt to disagree about the ordinary meaning of words and they are equally apt to form different opinions on the question whether there is sufficient doubt to warrant the application of a secondary meaning. This point was put very clearly by Lord Reid when dealing, in a later case,[3] with an argument that he should act on the presumption that penal statutes are to be construed strictly:

'But it only applies where after full inquiry and consideration one is left in real doubt. It is not enough that the provision is ambiguous in the sense that it is capable of having two meanings. The

---

20. A L Montrose, (1960) 76 LQR 359 at 361.
1. *Kirkness v John Hudson & Co Ltd* [1955] AC 696 at 712.
2. Odgers, *Construction of Deeds and Statutes*, 5th edn, p 449.
3. *Director of Public Prosecutions v Ottwell* [1970] AC 642 at 649.

imprecision of the English language (and, so far as I am aware, of any other language) is such that it is extremely difficult to draft any provision which is not ambiguous in that sense. This section [s 37 of the Criminal Justice Act 1967] is clearly ambiguous in that sense, the Court of Appeal (Criminal Division) attach one meaning to it, and your Lordships are attaching a different meaning to it. But if, after full consideration, your Lordships are satisfied, as I am, that the latter is a meaning which Parliament must have intended the words to convey, then this principle does not prevent us from giving effect to our conclusion.'

A secondary meaning may be wider than the ordinary meaning or it may be narrower. The appropriateness of a secondary meaning depends on the purpose of the statute.

An instance of the wide secondary meaning is the case of *South West Water Authority v Rumble's*,[4] where the word 'use' of drainage facilities was given a wide interpretation so as to include drainage into a sewer from the roof of a building in which a ground floor shop was situated, even though the shop itself had no direct water supply or drainage. A further example is provided by *Wills v Bowley*.[5] Section 28 of the Town Police Clauses Act 1847 (now repealed in this respect) provided that a police officer 'shall take into custody, without warrant, and forthwith convey before a justice, any person who within his view *commits*' any of a list of some 30 offences penalised by the section. The appellant was charged with the offence of using obscene language in a street 'to the annoyance of passengers' contrary to s 28. In resisting arrest, Mrs Wills assaulted three constables. The magistrates dismissed the charge against her under s 28 on the ground that no 'passengers' were annoyed by the language she used; however, they convicted her of assaulting police officers in the execution of their duty. The validity of this conviction depended upon the lawfulness of the arrest under s 28 which, on first sight, might appear to be limited to situations where a person actually 'commits' an offence. Nevertheless, by a majority, the House of Lords affirmed the conviction holding that the wording authorised an arrest where a police officer honestly believed that a person had been committing an offence within his view. This was one of a family of statutes permitting the arrest of people caught in the act of committing an offence and these statutes did not usually contain express language authorising arrest without warrant upon reasonable suspicion that an offence was being committed. It was necessary that

---

4. Supra, p 7.
5. [1983] 1 AC 57, [1982] 2 All ER 654.

the police should have clear guidance, and the legality of an arrest could not be made to depend on whether the person was subsequently convicted. These considerations and the analogy with police powers in more recent legislation, notably s 2 of the Criminal Law Act 1967 (now repealed), justified rebutting a presumption in favour of individual liberty despite the absence of clear express language. The minority, Lords Elwyn-Jones and Lowry, preferred a narrow construction of the section in favour of the liberty of the subject. A balance had to be struck between the liberty of the subject and the preservation of public order, and Lord Lowry argued[6]:

> 'in such a contest I would require the arguments to be clear and compelling before I could reject the literal meaning, which conduces to the liberty of the subject, in favour of reading into the statute words which it does not contain, with a view to promoting public order.'

The majority considered that they were not reading words into the section, but merely giving it a wide construction.

A secondary meaning may be chosen in preference to the ordinary meaning of a word. This is clearly illustrated by the controversial case of *Nottinghamshire County Council v Secretary of State for the Environment.*[7] Section 59 of the Local Government, Planning and Land Act 1980, as amended by Part II of the Local Government Finance Act 1982, empowered the Secretary of State to issue 'guidance . . . designed to achieve any reduction in the level of local authority expenditure (or any restriction on increases in that level) which he thinks necessary having regard to general economic conditions', which guidance could be used as a criterion for adjusting the block grant payable to local authorities. Section 59(11A) required that the guidance 'shall be framed by reference to principles *applicable* to all local authorities'. For the financial year 1985–6, the Secretary of State issued guidance which provided for an increase in expenditure according to two criteria, depending on whether the local authority's budget for the then current year (1984–5) exceeded or was below its Grant Related Expenditure assessment (a notional figure of necessary expenditure based on the authority's particular situation and functions). In a challenge by two local authorities to the legality of the guidance issued, the Court of Appeal held that the Secretary of State had unlawfully discriminated between authorities on the basis of their past expenditure records. Being based on budgets for the year which

---

6. Ibid, at 74.
7. [1986] AC 240, [1986] 1 All ER 199.

was, by the time of the announcement of the guidance, almost over, the two criteria were not 'applicable', ie capable of being applied, to all local authorities. However, the House of Lords unanimously reversed this decision. The Court of Appeal's interpretation led to two 'startling' consequences. First, the Secretary of State could only issue guidance permitting an overall increase or reduction in local government expenditure without regard to the situations and past records of individual authorities. Second, it would be illegitimate to mitigate the harsh effects of an overall increase or reduction in relation to those authorities which had conformed to government policy and kept their spending to a low level. These consequences were contrary to the policy of the Act in achieving a reduction in local government expenditure. Speaking for all their Lordships on this point, Lord Bridge adopted a purposive approach and held that 'applicable' in the context of s 59(11A) meant that the guidance was 'to be applied' to all authorities, rather than only to particular authorities. This interchangeability of 'applicable' and 'to be applied' could be demonstrated by an analysis of other sections of the Act.[8] On this interpretation, the guidance of the Secretary of State was valid since it applied to all local authorities. The ordinary meaning of 'applicable' was set aside in favour of an unusual, secondary meaning appropriate to the context and the purpose of the Act.

Wills v Bowley and *Nottinghamshire CC v Secretary of State for the Environment* are examples of the application of an extended meaning of words in order to avoid a result which was considered contrary to the purpose of the statutes in question. A further example of the same kind, though concerned with very different facts, is *Luke v Inland Revenue Commrs.*[9] Sections 160 and 161 of the Income Tax Act 1952 were aimed at preventing company directors from enjoying tax immunities in respect of expense allowances and payments in kind. The effect of s 161(1) was to render a director liable to tax in respect of expense incurred by the company 'in or in connection with the provision of living or other accommodation or of other benefits or facilities of whatsoever nature'. These words were wide enough to cover a case where a house was let by a company to one of its directors under a lease at a fair rent and, dry rot having been discovered, the company spent £5,000 on remedying it. This expenditure might be of no permanent benefit to the director whose tenancy might terminate shortly after the removal of the dry rot, yet he would be liable to tax on £5,000 in the absence of any saving clause to be found in some other provision of the

---

8. [1986] 1 All ER at 213.
9. [1963] AC 557.

statute. The House of Lords was none the less confronted with the question whether a director who leased a house from a company was liable for tax on expenses incurred by the company in carrying out repairs which are normally executed by a landlord. A majority of 3 to 2 found a saving clause in s 162(1) of the 1952 Act under which 'any expense incurred by a body corporate in the acquisition or production of an asset which remains its own property shall be left out of account for the purposes of the last preceding section'. It is almost an abuse of language to describe repairs as the production of an asset, but it is hard to believe that s 161 was intended to render a director liable to tax in respect of expenditure which was of no benefit to him personally. Considerations of this nature led Lord Reid to say:[10]

> 'To apply the words literally is to defeat the obvious intention of the legislation and to produce a wholly unreasonable result. To achieve the obvious intention and produce a reasonable result we must do some violence to the words. This is not a new problem, though our standard of drafting is such that it rarely emerges. The general principle is well settled. It is only where the words are absolutely incapable of a construction which will accord with the apparent intention of the provision and will avoid a wholly unreasonable result that the words of the enactment must prevail.'

In other circumstances a secondary meaning has a restrictive character. In some cases this will be required by the purpose of the Act itself. For example, in *Cooper v Motor Insurers' Bureau*,[11] a person suffered injuries when riding the motor cycle of a friend who had failed to warn him that the brakes were defective. The injured person obtained judgment for damages against the friend who owned the motor cycle, but the latter had not been insured against third party risks as required by s 143(1) of the Road Traffic Act 1972. The Motor Insurers' Bureau undertakes to satisfy judgments relating to road accidents, among others, against persons who have failed to take out compulsory insurance. The injured person sought a declaration that the Motor Insurers' Bureau was liable to satisfy the judgment he had obtained. Section 145(3)(a) provided that an insurance policy in relation to a motor vehicle 'must insure such person, persons or classes of persons as may be specified in the policy in respect of any liability which may be incurred by him or them in respect of the death of or bodily injury to any person caused by, or arising out of, the use of the

---

10. Ibid at 577.
11. [1985] QB 575, [1985] 1 All ER 449.

vehicle on a road'. The plaintiff argued that 'any person' here included the driver of the vehicle and that its owner was legally obliged to be insured in respect of his injuries. The Court of Appeal rejected this argument. Section 145 occurred in Part VI of the Act, headed 'Compulsory insurance or security against third-party risks', which began in s 143(1) by making it a criminal offence to use, or to cause or permit another to use, a motor vehicle on a road unless an insurance policy in respect of third-party risks was in force relating to the vehicle. The purpose of this Part of the Act was thus limited to protecting third parties and not the driver of a vehicle. Accordingly, read in this context, 'any person' in s 145(3)(a) was restricted to third parties and did not include the driver.[12] Any other interpretation would produce an inconsistency between the sections, and would have imposed an obligation to insure well beyond the stated policy of Part VI of the Act.

In other cases, an 'absurdity' or anomaly is perceived from the wider context of the purposes of the law in a particular area of social activity. Since the legislator is presumed to have intended a result which is coherent and consistent with the statutory and common law rules which he has left in force, the judge will seek an interpretation of statutory words which does not produce an incoherence or an inconsistency in the law as a whole and in the policies which the legislator is pursuing in a particular area. For example, *Richard Thomas and Baldwins Ltd v Cummings*[13] was concerned with the construction of s 16 of the Factories Act 1937 which required the fencing of dangerous parts of machines to be 'constantly maintained and kept in position while the parts required to be fenced or safeguarded are *in motion* or use'. There was an exception permitting exposure of the dangerous parts for examination and lubrication or adjustment shown by examination to be immediately necessary, but this clearly did not apply to repairs and Cummings had lost a finger in consequence of an injury sustained while repairing an unfenced machine which had been out of use for three weeks. He had turned the machine by hand in order to get it into position for repairing and repairs could not have been effected if the machine were fenced in accordance with the requirements of the Act. Clearly there was a sense in which the machine could be said to have been 'in motion', but the House of Lords interpreted these words restrictively so as to exclude a mere transitory manual turning. Referring to the impossibility of effecting repairs if 'in motion' were held to include any movement of the parts, however small, however brief and however caused, Lord Reid said:[14]

---

12. Cumming-Bruce LJ, [1985] 1 All ER at 452.
13. [1955] AC 321.
14. Ibid, at 334–5.

'The fact that the interpretation for which the respondent contends would lead to so unreasonable a result is, in my opinion, sufficient to require the more limited meaning of "in motion" to be adopted unless there is very strong objection to it, and none was suggested. It is true that the Factories Act is a remedial statute and one should therefore lean towards giving a wide interpretation to it, but that does not justify interpreting an ambiguous provision in a way which leads to quite unreasonable results.'

Since the law in general did not hinder the normal running of a factory, it was reasonable to interpret the section in a way which did not lead to such a result.

Despite these examples, the cases of a restrictive secondary meaning of statutory words are fewer than those where a wider secondary meaning has been adopted to give effect to the purpose of the statute. In many cases, the courts have taken the view of May LJ that:

'Whilst on modern principles of construction it is clearly legitimate to adopt a purposive approach and to hold that a statutory provision does apply to a given situation when it was clearly intended to do so, even though it may not also so apply on its strict literal interpretation, nevertheless I do not think that the converse is correct and that it is legitimate to adopt a purposive construction so as to preclude the application of a statute to a situation to which on its purely literal construction it would apply.'[15]

Jones v Wrotham Park Estates[16] could be cited as an example of a refusal to adopt a restrictive secondary meaning of the words used in the statute despite the fact that the result was contrary to the purpose of the statute.

We are now in a position to answer two questions which have been left open. (1) Does the word 'absurdity' used in various judicial statements mean something wider than repugnance or inconsistency with the rest of the instrument? (2) Do such words as 'repugnance', 'inconsistency', 'anomaly', 'contradiction' and 'absurdity' denote different issues, and how do they relate to a purposive construction of the statute?

It is submitted that the answer to the first question is in the affirmative; 'absurdity' in this context does mean something wider than repugnance or inconsistency with the rest of the instrument, although cases of repugnancy and inconsistency may be subsumed under the concep-

---

15. *R v Broadcasting Complaints Commission, ex p Owen* [1985] QB 1153 at 1174.
16. Supra, pp 18–19.

tion of absurdity.[17] *Richard Thomas and Baldwins Ltd v Cummings*[18] seems to afford conclusive support for the submission, since a holding, contrary to that of the House of Lords, to the effect that the machine was in motion would, so far from being inconsistent with, or repugnant to, the rest of the statute, have furthered its purpose, the protection of workmen. There are many similar cases. For example, in *Johnson v Moreton*[19] the anomaly which would have resulted from permitting the tenant to sign away his rights under s 24 of the Agricultural Holdings Act 1948 to appeal to the Agricultural Land Tribunal was perceived from the purpose of the Act. As Lord Hailsham remarked extra-judicially, 'There is nothing necessarily arbitrary or improper if judges select restricted or extended interpretations of an Act based less on language than on the nature and purpose of the legislation.'[20] But, as has been pointed out,[1] the context of a statutory provision includes the place which it occupies in relation to other legal provisions and values in the legal system as a whole. Accordingly, a secondary meaning of a statutory provision may be chosen to avoid an anomaly or repugnance in relation to those other provisions or values. Both the majority and the minority in *Wills v Bowley*[2] adopted this approach, differing merely on which legal value, public order or the liberty of the citizen, was to be given priority in the interpretation of the section.

Although the judge may proceed in this way with a view to securing coherence and consistency within the law as a whole, this approach is limited by the texts under consideration. This is clearly shown by the case of *R v Barnet London Borough Council, ex p Nilish Shah*.[3] Section 1(1) of the Education Act 1962 requires local education authorities to make grants to students who are 'ordinarily resident' in their area, so that they can attend courses of higher education. Regulations made under the Act required the student to have been 'ordinarily resident' in the United Kingdom for three years prior to his application. The question arose whether persons who had come to the United Kingdom for secondary or other education could count the period so spent as 'ordinary residence' so as to qualify for a mandatory grant under the Act. The Court of Appeal held that they could not.[4] Lord Denning MR

---

17. This view was once contested by E A Driedger, but he now supports the view stated in the text: see his 'Statutes: The Mischievous Literal Golden Rule' (1981) 59 Can Bar Rev 780 at 784.
18. Supra, p 91.
19. Supra, p 18.
20. *Hamlyn Revisited* (London, 1983) p 68.
1. Supra, p 48.
2. Supra, pp 87–8.
3. [1983] 2 AC 309, [1983] 1 All ER 226.
4. [1982] QB 688, [1982] 1 All ER 698.

and Eveleigh LJ were impressed by the need to relate this Act to the policy of the Commonwealth Immigrants Act 1962 and its successor, the Immigration Act 1971. Under the latter Act students coming only for study had a conditional leave to stay in the country limited to the purpose of study and this did not involve ordinary residence for the general purposes of everyday life. They considered that consistency with this Act required the term 'ordinarily resident' in the Education Act to be interpreted as living as an ordinary member of the community would, which could not include residence for the limited purpose of study. Lord Denning MR argued that 'We must do our best to legislate for a state of affairs for which Parliament has not legislated. We must say what is the meaning of the words 'ordinarily resident' in the context of the situation brought about by the Immigration Act 1971.'[5] The House of Lords unanimously reversed this decision. In its opinion, the Court of Appeal had given too much weight to the arguments drawn from the purposes of the Immigration Act 1971. Parliament's purpose expressed in the Education Act gave no hint of any restriction on the eligibility for a mandatory award other than ordinary residence in the United Kingdom for three years and a satisfactory educational record. There was nothing expressed in the Immigration Act which gave guidance as to the interpretation of the Education Act and, indeed, despite a series of immigration measures since 1962, nationality had not formed part of the regulations under the Education Act until 1980. Accordingly, the ordinary natural meaning of the Education Act prevailed to make the students eligible for a mandatory grant if they had resided in the United Kingdom for the purposes of study.[6] Lord Scarman stated that, 'It cannot be permissible in the absence of a reference (express or necessarily to be implied) by one statute to the other to interpret an earlier Act by reference to a later Act.'[7] The role of the judge is not to reconcile legislative provisions unless it is reasonable to infer that this is what the legislator intended.

If the answer to the first question is in the affirmative, then there would not appear to be a substantial difference in what is denoted by the words 'repugnance', 'inconsistency', 'anomaly', 'contradiction', and 'absurdity' as used by the judges. Our rules of interpretation have fortunately not reached such a degree of sophistication as to require distinctions of so great a subtlety to be drawn. The construction of s 59 of the Local Government, Planning and Land Act 1980 adopted by the

---

5. Ibid, at 721.
6. The law was altered on this point by the Education (Fees and Awards) Act 1983.
7. [1983] 2 AC at 348–9.

House of Lords in *Nottinghamshire County Council v Secretary of State for the Environment*[8] avoided a repugnancy between the requirement that guidance be determined by reference to criteria 'applicable to all local authorities' and the purpose of the Act in trying to reduce the expenditure of high spending local authorities; the construction of s 161(1) of the Income Tax Act 1952 adopted in *Luke v Inland Revenue Commrs*[9] avoided an anomaly; and the construction of s 145(3)(a) of the Road Traffic Act 1972 in *Cooper v Motor Insurers' Bureau*[10] avoided an internal consistency. In such cases the judges could also be described as avoiding an absurd result. Bennion argues[11] that 're-pugnancy, inconsistency and contradiction (all as between different enactments) raise conceptual problems different to those where the "absurdity" lies within a single provision.' Certainly problems of the internal consistency of a statute read as a whole may appear more readily resolved than those requiring consistency between a statutory provision and other legal provisions or values, where the choice of solutions may be greater and it may be more doubtful whether an attempt at consistency is appropriate. However, problems of internal consistency are sometimes resolved by appeal to other legal values, as was, for example, the case in *Johnson v Moreton*[12] where their Lordships referred to the general scheme of legislation in the area to determine the meaning of a section which appeared in contradiction to the purpose of the Act. This is often the effect of legal presumptions which are used to arbitrate between different possible meanings of statutory words. To this extent, the issues of internal and external consistency are not easily dissociated. Consistency with other provisions of the Act is but one instance of the wider obligation of judges to ensure that the provisions of the law are, as far as possible, interpreted in a way which is coherent and consistent.

Since these various words denote substantially the same issue, the use of different words may appear confusing. In the end, the issue always amounts to asking whether a construction is inconsistent with the purpose of the statute. Of course, the judge must have in view not merely the specific purpose of the statute, but also the general purposes of the law into which the purpose and provisions of the statute are presumed to have been intended to fit coherently. Given this double aspect of the consistency which the judge strives to achieve, it might be thought that a general word such as 'absurdity' best describes

---

8. Supra, pp 88–9.
9. Supra, pp 89–90.
10. Supra, p 90.
11. *Bennion*, p 337.
12. Supra, p 18.

all the conditions which permit the judge to depart from the primary meaning of statutory words. However, such a term has the inconvenience of failing to make it clear that it is only inconsistency with the purpose of the statute, understood in the light of other legal provisions and values, that justifies this departure and not a judge's more general views of what is an 'absurd' result. For this reason, the second basic rule talks of 'a result which is contrary to the purpose of the statute', rather than of 'an absurd result'.

E. READING WORDS IN AND OUT OF A STATUTE

This brings us to the illustration of the third of the basic rules set out on page 47; the judge may read in words which he considers to be necessarily implied by words which are already in the statute and he has a limited power to add to, alter or ignore statutory words in order to prevent a provision from being unintelligible, absurd or totally unreasonable, unworkable, or totally irreconcilable with the rest of the statute.

Words may be said to be necessarily implied by other words when their express statement merely clarifies a secondary meaning of those other words. Several instances of necessary implication have already been given. In *Adler v George*[13] the court took the view that, in the context of the obstruction of airfields, the words 'in the vicinity of' were apt to cover someone on a field; the words 'in or' were implied with the result that an offence could be committed by someone 'in or in the vicinity'. In *Johnson v Moreton*,[14] the whole context and purpose of the statute required the implication that the right to apply to the Agricultural Land Tribunal was to have effect 'notwithstanding any agreement to the contrary'. Similarly in *Wills v Bowley*[15] words permitting the arrest of someone reasonably believed to be committing the offence were treated as a necessary implication in the text. In many cases it is possible to apply the secondary meaning of a single word or phrase without there being any question of implying further words. Thus in *R v Webb*,[16] in the context of the Sexual Offences Act 1956, the offence of procuring a women to become a 'common prostitute' was held, without the necessity of supplying further words, to have been

---

13. Supra, p 33.
14. Supra, p 18.
15. Supra, pp 87–8.
16. [1964] 1 QB 357, [1963] 3 All ER 177.

committed by someone employing a masseuse who performed lewd acts with men although there was no suggestion of sexual intercourse. 'Lewd hireling' is a recognised secondary meaning of the word 'prostitute'. The reading in of statutory words is, however, a very frequent concomitant of giving a secondary meaning to a statutory provision of any length.

The reason why the process is mentioned in rule 3 is that there are inevitably cases in which it is debatable whether the court was giving effect to a secondary meaning or adding words in order to prevent unreasonable results. The construction of the proviso to s 38 of the Children and Young Persons Act 1933 mentioned on page 66 may be taken as an example. The proviso reads:

> 'Provided that where evidence admitted by virtue of this section is given on behalf of the prosecution the accused shall not be liable to be convicted of the offence unless that evidence is corroborated by some other material evidence in support thereof implicating him.'

When, in *Director of Public Prosecutions v Hester*,[17] the House of Lords treated the words 'some other material evidence in support thereof' as the equivalent of 'some other material evidence admitted otherwise than by virtue of this section', they were certainly doing no more than stating expressly what was already implied in the statutory words; but what about the reading in of some such words as 'in consequence of such evidence' after the word 'offence' in order to prevent the preposterous result that an accused would, on a literal construction of the proviso, not be liable to be convicted in a case in which there was an abundance of evidence against him admissible otherwise than by virtue of s 38 and some peripherally relevant evidence of an uncorroborated unsworn child? The phrase 'that evidence' means, in its verbal context, 'any evidence admitted by virtue of s 38'. If a court holds that, in its legal context, 'that evidence' means 'evidence in consequence of which the accused is liable to be convicted', is it giving effect to a secondary meaning, or is it exercising a power to add words in order to prevent a wholly unreasonable result? This is a silly question in the context of the present discussion because it makes no difference what the answer is. The words 'in consequence of such evidence' must be read into the proviso in either event.

An example of the exercise of the power to add to the words of a statute in order to prevent a provision from having a result clearly contrary to the plain intention of the rest of the statute was the decision of

---

17. [1973] AC 296, [1972] 3 All ER 1056.

the Court of Appeal in *Deria v General Council of British Shipping*.[18] There s 8(1) of the Race Relations Act 1976 was read as providing that 'employment is to be regarded as being at an establishment in Great Britain unless the employee does *or is to do* his work wholly outside Great Britain', the italicised words being necessary to prevent initially permissible discrimination from being rendered unlawful by changes in the location of employment several months later. Such a case demonstrates that the criticisms of judicial legislation in *Duport Steels*[19] and *ex p Shah*[20] should not be treated as precluding a judicial power to read words into statutes beyond those which are already there by necessary implication. A more elaborate attempt to lay down the limits of the power to read words into a statute was made in *Western Bank Ltd v Schindler*.[1] The defendant had entered into a mortgage under which he was liable to repay the capital, with interest, after 10 years, but was under no obligation to pay any interest until then. The mortgagee applied to the court to take possession of mortgaged property under his common law right to possession, exercisable irrespective of any default. Section 36(1) of the Administration of Justice Act 1970 gives the court a power to defer a possession order 'if it appears to the court that in the event of its exercising the power the mortgagor is likely to be able within a reasonable period to pay any sums due under the mortgage or to remedy a default consisting of a breach of any other obligation arising under or by virtue of the mortgage'. A literal reading would suggest that the court's powers are limited to cases where the mortgagor is in default under the mortgage agreement. Here, the defendant mortgagor was held not to be in default under the mortgage, because the 10 years had not elapsed at the end of which the repayment of the capital with interest was required; and the mortgagee argued that, there being no default, s 36 was inapplicable. The Court of Appeal rejected this argument. Both Buckley and Scarman LJJ considered that it would be manifestly unfair if the court were to have a discretionary power to defer an order for possession where the mortgagor was in default, but no such power where he was not. They considered that the conditional clause in the subsection must be read as applying only in cases involving a default, and that its meaning would be clear if it had read 'but, if any sum is due under the mortgage or the mortgagor is in default . . . [the court may exercise its power to defer possession] only if it appears to the court . . .'. Scarman LJ distinguished this approach from judicial legislation:

---

18. Supra, p 34.
19. Supra, p 29.
20. Supra, pp 93–4.
1. [1977] Ch 1.

'Judicial legislation is not an option open to an English judge. Our courts are not required, as are, for instance, the Swiss courts (see the Swiss Civil Code, articles 1 and 2), to declare and insert into legislation rules which the judge would have put there, had he been the legislator. But our courts do have the duty of giving effect to the intention of Parliament, if it be possible, even though the process requires a strained construction of the language used or the insertion of words in order to do so . . . The line between judicial legislation, which our law does not permit, and judicial interpretation in a way best designed to give effect to the intention of Parliament is not an easy one to draw. Suffice it to say that before our courts can imply words into a statute the statutory intention must be plain and the insertion not too big, or too much at variance with the language used by the legislature. The courts will strain against . . . leaving unfilled the "casus omissus".'[2]

This approach seems to go further than what might be added to a text by necessary implication.

Some allowance must at least be made for obvious drafting errors. For example, s 33 of the Fines and Recoveries Act 1833 provided that, if the protector of a settlement should be convicted of felony, or an infant, the Court of Chancery should be the protector in lieu of the infant. The convicted felon was obviously omitted in error, and, in *Re Wainewright*,[3] Lord Lyndhurst held that the omission should be made good by supplying the words 'in lieu of the person who shall be convicted' before the reference to the infant.

Even in this class of case judges will sometimes go to remarkable lengths in order to avoid saying that they are adding words to a statute. In *A-G v Beauchamp*[4] the defendant was charged under a statute which provided that:

'Every person who shall print any paper . . . which shall be meant to be published or dispersed and who shall not print upon . . . such paper . . . his or her name and place of abode or business, and every person who shall publish or disperse . . . any printed paper . . . on which the name and place of abode of the person printing the same shall not be printed as aforesaid, shall for every copy so printed by him or her, forfeit a sum of not more than £5.'

---

2. Ibid, at 18.
3. (1843) 1 Ph 258.
4. [1920] 1 KB 650.

The defendant was the publisher, but not the printer, of a paper which did not bear the name and place of abode or business of the printer. He was held liable to a penalty under the statute by the Divisional Court notwithstanding the omission of the words 'or published or dispersed' before the words 'by him or her' at the end of the section. Rowlatt J thought the omission was an obvious error which could be made good; but the other two members of the court preferred to treat the words 'so printed by him or her' as referring to the 'person printing the same' in order to avoid adding words. Rowlatt J's retort, not accepted by the other members of the court, was that their construction would mean that anyone who only published one copy of an offending paper would be liable to a penalty in respect of every copy printed by the printer.

Although most of the cases happen to be concerned with the substitution rather than the addition of words, modern judges are generally prepared to describe what they are doing in more realistic terms than their predecessors. All the same, many of them will prefer not to express what they are doing as a rectification of the statutory words. Thus in *Johnson v Moreton*,[5] all their Lordships preferred to say that the granting of the right to apply to the Agricultural Lands Tribunal should be construed as a mandatory provision of the Agricultural Holdings Act 1948, rather than to say that they were adding words to the section.

One of the frankest statements concerning the power to go further than merely giving a statutory provision a secondary meaning and stating expressly what was already implied is that of MacKinnon LJ in *Sutherland Publishing Co Ltd v Caxton Publishing Co Ltd*:[6]

> 'When the purpose of an enactment is clear, it is often legitimate, because it is necessary, to put a strained interpretation upon some words which have been inadvertently used, and of which the plain meaning would defeat the obvious intention of the legislature. It may even be necessary, and therefore legitimate, to substitute for an inept word or words that which such intention requires. The most striking example of this I think is one passage in the Carriage of Goods by Sea Act 1924, where to prevent a result so nonsensical that the legislature cannot have intended it, it has been held necessary and legitimate to substitute the word "and" for the word "or". The violence of this operation has, I think, been minimised by saying that in this place the word "or" must be taken to mean "and". That is a cowardly evasion. In

---

5. Supra, p 18.
6. [1938] Ch 174 at 201.

truth one word is substituted for another. For "or" can never mean "and".'

MacKinnon LJ was presumably referring to *R F Brown & Co Ltd v T and J Harrison*[7] where, as MacKinnon J he had held that, in a provision of the Carriage of Goods by Sea Act 1924, 'or' could not be read as conjunctive, although he was prepared to treat 'and' as substituted for 'or'. He omitted to say that, although the Court of Appeal affirmed his decision, they did so on the ground that 'or' could sometimes be construed conjunctively in order to avoid an absurdity, Atkin LJ feeling constrained to characterise the argument that 'or' could never mean 'and' as the worst point that had ever been taken in the Court of Appeal in his time. MacKinnon LJ was partially vindicated by the decision of the House of Lords in *Federal Steam Navigation Co Ltd v Department of Trade and Industry*,[8] where Lord Reid agreed that 'or' can never mean 'and', adding that decisions suggesting that, as a matter of construction, it could do so were wrong; but he reaffirmed the existence of a power to substitute 'and' for 'or' although he was one of the two dissentients who thought that it ought not to have been exercised on the particular facts. Both defendants were charged with contravening s 1 of the Oil in Navigable Waters Act 1955 which read in part as follows: 'If any oil . . . is discharged from a British ship . . . into a part of the sea which is a prohibited sea area . . . *the owner or master* of the ship shall be guilty of an offence.' The defendants were respectively the owner and master of a British ship from which oil had been discharged into a prohibited sea area. Both of them were convicted and they appealed unsuccessfully to the Court of Appeal. In the House of Lords a majority of 3 to 2 was in favour of dismissing their appeals. All the law lords agreed that the House had power to treat the section as though the relevant words were 'the owner and the master or each of them' or, to put it more shortly, 'the owner and or the master'. What divided the House was the question whether the concept of a criminal offence with regard to which the prosecution had an unfettered discretion to select which of two persons should be proceeded against was such a legal monstrosity that it had to be avoided by the application to the section of what Lord Wilberforce, a member of the majority, regarded as 'surgery rather than therapeutics'.[9] MacKinnon LJ's vindication has been described as partial because Lord Salmon expressly, and Lords Morris and Simon by implication, did not commit themselves on the linguistic question whether 'or' could ever mean

---

7. (1927) 43 TLR 394, affirmed by the Court of Appeal at 633.
8. [1974] 2 All ER 97.
9. Ibid, at 111.

'and'. Granted that a court has power to substitute 'and' for 'or' in the reading of a statute the linguistic question is legally irrelevant.

R v Oakes[10] is the converse of *Federal Steam Navigation Co Ltd v Department of Trade and Industry*, for 'or' was substituted for 'and'. Oakes was charged with doing an act preparatory to the commission of an offence under the Official Secrets Act 1911. Section 7 of the Official Secrets Act 1920 reads:

> 'Any person who attempts to commit any offence under the Official Secrets Act 1911, or this Act, or solicits or incites or endeavours to persuade another, or aids or abets *and* does any act preparatory to the commission of an offence under the Official Secrets Act 1911 or this Act shall be guilty. . . .'

It was unsuccessfully argued at first instance and on appeal that the indictment disclosed no offence because Oakes was not charged with attempting, inciting, aiding or abetting the commission of an offence in addition to doing a preparatory act. Lord Parker's answer was:[11]

> 'It seems to this court that where the literal reading of a statute, and a penal statute, produces an intelligible result, clearly there is no ground for reading in words or changing words according to what may be the supposed intention of Parliament. But here we venture to think that the result is unintelligible.'

The courts seem to have had fewer inhibitions about ignoring statutory words than about adding to and altering them. It is only necessary to mention two very strong cases, *Salmon v Duncombe* and *Re Lockwood*. The first is a strong case because some words were ignored and others treated as necessarily implied by the words that were left, and the second is a strong case because an entire subsection of a modern statute was totally disregarded.

Salmon v Duncombe[12] was concerned with the construction of a Natal Ordinance of 1856. The title and preamble made it clear that the purpose of the Ordinance was to enable natural-born British subjects resident in Natal to make wills free from the restrictions on testation imposed by Roman Dutch law. Mrs Duncombe, a natural-born British subject, had made a will in favour of her second husband while she was resident in Natal. Her estate consisted of real property situated in Natal, and the question was whether the second husband was entitled to the entire estate or whether the children of Mrs Duncombe's first

---

10. [1959] 2 QB 350, [1959] 2 All ER 92.
11. Ibid, at 354.
12. (1886) 11 App Cas 627.

marriage were entitled to portions of it in accordance with Roman Dutch law which had been adopted in Natal. Section 1(1) of the Ordinance read:

> 'Any natural-born subject of Great Britain and Ireland resident within this district may exercise all and singular the rights which such natural-born subject could or might exercise according to the laws and customs of England in regard to the disposal by last will and testament of property, both real and personal, situated in this district, *to all intents and purposes as if such natural-born subject resided in England.*'

The draftsman had failed to make allowance for the provisions of English private international law according to which gifts by will of immovable property are governed by the law of the country where the property is situated. If Mrs Duncombe had been resident in England when she made her will it would have been subject to the restrictions of Roman Dutch law in favour of the children of her first marriage so far as her real property in Natal was concerned. There was no finding with regard to Mrs Duncombe's domicile at the time of her death. But it may be added that, by English law, the validity of dispositions of movable property is governed by the law of the testator's last domicile, so that the will of a natural-born British subject resident and domiciled in Natal would be subject to the restrictions imposed by Roman Dutch law on account of the last nine words of the Ordinance. The judicial committee of the Privy Council got over the difficulties occasioned by the draftsman's apparent ignorance of English private international law by disregarding the last nine words of the Ordinance and implying the words 'over property subject to such laws and customs' after the word 'England'. In justification of this course Lord Hobhouse said: 'It is very unsatisfactory to be compelled to construe a statute in this way, but it is much more unsatisfactory to deprive it altogether of meaning'.[13]

In *Re Lockwood*[14] Lockwood died intestate and his only next of kin were issue of uncles and aunts of the whole blood. Under s 46 and the early part of s 47 of the Administration of Estates Act 1925, the issue of deceased uncles and aunts of the intestate are entitled to share in his estate, but s 47(5) (inserted by the Intestate Estates Act 1952) raises doubts with regard to cases in which there are no surviving uncles and aunts. The subsection reads:

> 'It is hereby declared that, where the trusts in favour of any class of the relatives of the intestate, other than issue of the intestate, fail by reason of no member of that class acquiring an absolutely

---

13. 11 App Cas at 635.
14. [1958] Ch 231, [1957] 3 All ER 520.

vested interest, the residuary estate of the intestate . . . shall . . . go devolve and be held under the provisions of this Part of this Act as if the intestate had died without leaving any member of that class, *or issue of any member of that class*, living at the death of the intestate.'

On the strength of this subsection the Crown claimed the deceased's estate as *bona vacantia*. *Prima facie* its case was unanswerable. The trusts in favour of Lockwood's uncles and aunts had failed because none of them had acquired a vested interest, accordingly the estate was to go and devolve as if no issue of uncles and aunts had been living at the date of Lockwood's death. There were no next of kin of the half blood, hence the Crown must succeed on the strength of the plain language of s 47(5). This conclusion is sufficiently odd to give pause for thought, but consequences thought by some to be even more capricious would follow from giving effect to the subsection. If one uncle of the whole blood had survived, the issue of dead uncles and aunts would have been entitled to the shares their parents would have received had they survived; if Lockwood had been survived by an uncle of the half blood in addition to the issue of uncles and aunts of the whole blood, that uncle would have been entitled to the whole estate. Harman J decided to disregard the italicised words, saying: 'I take this course because I am convinced that Parliament, in laying down rules for ascertaining next-of-kin, cannot have intended to promote those more remote over those nearer in blood'.[15] The chosen course was rendered all the more bold by the fact that Harman J was unable to think of any situation to which the subsection without those words might properly be applied.

The power to add to, alter or ignore statutory words is an extremely limited one. Generally speaking it can only be exercised where there has been a demonstrable mistake on the part of the draftsman or where the consequence of applying the words in their ordinary, or discernible secondary, meaning would be utterly unreasonable. Even then the mistake may be thought to be beyond correction by the court, or the tenor of the statute may be such as to preclude the addition of words to avoid an unreasonable result. *Inland Revenue Commrs v Ayrshire Employers' Mutual Insurance Association Ltd*[16] is a case in which the draftsman's mistake was treated as being past correction by the addition of words. It was not disputed that s 31 of the Finance Act 1933 was intended to provide that mutual insurance companies were liable to income tax on the annual surplus arising from transactions with their members; but the draftsman had mistakenly assumed that these com-

---

15. Ibid, at p 238.
16. [1946] 1 All ER 637.

panies were already liable to tax on profits derived from insurance transactions with non-members and this assumption formed the basis of subsection (1):

> 'In the application to any society or company of any provision or rule relating to profits or gains chargeable under Case I of Schedule D (which relates to trades), . . . any reference to profits or gains shall be deemed to include a reference to a profit or surplus arising from transactions of the company or society with its members which would be included in profits or gains for the purpose of that provision or rule if those transactions were transactions with non-members. . . .'

A unanimous House of Lords held that the Association's profits from transactions with its members were not liable to tax because, according to the case law, profits of mutual insurance companies were immune from tax on the ground that they belonged to the contributors whether they were members of the Association or not. Lord Macmillan said that the legislature had 'plainly missed fire'.[17] To this Lord Diplock has since retorted extrajudicially that if, as in this case, the courts can identify the target of Parliamentary legislation, 'their proper function is to see that it is hit; not merely to record that it has been missed'.[18] There is obvious force in this remark but there is also much to be said for the following observations of Lord Simonds in the *Ayrshire Insurance* case itself:[19]

> 'The section . . . is clearly a remedial section, if that is a proper description of a section intended to bring further subject matter within the ambit of taxation. It is at least clear what is the gap that is intended to be filled and hardly less clear how it is intended to fill that gap. Yet I can come to no other conclusion than that the language of the section fails to achieve its apparent purpose and I must decline to insert words or phrases which might succeed where the draftsman failed.'

Lord Diplock's comment implies that it is the courts' sole function to ascertain the intention of Parliament and give effect to it. No doubt this is true so far as most statutes are concerned, but, in the case of some statutes, notably those creating crimes but possibly also those imposing taxes, surely the courts have the further function of ensuring that citizens are only deprived of their liberty or their money by

---

17. Ibid, at 641.
18. *Courts and Legislators* (Birmingham, 1965) p 10, reprinted in B Harvey (ed), *The Lawyer and Justice* (London, 1978) 265 at 274.
19. [1946] 1 All ER at 641.

reasonably clearly worded provisions or at least by provisions which, though poorly phrased, are susceptible of comparatively easy rectification. With the best will in the world rectification of s 31 of the Finance Act 1933 would have been far from easy. Lord Diplock's own speech in *Jones v Wrotham Park Estates Ltd*[20] should sound a note of caution here. In that case it was clear that the legislation had failed to cover a possible method of evasion, yet their Lordships refused to rectify the Act in the absence of a clear indication of what the substituted words should be.

R v Northampton Borough Council, ex p Quietlynn Ltd[1] is a case in which the clear wording of express provisions of a statute precluded any addition to its words in order to avoid an unreasonable result. Paragraph 29 of Sch 3 to the Local Government (Miscellaneous Provisions) Act 1982 applies to applications for licences to use premises as a sex establishment made before 'the appointed day' (the day on which the Schedule comes into force in the area of the local authority concerned). Sub-paragraph (2) prohibits the local authority from considering any application to which the paragraph applies before the appointed day, and sub-paragraph (3) prohibits them from granting any such application 'until they have considered all such applications'. In two cases, because of administrative difficulties, local authorities had granted licences to use premises as sex establishments in respect of applications made *after* the appointed day, but had refused to grant licences in respect of applications made *before* that day until they could consider all these latter applications. A company which had made applications before the appointed day sought judicial review to quash these refusals to grant licences. The Court of Appeal concluded that Parliament had assumed that, on the appointed day, the local authority would gather up and consider all the applications for licences received before that day and decide on them, so that subsequent applications would necessarily be processed at a later date. This assumption had been falsified by the administrative difficulty of having to consider all the applications received before the appointed day prior to a determination on any of them. The lack of a provision requiring priority to be given to applications made before the appointed day over those made later resulted from a failure of Parliament to foresee the situation which arose, and not just from a failure to spell out its intentions clearly. The Court of Appeal thus felt constrained to construe the wording of paragraph 29(3) according to its plain terms which required the local authority to delay granting any licences to those who

---

20. Supra, p 19.
1. (1986) 85 LGR 249.

had applied before the appointed day until all such applications could be decided upon together. Accordingly the local authorities had acted properly and the applications for judicial review failed. A clear objection to action by the courts in such a situation is the difficulty of specifying the precise words which should be added. Should the local authorities have granted no licences at all until they had decided on all the applications made before the appointed day?

Were it not for a passage in Lord Reid's speech in *Federal Steam Navigation Co Ltd v Department of Trade and Industry*[2] no attempt would have been made in the formulation of rule 3 of the basic rules set out on page 47 to classify the cases to which it applies. It confers a wholly exceptional power of what is in effect rectification of a statute, and the wiser course might have been to refrain from further formulation. Lord Reid said:[3]

> 'Cases where it has properly been held that a word can be struck out of a deed or statute and another substituted can as far as I am aware be grouped under three heads: where without such substitution the provision is unintelligible or absurd or totally unreasonable; where it is unworkable; and where it is totally irreconcilable with the plain intention shown by the rest of the deed or statute.'

Perhaps it is permissible to extend these remarks to cases of addition and alteration. Examples have been given of all three of the categories mentioned by Lord Reid. Section 7 of the Official Secrets Act 1920 is unintelligible without the substitution of 'or' for 'and' adopted in *R v Oakes*;[4] the addition of the reference to a convicted felon in *Re Wainewright*[5] prevented an absurdity; and the effect of s 36 of the Administration of Justice Act 1970 would have been totally unreasonable without the emendation agreed by Buckley and Scarman LJJ in *Western Bank Ltd v Schindler*.[6] *Wills v Bowley*[7] may properly be regarded as adding words to s 28 of the Town Police Clauses Act 1847 in order to prevent it being unworkable for police officers. Section 47(5) of the Administration of Estates Act 1925 is plainly at variance with the scheme of the Act under which relations of the whole blood

---

2. Supra, p 101.
3. [1974] 2 All ER at 100.
4. Supra, p 102.
5. Supra, p 99.
6. Supra, pp 98–9.
7. Supra, pp 87–8; but see the contrary views of Lord Lowry in the same case, [1983] 1 AC at 89. It is not sufficient that the result is merely inconvenient: *Pollway Nominees Ltd v Croydon London Borough Council* [1985] 3 All ER 24, CA, and *Bennion*, p 683.

are preferred to relations of the half blood and this was the justification of the action of Harman J in *Re Lockwood*.[8]

Lord Reid also made the point that it would not always be proper to strike words out even when the case fell within one of the above categories. In this context it is worth recalling the three conditions for the exercise of the analogous power of adding words to a statute laid down by Lord Diplock in *Jones v Wrotham Park Estates Ltd*:[9]

'First, it [must be] possible to determine from a consideration of the provisions of the Act read as a whole what the mischief was that it was the purpose of the Act to remedy; secondly, it [must be] apparent that the draftsman and Parliament had by inadvertence overlooked, and so omitted to deal with, an eventuality that required to be dealt with if the purpose of the Act was to be achieved; and thirdly, it [must be] possible to state with certainty what were the additional words that would have been inserted by the draftsman and approved by Parliament had their attention been drawn to the omission before the Bill passed into law.'

To these might be added a fourth condition drawn from the judgment of Scarman LJ in *Western Bank Ltd v Schindler*,[10] namely that the insertion should not be 'too big, or too much at variance with the language used by the legislature'. In omitting or inserting words the judge is not really engaged in a hypothetical reconstruction of the intentions of the draftsman or the legislature, but is simply making as much sense as he can of the text of the statutory provision read in its appropriate context and within the limits of the judicial role.

There can be little doubt that different judges have taken different views with regard to the exercise of the exceptional power of rectification. It is far from clear that all judges would give their blessing to the emendation of s 8(1) of the Race Relations Act 1976 approved by the Court of Appeal in *Deria v General Council of British Shipping*.[11] On the other hand there are reported decisions in which the power was not exercised although other judges might have acted differently. In support of this statement it is only necessary to refer to *Altrincham Electric Supply Ltd v Sale Urban District Council*,[12] a case which excited a remarkable difference of judicial opinion. The company supplied electricity to the urban district of Sale and to parts of the rural

---

8. Supra, pp 103–4.
9. Supra, p 19.
10. Supra, p 99.
11. Supra, pp 97–8.
12. (1936) 154 LT 379.

district of Bucklow. The Sale Urban District Council served notice exercising its statutory option to purchase so much of the company's undertaking as operated in the area of Sale. The case turned on the assessment of the purchase price which depended on the true construction of the following extract from s 58 of the Ashton-on-Mersey Electric Lighting Ordinance 1896:

'The price payable by the Local Authority shall be ascertained as follows: If the accumulated profits of the undertaking shall at the expiration of notice amount to or exceed a return of 7½% per annum on the total expenditure of the undertakers upon the undertaking, including the cost of additions and alterations, the purchase money shall be a sum equal to such total expenditure.'

If, as the company contended, 'the total expenditure of the undertakers upon the undertaking' meant the expenditure of the whole of its undertaking, including those parts of it which operated in Bucklow, the sum due was nearly twice as much as would have been due if the words were so construed (or altered) as to mean 'the total expenditure of the undertakers upon the undertaking or such parts thereof as are included in the notice'. It was of course the contention of the Sale Urban District Council that the Order should be so construed. The arbitrator and Farwell J decided in favour of the company on the ground that the words were clear and unambiguous. A majority of the Court of Appeal decided in favour of the Urban District Council and the House of Lords allowed the company's appeal by a majority of 3 to 2. It is true that the minority in the House of Lords appears to have treated the case as one in which the limitation on the meaning of undertaking was necessarily implied, but it is difficult to escape the conclusion that some modern judges would have regarded the case as one in which the power of rectification might be exercised on the ground that adhering to the ordinary meaning of the words would have been something that was totally unreasonable. However the contrary view was expressed with great force by Lord Russell who said:[13]

'In the present case, notwithstanding the alleged impossible results which are said to flow from the plain meaning of the words used (eg the duplication which would necessarily accompany the hypothetical case of simultaneous notices and purchases by Sale and Bucklow), I find myself without any materials, evidential or otherwise, which enable me to assert that the words in s 58 cannot possibly have been intended by their authors to bear the only meaning which they naturally convey.'

---

13. Ibid, at 388.

Lord Macmillan pinned his faith to the following passage from Lord Halsbury's speech in *Income Tax Special Purposes Commissioner v Pemsel*:[14]

'Whatever the real fact may be I think a court of law is bound to proceed on the assumption that the legislature is an ideal person that does not make mistakes. It must be assumed that it has intended what it has said, and I think any other view of the mode in which we must approach the interpretation of a statute would give authority for the interpretation of the language of an Act of Parliament which would be attended with the most serious consequences.'

What, it may be asked, would Lord Halsbury have done in *Salmon v Duncombe*?[15] Would he have acquitted the accused in *R v Vasey and Lally*[16] on the ground that the statutory provision under which they were charged was gibberish which did not define a crime in relation to salmon rivers? Section 13 of the Salmon Fisheries Act 1873 read:

'The provisions of s 32 of the Malicious Injuries to Property Act 1861 so far as they relate to poisoning any water with intent to kill or destroy fish shall be extended and apply to salmon rivers, as if the words "or in any salmon river" were inserted in the said section in lieu of the words "private rights of fishery" after the words "noxious material in any such pond or water".'

Unfortunately the words 'any private rights of fishery' did not follow the words 'noxious material in any pond or water' but occurred at a point in the verbiage of s 32 before the putting of noxious material into water with intent to kill or destroy fish had been reached. The Court for Crown Cases Reserved did not care whether the words in s 13 of the 1873 Act from 'as if' on were ignored or whether the proposed amendment was inserted at a point at which it made sense. But the Court did carry out the obvious intention of the legislature and held that in consequence of s 13 of the 1873 Act, it was a misdemeanour under s 32 of the 1861 Act unlawfuly and maliciously to put noxious materials into any salmon river with intent to destroy fish.

Would Lord Halsbury have concluded that, on the true construction of the Criminal Appeal Act 1907, an accused who pleaded guilty could appeal against sentence although the Court of Criminal Appeal had no power to substitute another sentence if the original one were quashed?

---

14. [1891] AC 531 at 549. For a draftsman's view of his own fallibility compare F Bennion, *Statute Law* (2nd edn, London, 1983), Chs 16–18.
15. Supra, pp 102–3.
16. [1905] 2 KB 748.

This certainly appeared to be the effect of the words of the Act. Under s 3 a person convicted on indictment might appeal against a sentence passed on his conviction. Section 4(3) provided that 'on an appeal against sentence the Court of Criminal Appeal shall, if they think that a different sentence should have been passed, quash the sentence passed at the trial, and pass such other sentence warranted in law by the *verdict* (whether more or less severe) in substitution therefor as they think ought to have been passed'. Plainly no other sentence is warranted in law 'by the verdict' in the case of someone who pleaded guilty, but the Court of Criminal Appeal avoided this difficulty in *R v Ettridge*[17] by 'striking out' those words. Although it could be said that the questions posed here reflect a recent change in what is expected of the judges, the cases demonstrate that even Lord Halsbury's contemporaries were not slow to correct mistakes which the legislature had made.

Of course there must be an exceptionally strong case for the exercise of the wholly exceptional power of rectification, and of course it is essential that the courts should so far as possible stick to the ordinary meaning of statutory words, but this does not mean that they should throw their hands up in despair, not always unmingled with satisfaction, when the ordinary meaning produces a preposterous result. It is difficult to see any difference between the literal meaning approved by the majority in the *Altrincham* case and the interpretation in Alberta[18] of the bye-law requiring all drug shops to be closed at 10 pm on each and every day of the week as permitting a momentary closure at 10 pm to be followed by a reopening on the same day. It was said that no one but a lawyer would ever have thought of imputing such an intention to the bye-law. Who but a lawyer would have thought of imputing to Parliament the intention attributed to it by the majority in the *Altrincham* case? As often as not it is a matter of taste whether such results are avoided by the technique of necessary implication or by rectification, but avoided they should be like the plague.

17. [1909] 2 KB 24.
18. Supra, p 67.

Chapter 5
Internal aids to construction

The internal aids to construction will be briefly discussed under the heads of the enacting parts of the same statute, other parts of the same statute (preamble, headings, title etc) and rules of language such as the *ejusdem generis* rule.

A. ENACTING PARTS OF THE SAME STATUTE

It is scarcely necessary to cite authority for the proposition that Acts must be construed as a whole. Guidance with regard to the meaning of a particular word or phrase may be found in other words and phrases in the same section or in other sections although the utility of an extensive consideration of other parts of the same statute will actually vary from case to case. Speaking of the Income Tax Act 1952 (which consolidated a large number of enactments passed between 1918 and 1951), Lord Reid said:[1]

> 'It is no doubt true that every Act should be read as a whole, but that is, I think, because one assumes that in drafting one clause of a Bill the draftsman had in mind the language and substance of other clauses, and attributes to Parliament a comprehension of the whole Act. But where, as here, quite incongruous provisions are lumped together and it is impossible to suppose that anyone, draftsman or Parliament, ever considered one of these sections in the light of another, I think it would be just as misleading to base conclusions on the different language of different sections as it is to base conclusions on the different language of sections in different Acts.'

---

1. *Inland Revenue Commrs v Hinchy* [1960] AC 748 at 766.

Changes of language do, however, frequently have a decisive effect on the construction of the statutory provision. For example, s 102 of the Mental Health Act 1959 empowered the judge to do or secure the doing of all such things with respect to the property and affairs of a patient as appear necessary or expedient: '(b) for the maintenance or other benefit of members of the patient's family; or (c) for making provision for other persons or purposes for whom or which the patient might be expected to provide if he were not mentally disordered'. In *Re D M L*[2] Cross J said: 'The contrasting language of sub-clauses (*b*) and (c) suggests to my mind that the legislature considered that the word 'family' consisted of persons for all of whom the patient might *prima facie* be expected to make some provision. This, I think, indicates that the word does not include collateral relatives'. The result was that a scheme to avoid death duties under which benefits were conferred on the patient's nephews and nieces could not be sanctioned under s 102(b) although it was sanctioned under s 102(c).

There is a presumption that the same word or phrase bears the same meaning throughout the same statute. For example, in *Dixon v British Broadcasting Corporation*,[3] para 5(2) of Sch 1 to the Trade Union and Labour Relations Act 1974[4] provided that an employee was to be treated as dismissed by his employer only if '(a) the contract under which he is employed by the employer is terminated by the employer, whether it is terminated by notice or without notice, or (b) where under that contract he is employed for a fixed term, that term expires without being renewed under the same contract'. In an earlier case, *British Broadcasting Corporation v Ioannou*,[5] the Court of Appeal had expressed the opinion in relation to para 12 of the same Schedule[6] that a 'fixed term contract' was one whose term could not be unfixed by notice. If applied to paragraph 5(2), such an interpretation would mean that a contract for a stated period which contained a clause permitting either party to terminate it upon notice would not be a 'fixed term' contract, which would stultify the purpose of the Act in protecting employees against the premature or unfair termination of their employment. Accordingly, in deciding that contracts of two months and four weeks respectively, containing a clause permitting termination on notice, were 'fixed term' contracts, the Court of Appeal in *Dixon* felt obliged to declare the interpretation given in *Ioannou* as wrong, for both para 5 and para 12 were in the same Part II

---

2. [1965] Ch 1113 at 1137.
3. [1979] QB, [1979] 2 All ER 112.
4. Now s 55 of the Employment Protection (Consolidation) Act 1978.
5. [1975] QB 781, [1975] 2 All ER 999.
6. Now s 142 of the Employment Protection (Consolidation) Act 1978.

of the Schedule and the phrase should have the same meaning in each. The presumption is, however, of the mildest kind for it is easy to point to cases in which the same word has been held to have different meanings in different sections, or even the same section, of a single statute. A stock example of the first type of case is provided by the different meanings of the word 'premises' in the Landlord and Tenant Act 1954. Sometimes it is used in its popular sense of buildings while at other points in the statute it bears the technical meaning of that which may form the subject matter of the habendum of a lease with the result that land with or without buildings on it may be included.[7] The stock example of the use of the same verb in different senses in the same section is s 57 of the Offences Against the Person Act 1861 which provides that: 'whosoever, being *married*, shall *marry* any other person during the life of the former husband or wife' shall be guilty of bigamy. Although 'being married' means being validly married, 'shall marry' necessarily means no more than 'go through a marriage ceremony'.[8]

Bennion[9] raises the corollary that different words, should, *prima facie*, be given a different meaning. The draftsman should never be presumed to have been gratuitous in his changes of wording. However, the *Nottinghamshire County Council*[10] case shows that this is merely a presumption, for there the House of Lords treated 'applicable' and 'to be applied' as being interchangeable expressions. That case well illustrates the problems that may be caused by provisions textually inserted into an Act by subsequent legislation. The controversial word 'applicable' occurred in a subsection inserted into the Local Government Planning and Land Act 1980 by the Local Government Finance Act 1982. The various judges in the case had to consider whether the word was intended to be different from 'to be applied' used in the original section. As Balcombe J put it in *Chaudhary v Chaudhary*:[11]

> 'the principle of giving a word or phrase the same construction when it appears in different sections of the same Act, which in any event is not an absolute rule, is of limited application when the section relied on for the purpose of comparison has been introduced by subsequent legislation.'

It would be pointless to multiply examples of the effect of a change of language, or the use of identical language, within the same section or statute. Everything depends on the context, and it is impossible to make

---

7. *Bracey v Read* [1963] Ch 88, [1962] 3 All ER 472.
8. *R v Allen* (1872) LR 1 CCR 387.
9. *Bennion*, p 376.
10. *Supra*, pp 88–9.
11. [1984] 3 All ER 1017 at 1035.

useful generalisations; but something must be said about the effect that one section of a statute may have on the construction of another section of the same statute as a matter of substance rather than language. To begin with, two sections may be repugnant to each other. If the repugnancy is total and wholly inescapable, a rule of thumb has to be applied under which the later section prevails in accordance with the maxim that 'later laws repeal earlier contrary laws' (*'leges posteriores priores contrarias abrogant'*). But this is very much a last resort and there are various techniques of construction which may be employed in order to avoid a repugnancy. One of these, the technique of finding a secondary meaning for one or more of the words or phrases in question, has already been discussed. Two others are the technique of treating apparently conflicting provisions as dealing with distinct matters, and the technique of holding that one section apparently in conflict with another merely provides for an exception to the general rule contained in that other. The first is illustrated by *Windsor & Maidenhead Royal Borough Council v Brandrose Investments Ltd*, the second by *Steeples v Derbyshire County Council*, both cases concerning the interpretation of the Town and Country Planning Act 1971.

Windsor & Maidenhead Royal Borough Council v Brandrose Investments Ltd,[12] concerned the relationship between ss 52 and 277A of the Act. The former confers on a local planning authority power to enter into an agreement with any person regulating the use of that person's land. The Windsor & Maidenhead Council entered into such an agreement with a landowner allowing it to develop its site, which could not be done without the demolition of the buildings then on it. Section 52(3) expressly provides that—

> 'Nothing in this section or in any agreement made thereunder shall be construed—(a) as restricting the exercise, in relation to land which is the subject of any such agreement, of any powers exercisable by any Minister or authority under this Act so long as those powers are exercised in accordance with the provisions of the development plan, or in accordance with any directions which have been given by the Secretary of State . . .'

There was no development plan or direction of the Secretary of State affecting the site. Subsequently, the authority included the site within a conservation area and invoked the provision in s 277A(2) of the Act that no building in the area could be demolished without its consent. The Court of Appeal held that the two powers were distinct and that

---

12. [1983] 1 All ER 818.

the power to create a conservation area was not limited by the exercise of the power under s 52. Accordingly the Council was entitled to insist that no demolition on the site took place without its consent. In *Steeples v Derbyshire County Council*,[13] two further sections of the same Act were in conflict. Section 26 sets out the procedure for applications for planning permission relating to 'any class of development' designated under that section. Section 270(1) provides that, 'in relation to land of local planning authorities and to the development by local authorities of land in respect of which they are the local planning authorities', certain specified sections (not including s 26) shall have effect, subject to any exceptions or modifications prescribed in regulations. In a challenge to a planning application by a local planning authority for the creation of an amusement park on its own land, it was argued that the application was invalid, inter alia, because the authority had not complied with the formalities specified in s 26. Webster J rejected the argument on the ground that s 270(1) should be construed as exempting local planning authorities from the obligations of the Act except in respect of the sections which it expressly mentions.

One section may affect the construction of another as a matter of substance when account is taken of the fact that a particular construction of the section before the court, which does not produce a result contrary to the purpose of the statute, would lead to a construction of other sections which would produce such a result. Whether considerations of this nature are proper in a criminal case is perhaps questionable, but the outstanding instance is undoubtedly *R v Prince*.[14] Prince was charged with abduction contrary to s 55 of the Offences Against the Person Act 1861 according to which it was an offence to 'unlawfully take . . . any unmarried girl, being under the age of 16 years, out of the possession and against the will of her father or mother. . . .' He was found by the jury to have believed on reasonable grounds that the girl he abducted was over 16, but by a majority of 14 to 1, the Court for Crown Cases Reserved held that this was no defence. Under s 50 of the 1861 Act it was a felony to 'carnally know and abuse any girl under the age of 10 years', and s 51 made it a misdemeanour to 'carnally know and abuse any girl being above the age of 10 years and under the age of 12 years'. The principal argument used in the leading majority judgment delivered by Blackburn J is contained in the following passage:[15]

'It seems impossible to suppose that the intention of the legislature in those two sections [ss 50 and 51] could have been to make

---

13. [1984] 3 All ER 468.
14. (1875) LR 2 CCR 154.
15. Ibid, at 171–2.

the crime depend upon the knowledge by the prisoner of the girl's actual age. It would produce the monstrous result that a man who had carnal connection with a girl, in reality not quite 10 years old, but whom he on reasonable grounds believed to be a little more than 10, was to escape altogether. He could not, in that view of the statute, be convicted of the felony, for he did not know her to be under 10. He could not be convicted of the misdemeanour because she was in fact not above the age of 10. It seems to us that the intention of the legislature was to punish those who had connection with young girls, though with their consent, unless the girl was in fact old enough to give a valid consent. . . . The 55th section, on which the present case arises, uses precisely the same words as those in ss 50 and 51, and must be construed in the same way.'

In a sense Prince was the victim of bad drafting, for, quite apart from any issue concerning the niceties of *mens rea*, there is something seriously wrong with two such provisions as ss 50 and 51 of the Offences Against the Person Act 1861 if a man charged with unlawful intercourse with a girl above 10 and under 12 should have the cast iron defence that she was in fact under 10. Section 51 should simply have prohibited intercourse with girls under 12. Allowing for the substitution of the ages of 13 and 16 for 10 and 12, this is the result achieved by ss 5 and 6 of the Sexual Offences Act 1956, as amended by the Criminal Law Act 1967. Section 5 punishes intercourse with girls under 13 with a maximum of imprisonment for life, and s 6 punishes intercourse with girls under 16 with a maximum of two years' imprisonment. The failure of the draftsman of the 1861 Act to appreciate the merits in certain situations of a statutory overlap may have been a significant cause of the proliferation of offences of strict liability.

Three types of provision to be found in the enacting parts of many statutes require special consideration as aids to interpretation. They are the interpretation (or definition) section, the proviso and the saving.

1. Interpretation sections

Modern statutes frequently contain (usually, in the case of English statutes, at the end) a set of provisions with the marginal note 'Interpretation'. These usually take one of two forms, stating either that a particular word or phrase 'means . . .' (or 'has the meaning hereby assigned to it') or that a particular word or phrase 'includes . . .'. Both forms are found in s 61(1) of the Sale of Goods Act 1979: '"buyer" means a person who buys or agrees to buy goods'; '"goods" includes all personal chattels other than things in action and money'. There are usually qualifying words such as 'unless the context otherwise requires', nevertheless the distinction is important because, when an interpretation section states that a word or phrase 'means . . .', any other meaning is excluded, whereas the word 'includes' indicates an extension of the ordinary meaning which continues to apply in appropriate cases.

> 'The word "include" is very generally used in interpretation clauses in order to enlarge the meaning of words or phrases occurring in the body of the statute; and when it is so used these words or phrases must be construed as comprehending, not only such things as they signify according to their natural import, but also those things which the interpretation clause declares that they shall include.'[16]

The justices' failure to appreciate the implications of the distinction between 'means' on the one hand, and 'includes' on the other hand, was partly responsible for the appeal in *Carter v Bradbeer*.[17] According to s 201(a) of the Licensing Act 1964 '"bar" includes any place exclusively or mainly used for the consumption of intoxicating liquor'. Carter was the holder of a special hours' certificate under which he was permitted to serve drinks in a club outside the normal licensing hours, but s 76(5) of the Act provides that a special hours' certificate does not permit the service of drinks at a 'bar'. Two rooms in a club managed by Carter contained a counter across which drinks were served outside normal licensing hours. These rooms were also used for dancing and the consumption of meals. The justices concentrated on s 201(a) and convicted Carter on the ground that the rooms could be subdivided into different areas, those near the counters being places exclusively or mainly used for the consumption of intoxicating liquor. The conviction was affirmed by the House of Lords, but not on the basis of the distinction drawn by the justices. The counters were treated as bars within the ordinary meaning of the term.

Interpretation sections may bring the most incongruous things within the operation of a statute. This point was made by Channell J in the course of holding that the Savoy Hotel was a shop.[18] In spite of its seeming oddity, the effect of the decision was beyond criticism for it

---

16. *Dilworth v Stamp Commissioner* [1899] AC 99 at 105–6 per Lord Watson.
17. [1975] 3 All ER 158.
18. *Savoy Hotel Co v London County Council* [1900] 1 QB 665 at 669. For a more recent example see *Dunsby v British Broadcasting Corporation*, (1983) Times, 25 July (a film studio is a 'factory' within s 175(1)(c) of the Factories Act 1961).

brought persons under 18 within the protection against excessive working hours accorded by the Shops Act 1892 under which 'shop' included 'licensed public houses and refreshment houses of any kind'. None the less, it is presumably the apparently bizarre nature of conclusions of this sort which have led to criticisms of interpretation sections. Lord Brougham spoke of them as 'the famous freak of modern lawgivers',[19] and Blackburn J said that they frequently do a great deal of harm because they give a non-natural sense to words which are afterwards used in a natural sense.[20] Blackburn J was speaking of 'the expression . . . includes' type of clause, but his observation would equally apply to the 'means' type. Interpretation sections are comparatively modern, but they have been a common form of legislation for the last 100 years and have been responsible for a great deal of economy of drafting.

2. Provisos

A proviso is frequently not an aid to construction, although the terms of the provision to which it is a proviso are usually of considerable aid to its construction. To discuss the subject under the head of aids to construction is rather like putting the cart before the horse. But the adoption of this course has its conveniences. The reason why the main provision affects the construction of the proviso is that there is a presumption based on the ordinary use of language that the scope of the proviso is affected by the scope of the main provision. The leading case is *Thompson v Dibdin*.[1] After enacting that no marriage between a man and his deceased wife's sister should be, or be deemed to have been, void or voidable as a civil contract by reason of such affinity, s 1 of the Deceased Wife's Sister's Marriage Act 1907[2] continued:

> 'Provided always that no clergyman in holy orders of the Church of England shall be liable to any suit, penalty or censure, whether civil or ecclesiastical, for anything done or omitted to be done by him in the performance of the duties of his office to which suit, penalty or censure he would not have been liable if this Act had not been passed.'

Did this mean that a clergyman could refuse holy communion to a man and his deceased wife's sister who had intermarried, as he could have

19. *Parliamentary Debates*, 3rd series, vol 98, col 888 (12 May, 1848).
20. *Lindsay v Cundy* (1876) 1 QBD 348 at 358.
1. [1912] AC 533.
2. See now Marriage (Enabling) Act 1960.

done before the Act? Read without reference to what preceded it, this would have been the effect of the proviso, but, having regard to the fact that s 1 was solely concerned with the contract of marriage, the Court of Appeal and House of Lords held that a clergyman was not entitled to refuse holy communion in the circumstances:

> '. . . A proviso must *prima facie* be read and considered in relation to the principal matter to which it is a proviso, that is the marriage contract. It is not a separate or independent enactment. The words are dependent on the principal enacting words to which they are tacked as a proviso. They cannot be read as divorced from their context.'[3]

It has been said that if Parliament had in plain terms stated in the proviso that a clergyman might do just what the clergyman in *Thompson v Dibdin* had claimed to do, the courts would not have been entitled to refuse to give effect to that enactment on the ground that the draftsman had broken a rule which he should have observed. This is of course perfectly true, but such draftsmanship invites misunderstanding. The point is that the ordinary reader would expect a proviso to qualify in some way the words which precede it.

Enactments containing provisos must be construed as a whole and it is not permissible to separate the principal part of the enactment from the proviso.[4] Nevertheless, the ordinary reader would not expect the proviso to control the construction of the main provision. Warnings have from time to time been given against allowing a proviso to exercise an undue influence over the construction of the main section. To quote Lord Watson:[5]

> 'I am perfectly clear that if the language of the enacting part of the statute does not contain the provisions which are said to occur in it, you cannot derive those provisions by implication from a proviso, . . . I perfectly admit that there may be and are many cases in which the terms of an intelligible proviso may throw considerable light on the ambiguous import of the statutory words.'

---

3. [1912] AC at 544 per Lord Ashbourne.
4. See *Gubay v Kington (Inspector of Taxes)* [1984] 1 All ER 513, HL.
5. *West Derby Union v Metropolitan Life Assurance Society* [1897] AC 647 at 652. *Bennion* (p 572) suggests that such warnings resulted from the fact that provisos in the nineteenth century were frequently added by a Bill's opponents and were not an integral part of the original scheme of the Bill.

3. Savings

A saving resembles a proviso in its function of qualifying the main provision, but has no particular form.[6] It often begins with a phrase such as 'Nothing in this section shall be construed as . . .'. Section 52(3) of the Town and Country Planning Act 1971, discussed in the *Windsor and Maidenhead* case,[7] is an example. Being, like a proviso, a qualification of the generality of the main provision, it is subject to similar principles of interpretation. In *Ealing London Borough Council v Race Relations Board*,[8] Lord Simon of Glaisdale expressed some hesitation about savings:

'. . . considerable caution is needed in construing a general statutory provision by reference to its statutory exceptions. 'Saving clauses' are often included by way of reassurance, for avoidance of doubt or from abundance of caution. Section 27(9)(a) [of the Race Relations Act 1968] itself provides a striking example: it provides that nothing in the Act shall invalidate certain rules restricting certain classes of employment to "persons of particular birth, citizenship, nationality, descent or residence", and "residence", at least, is not conceivably within the ambit of s 1(1).'

The function of a saving provision is not to alter existing rights or powers, but to preserve them. All the same, this may lead to surprising results. Thus, in *R v Brent Health Authority, ex p Francis*,[9] s 1(8) of the Public Bodies (Admission to Meetings) Act 1960 was successfully used to justify the exclusion of the public from a meeting which the Act required to be open. The subsection provided that:

'The provisions of this section shall be without prejudice to any power of exclusion to suppress or prevent disorderly conduct or other misbehaviour at a meeting.'

The applicant claimed that this did not include a power to exclude the public altogether. Drawing on a precedent of 1866 in relation to a colonial legislature, it was held that the common law conferred on a body all powers without which it could not perform its functions, and that this included a power to remove people for obstructing debates. On this basis, the common-law power to exclude the public from meetings, where members of the public create a disorder, was held to

---

6. *Bennion*, pp 573–4.
7. Supra, p 115.
8. [1972] AC 342 at 363; supra, pp 69–70.
9. [1985] QB 869, [1985] 1 All ER 74.

be preserved by the saving, even though the legislature had probably been unaware of the existence of such an obscure common-law power.

B. OTHER PARTS OF THE SAME STATUTE

Matters calling for discussion under this head are the long title, preamble (if any) and short title, cross-headings, side-notes (or marginal notes) and punctuation. Nowadays it is probably true to say that each one of the above items has some value as an aid to construction in some circumstances, but they all have less value than the items mentioned in the previous section simply because they do not enact anything. Certainly the provisions of Lord Scarman's Interpretation of Legislation Bills of 1980 and 1981 which sought to give statutory effect to the admissibility of such items as aids to interpretation encountered no objections.[10] There is a distinction between the first and second groups of items because the first three items can be amended by Parliament when dealing with a Bill whereas this is not true of the last three. All the same, the content of the last three is determined by the Parliamentary clerks, on the advice of the draftsman, in accordance with Parliamentary practice, and is fixed before royal assent. Thus, in their different ways, all of the items listed can fairly be regarded as representing the intention of Parliament, and it would be wrong to reject the last three as merely indicating the intention of the draftsman.[11]

There is a bewildering mass of conflicting dicta on the question whether some of the above items can be treated as aids to construction at all and, when it is conceded that they may be so treated, upon their weight. This is due to a failure to distinguish between two stages in the process of interpretation at which the aids may be relevant. The first stage is that at which the judge has to decide whether he has any real doubt about the meaning of the word, phrase or passage which he is called upon to interpret. At this point it is hard to believe that he can or should have any inhibitions concerning the parts of the statute which he will read. No doubt he will begin with the section containing the word, phrase or passage in dispute. He can hardly help taking account of the punctuation and side-note. If he is to fulfil his duty of reading the whole Act, when it is necessary to do so in order to determine whether there is an ambiguity, he must look at the long title, preamble (if any),

---

10. See 405 HL Deb, cols 276–306 (13 February, 1980); 418 HL Deb, cols 64–83 (9 March, 1981).
11. See *Bennion*, p 272; cf the first edition of this work p 107.

short title and cross-headings. If, after this performance, the judge is satisfied that the word, phrase or passage the meaning of which is in dispute really only has one meaning in the context, he must apply that meaning; but if he has doubts on the subject he will think again. It is at this point that the distinction between the enacting parts of a statute and the other parts becomes crucial. If the sole cause of doubt is a disparity between the otherwise clear and unambiguous words and a title, preamble, heading or side-note, the judge must disregard his doubts and apply the otherwise clear and unambiguous words. This is because there is a rule of law according to which, although the parts of the statute which do not enact anything may be consulted as a guide to Parliamentary intent and hence to the meaning of the enacted words, effect must not be given to any doubts which they may raise about the meaning of those words. If, however, the judge has doubts about the meaning of the statutory provision he is considering for some other reason such as its lack of clarity or apparent pointlessness, he may take the title, preamble, heading or side-note into consideration in determining how those doubts should be resolved. As we shall see, reservations have been expressed about the propriety of taking any of the above items into consideration, and it is necessary to be especially cautious when endeavouring to state the law with regard to the extent to which the short title and side-notes, not to mention punctuation, may be taken into consideration; but it is submitted that the following remarks of Lord Upjohn in *Director of Public Prosecutions v Schild-kamp*[12] amply justify the above general account of the relevance of the items mentioned at the beginning of this section to the judicial process of interpretation. The remarks were made with special reference to cross-headings:

> 'When the court construing the statute is reading it through to understand it, it must read the cross-headings as well as the body of the statute and that will always be a useful pointer to the intention of Parliament in enacting the immediately following sections. Whether the cross-heading is no more than a pointer or label, or is helpful in assisting to construe, or even in some cases to control, the meaning or ambit of those sections must necessarily depend on the circumstances of each case, and I do not think it is possible to lay down any rules.'

The matter must now be considered in slightly greater detail.

---

12. [1971] AC 1 at 28.

1. Long title and preamble

The long title of an Act is set out at the beginning and usually contains a general indication of the legislative purpose. For example the long title of the Cable and Broadcasting Act 1984 reads:

> 'An Act to provide for the establishment and functions of a Cable Authority and to make other provision with respect to cable programme services; to amend the Broadcasting Act 1981, to provide for the establishment and functions of a Satellite Broadcasting Board and to make other provision with respect to broadcasting services; and for connected purposes.'

Rules of Parliamentary procedure require no more than that the long title should cover everything in the Bill as introduced; and, if necessary, it is amended to accommodate changes made in the content of the Bill before it is enacted. In modern times all Acts have long titles, but preambles have for a long time been something of a rarity. An exception is the Canada Act 1982, the preamble to which reads:

> 'Whereas Canada has requested and consented to the enactment of an Act of the Parliament of the United Kingdom to give effect to the provisions hereinafter set forth and the Senate and the House of Commons of Canada in Parliament assembled have submitted an address to Her Majesty requesting that Her Majesty may graciously be pleased to cause a Bill to be laid before the Parliament of the United Kingdom for that purpose'.

When there is a preamble, it sets out the facts and assumptions upon which the statute is based. The long title and preamble are discussed together because the law with regard to the use which may be made of each is the same, and what is strictly a long title is sometimes erroneously referred to as a preamble.[13]

The commonly accepted position as regards the use that may be made of the long title was succinctly stated by Donovan J in *R v Bates*:[14]

> 'In many cases the long title may supply the key to the meaning. The principle, as I understand it, is that where something is doubtful or ambiguous the long title may be looked to to resolve the doubt or ambiguity, but, in the absence of doubt or ambiguity, the passage under construction must be taken to mean what it says, so that, if its meaning be clear, that meaning is not to be narrowed or restricted by reference to the long title.'

---

13. Eg *Ward v Holman*, infra, p 126.
14. [1952] 2 All ER 842 at 844; *Manuel v A-G* [1982] 3 All ER 822 at 831 per Slade LJ.

However, this has been challenged by some other judicial statements and is rejected by Bennion as too restrictive. On this wider view, the long title may always be consulted as 'the plainest of all guides to the general objectives of a statute. But it will not always help as to particular provisions'.[15] However, even if this wider view is adopted, it does not contradict the fundamental point made by Donovan J that, once their full context is considered in the light of the purposes of the Act, it is the unambiguous words of a section which will prevail over the long title.

The accepted position as regards the use that may be made of a preamble was stated by Lord Normand in the following terms in *A-G v Prince Ernest Augustus of Hanover*:[16]

'When there is a preamble it is generally in its recitals that the mischief to be remedied and the scope of the Act are described. It is therefore clearly permissible to have recourse to it as an aid to construing the enacting provisions. The preamble is not, however, of the same weight as an aid to construction of a section of the Act as are other relevant enacting words to be found elsewhere in the Act or even in related Acts. There may be no exact correspondence between preamble and enactment, and the enactment may go beyond or it may fall short of the indications that may be gathered from the preamble. Again, the preamble cannot be of much or any assistance in construing provisions which embody qualifications or exceptions from the operation of the general purpose of the Act. It is only when it conveys a clear and definite meaning in comparison with relatively obscure or indefinite enacting words that the preamble may legitimately prevail. The courts are concerned with the practical business of deciding a *lis*, and when the plaintiff puts forward one construction of an enactment and the defendant another, it is the court's business in any case of some difficulty, after informing itself of what I have called the legal and factual context including the preamble, to consider in the light of this knowledge whether the enacting words admit of both the rival constructions put forward. If they admit of only one construction, that construction will receive effect even if it is inconsistent with the preamble, but if the enacting words are capable of either of the constructions offered by the parties, the construction which fits the preamble may be preferred.'

---

15. *Black-Clawson International Ltd v Papierwerke Waldhof-Aschaffenberg AG* [1975] AC 591 at 647 per Lord Simon of Glaisdale; *Bennion*, pp 576–8.
16. [1957] AC 436 at 467; *supra*, p 52.

Lord Normand was speaking in a case in which the section of the statute of Anne which conferred British citizenship on the lineal descendants of the Electoress Sofia 'born or hereafter to be born' was held to be unaffected by the reference to naturalisation in Queen Anne's lifetime in the preamble. The preamble itself was none too clear, but the Hanover case is clear authority for the proposition that the fact that the enacting words under consideration go beyond the scope of the purposes mentioned in the preamble is not a reason for declining to give effect to otherwise unambiguous statutory words.[17] It will be recollected that the case is also authority for the proposition that no one is entitled to assert that statutory words are unambiguous until he has read them in their full context which includes the long title and, if there is one, the preamble.[18]

A further illustration of the rule that these parts of a statute cannot control otherwise unambiguous enacting words merely because those words fall outside their scope is provided by *Ward v Holman*.[19] The long title of the Public Order Act 1936 is:

'An Act to prohibit the wearing of uniforms in connection with political objects and the maintainance by private persons of associations of military or similar character; and to make further provision for the preservation of public order on the occasion of public processions and meetings and in public places.'

Under s 5 (as originally enacted):

'Any person who in any public place or any public meeting uses threatening, abusive or insulting words or behaviour with intent to provoke a breach of the peace or whereby a breach of the peace is likely to be occasioned, shall be guilty of an offence.'

Holman broke a window of a neighbour's house, stood in the street shouting abuse towards the house and, when members of the neighbour's family congregated in the street, challenged them to a fight. He was charged with an offence against s 5 of the Act. Quarter Sessions, on the hearing of an appeal from the magistrates, held that he was not guilty because the Act was confined to public meetings, processions and the like; but the Divisional Court re-instated his conviction. Lord Parker CJ said: 'It is impossible to look at the preamble [*sic*] of the Act as controlling the operative words of the Act itself unless those words are ambiguous', adding (correctly) that there was anyway no inconsistency between the 'preamble' and the words of the section.

---

17. See also *The Norwhale* [1975] QB 589, [1975] 2 All ER 501.
18. Supra, pp 54–5.
19. [1964] 2 QB 580, [1964] 2 All ER 729, DC.

This case may be contrasted with *Brett v Brett*[20] which shows that the long title and preamble may be allowed to play their part in controlling apparently unambiguous enacted words when doubts about the meaning of those words arise from some other source. The Wills Act 1751 provided that beneficiaries who attested 'any will or codicil' should be good witnesses but that gifts made to them in the will or codicil should be void. The words 'any will or codicil' were of course apt to cover wills of personalty as well as realty, but the then state of the law naturally gave rise to doubts about their applying to wills of personalty because such wills did not require attestation at all. These doubts, coupled with the terms of a later section of the Act, and a reference to the long title and preamble both of which spoke only of wills and codicils of real estate were held by Sir John Nicholl to warrant the reading in of the words 'of real estate' after the word 'codicil'.

One of several examples of modern cases in which reference has been made to the long title as something which resolved a doubt about the meaning of an enacted word is *R v Wheatley*.[1] The appellant was charged with the unlawful possession of an 'explosive substance', namely a metal pipe bomb filled with fire-dampened sodium chlorate mixed with sugar, contrary to s 4 of the Explosive Substances Act 1883. While expert evidence for the Crown contended that the bomb was capable of producing an explosive effect, expert evidence for the accused contended that it would only produce a pyrotechnic effect and was therefore not an 'explosive substance'. In his direction to the jury, the trial judge held that the words 'explosive substance' were to be construed by reference to the definition of 'explosive' in s 3(1) of the Explosives Act 1875 which covered substances 'used or manufactured with a view to produce a practical effect by explosion or a pyrotechnic effect'. The Court of Appeal upheld the conviction on the ground that the 1883 Act had properly been construed in the light of the 1875 Act. The long title of the 1883 Act was 'An Act to amend the law relating to Explosive Substances', and that of the 1875 Act was 'An Act to amend the law with respect to manufacturing, keeping, selling, carrying, and importing Gunpowder, Nitro-glycerine, and other Explosive Substances'. From a comparison of these long titles, it was clear that they dealt with the same subject matter, and this sufficed to justify the judge's application of the definition of 'explosive substance' contained in the earlier Act.

---

20. (1826) 3 Add 210.
1. [1979] 1 All ER 954.

2. Short title

The short title is usually stated in a separate subsection towards the end of the statute. For example s 36(1) of the Theft Act says 'This Act may be cited as the Theft Act 1968'. As it is contained in the body of the Act and is, like the long title and preamble, subject to amendment by Parliament while the Bill is being passed, one might think that the short title should be treated in the same way as a guide to interpretation. However, its sole purpose being to serve as a brief identifying label, it is by no means as helpful as the long title or a preamble. The need for brevity often results in a short title that does not cover everything in the Act. Thus, for example, s 10 of the Contempt of Court Act 1981 confers on the press a general privilege not to disclose its sources (this being one of the 'related matters' mentioned in the long title).[2] The draftsman may occasionally seek to make the short title formally comprehensive, as in the 'Health and Safety at Work *etc* Act 1974', but this is not usual. However, despite its limitations, there is no reason why the short title should not sometimes be used as a guide to interpretation. As Scrutton LJ put it, with reference to the issue whether the Vexatious Actions Act 1896 applied to criminal proceedings:[3]

> 'I agree that the court should give less importance to the title than to the enacting part, and less to the short title than to the full title, for the short title being a label, accuracy may be sacrificed to brevity; but I do not understand on what principle of construction I am not to look at the words of the Act itself to help me to understand its scope in order to interpret the words Parliament has used, by the circumstances in respect of which they were legislating. It is by no means conclusive, but it is striking that if they were intending to deal with criminal proceedings they should call their Act the Vexatious Actions Act.'

3. Headings

Headings are not voted upon by Parliament, but they are included in the Bill and form part of the text entered on the Parliament Roll. Despite dicta to the contrary, they have Parliamentary authority and are appropriately consulted to resolve an ambiguity in the text. Thus in

---

2. See *Secretary of State for Defence v Guardian Newspapers Ltd* [1985] AC 339, [1984] 3 All ER 601.
3. *Re Boaler* [1915] 1 KB 21 at 40–1.

Dixon v British Broadcasting Corporation[4] both Shaw and Brandon LJJ referred to the heading 'Unfair Dismissal' of Part II of Sch 1 to the Trade Union and Labour Relations Act 1974 and to the heading 'Right of employee not to be unfairly dismissed' underneath as giving the purpose in the light of which paras 5 and 12 were to be interpreted. Equally, in *R v Bates*[5] Donovan J equated headings with the long title, at any rate for the purposes of the case before him. We have already seen that great importance was attached to the headings in the Companies Act 1948 by the majority of the House of Lords in *Director of Public Prosecutions v Schildkamp*.[6] The fact that the heading of the group of sections which included s 332 was 'Offences antecedent to or in the course of Winding-Up' supported the conclusion that the offence under s 332(3) could only be charged in a case in which a winding-up order had been made. The uncertainty concerned the scope rather than the meaning of the statutory words.

4. Side-notes

Chandler v Director of Public Prosecutions[7] might be thought conclusive authority for the proposition that side-notes (frequently spoken of as 'marginal notes') cannot be used as aids to construction in any circumstances. The defendants, members of the Committee of 100, the aim of which was to further nuclear disarmament, participated in a demonstration at an airfield with the object of grounding all aircraft. They were charged with and convicted of an offence against s 1(1) of the Official Secrets Act 1911 which punishes those who approach prohibited places for a purpose prejudicial to the safety of the state. The side-note reads 'Penalties for spying' and it was conceded that the defendants were not spying, but their appeal to the House of Lords was dismissed on the ground that they were acting for a purpose prejudicial to the safety of the state within the meaning of s 1(1). Lord Reid said:[8]

> 'In my view side-notes cannot be used as an aid to construction. They are mere catch-words and I have never heard of it being supposed in recent times that an amendment to alter a side-note could be proposed in either House of Parliament. Side-notes in the original Bill are inserted by the draftsman. During the pas-

---

4. Supra, p 113.
5. [1952] 2 All ER 842.
6. [1971] AC 1; supra, p 55.
7. [1964] AC 736, [1962] 3 All ER 142.
8. Ibid, at 789.

sage of the Bill through its various stages amendments to it or other reasons may make it desirable to alter a side-note. In that event I have reason to believe that alteration is made by the appropriate officer of the House—no doubt in consultation with the draftsman. So side-notes cannot be said to be enacted in the same sense as the long title or any part of the body of the Act.'

In spite of its great weight, three remarks may be made with regard to this passage. In the first place what Lord Reid said would seem to be equally applicable to cross-headings, yet we have just seen that this has not prevented these from being treated in much the same way as the long title and preamble. Secondly, even if it is the case that side-notes cannot be called in aid in order to resolve doubts, it can hardly be the law that they are to be disregarded by the judge when he is perusing the Act with a view to ascertaining whether he has any doubts. No judge can be expected to treat something which is before his eyes as though it were not there. In the words of Upjohn LJ: 'While the marginal note to a section cannot control the language used in the section, it is at least permissible to approach a consideration of its general purpose and the mischief at which it is aimed with the note in mind'.[9] Finally, Lord Reid's remarks in *Chandler v Director of Public Prosecutions* must be read in the light of his subsequent remarks in *Director of Public Prosecutions v Schildkamp*:[10]

'But it may be more realistic to accept the Act as printed as being the product of the whole legislative process, and to give due weight to everything found in the printed Act. I say more realistic because in very many cases the provision before the court was never even mentioned in debate in either House, and it may be that its wording was never closely scrutinised by any member of either House. In such a case it is not very meaningful to say that the words of the Act represent the intention of Parliament but the punctuation, cross-headings and side-notes do not.'

Thus the side-note may be more useful as an indication of the purpose of the provision than as a guide to its meaning.

5. Punctuation

As the remark of Lord Reid suggests, punctuation forms part of the statute and, even if the reader has to be wary of older Acts, in which

---

9. *Stephens v Cuckfield RDC* [1960] 2 QB 373 at 383.
10. [1971] AC at 10.

punctuation was inserted after enactment by the printer, the punctuation of modern statutes must be given the significance it has to the ordinary user of the English language. As Lord Lowry put it:[11]

'I consider that not to take account of punctuation disregards the reality that literate people, such as Parliamentary draftsmen, punctuate what they write, if not identically, at least in accordance with grammatical principles. Why should not other literate people, such as judges, look at the punctuation in order to interpret the meaning of the legislation as accepted by Parliament?'

Or, as Thornton more trenchantly observes,[12]

'It is a curious paradox that judges, whose entire reading is punctuated, should, in carefully punctuated judgments, consider themselves obliged to proclaim that the punctuation in carefully punctuated statutes is no part of the law.'

While older dicta[13] suggested that the punctuation should not be regarded as decisive of meaning, this does not represent the modern view. All the same, the judge may in some cases be compelled to correct errors in punctuation, a course which the courts are prepared to adopt more readily than amendment of the wording of the statute.

For example, in *Luby v Newcastle-under-Lyme Corporation*,[14] s 113(4) of the Housing Act 1957 provided that 'the local authority shall from time to time review rents and make such changes, either of rents generally or of particular rents, and rebates (if any) as circumstances may require.' The comma after the word 'rents' where it occurs for the third time suggests that the authority has power to make rebates rather than to make changes in rebates, but the subsection was read as though the comma was not there. As Bennion points out, the obscurity really results from the omission of the word 'of' before 'rebates' and not so much from the comma used.[15] Nevertheless, by focussing on the punctuation, the judges are able to appear to be interfering less with the Parliamentary text than if words were added.

---

11. *Hanlon v Law Society* [1981] AC 124 at 198.
12. *Legislative Drafting* (3rd edn) pp 33–4.
13. Eg *Duke of Devonshire v O'Connor* (1890) 24 QBD 468 at 478 per Lord Esher MR.
14. [1965] 1 QB 214, [1964] 3 All ER 169.
15. *Bennion*, pp 597–8.

C.   RULES OF LANGUAGE

Something must now be said about the rule of *ejusdem generis* ('of the same kind'), the maxim *noscitur a sociis* ('a thing is known by its associates'), the rule of rank and the maxim *expressio unius exclusio alterius* ('the mention of one thing is the exclusion of another'). *Noscitur a sociis* and the rule of rank can, roughly speaking, be respectively regarded as extended and attenuated versions of the *ejusdem generis* rule. These rules or maxims have attracted an unduly large quantity of case law because they are neither legal principles nor legal rules. It is hardly correct to speak of them as rules of language, for they simply refer to the way in which people speak in certain contexts. They are no more than rough guides to the intention of the speaker or writer. To quote from an article by E A Driedger:[16] 'Ordinarily a husband who authorised his wife to purchase a hat, coat, shoes and "anything else you need" would not expect her to buy anything but clothes.' To exemplify the *expressio unius* maxim by the words of an even more generous hypothetical speaker, if someone were to say 'I am going to give you my houses in London and York and the fixtures in my London house', the prospective donee could hardly hope for the fixtures in the York house.

1.   Ejusdem generis ('of the same kind')[17]

The words of E A Driedger may again be quoted for a full formulation of the *ejusdem generis* rule:[18]

> 'Where general words are found, following an enumeration of persons or things all susceptible of being regarded as specimens of a single genus or category, but not exhaustive thereof, their construction should be restricted to things of that class or category, unless it is reasonably clear from the context or the general scope and purview of the Act that Parliament intended that they should be given a broader signification.'

16. 'A New Approach to Statutory Interpretation' (1951) 29 Can Bar Rev 838, 841.
17. See G Williams, 'The Origin and Logical Implications of the *Ejusdem Generis* Rule' (1943) 7 Conv (NS) 119; A Samuel, 'The Ejusdem Generis Rule in Statutory Interpretation' [1984] Stat LR 180.
18. *Construction of Statutes* (2nd edn) p 116.

In *Quazi v Quazi*, Lord Diplock explained the rule in the following way:[19]

'The presumption then is that the draftsman's mind was directed only to [the genus indicated by the specific words] and that he did not, by his addition of the word "other" to the list, intend to stray beyond its boundaries, but merely to bring within the ambit of the enacting words those species which complete the genus but have been omitted from the preceding list either inadvertently or in the interests of brevity.'

An example is s 2(4) of the Land Charges Act 1972 which requires the registration as a Class C(iv) land charge of any 'estate contract', 'including a contract conferring either expressly or by statutory implication, a valid option to purchase, a right of pre-emption *or any other like right*'. The italicised words have been held to cover a conditional contract,[20] a contract to transfer land to any third person the contracting party specifies,[1] an obligation on the tenant to offer to surrender the lease before requesting the landlord's consent to its transfer,[2] and the right of a council to repurchase a council house it had sold.[3] However, the words have been held not to cover a notice to treat served under a compulsory purchase order,[4] nor an equitable right to re-entry,[5] nor a proprietary estoppel.[6] They are concerned with rights created voluntarily by contract, and not with rights created in other ways. Although, as Lord Diplock indicated, one reason for the rule is that the draftsman must be taken to have inserted the general words in case something which ought to have been included among the specifically enumerated items had been omitted; a further reason is that, if the general words were intended to have their ordinary meaning, the specific enumeration would be pointless. For instance, in *Re Stockport Ragged, Industrial and Reformatory Schools*[7] the question was whether Industrial Schools fell within the proviso to s 62 of the Charitable Trusts Act 1853. If they did not, the consent of the Charity Commissioners to their mortgages was required. The proviso referred to 'any cathedral, collegiate, chapter, or *other* schools'; but it was held

---

19. [1980] AC 744 at 807–8.
20. *Haselmere Estates Ltd v Baker* [1982] 3 All ER 525.
1. *Turley v Mackay* [1944] Ch 37, [1943] 2 All ER 1.
2. *Green v Church Commissioners for England* [1974] Ch 467, [1974] 3 All ER 609, CA.
3. *First National Securities Ltd v Chiltern DC* [1975] 2 All ER 766.
4. *Capital Investments Ltd v Wednesfield UDC* [1965] Ch 774, [1964] 1 All ER 655.
5. *Shiloh Spinners Ltd v Harding* [1973] AC 691, [1973] 1 All ER 90.
6. *E R Ives Investments Ltd v High* [1967] 2 QB 379, [1967] 1 All ER 504, CA.
7. [1898] 2 Ch 687.

to be applicable only to schools of the specified kinds and those of a similar type. Lindley MR said that he could not conceive why the legislature should have taken the trouble to specify particular kinds of schools except in order to show the type of school to which reference was being made.

For the rule to apply, it must be possible to construct a category (commonly called a 'genus') out of the specific words to delimit what is to be considered as 'of the same kind'. *Quazi v Quazi*[8] concerned s 2 of the Recognition of Divorces and Legal Separations Act 1971, which requires recognition to be given to foreign divorces and legal separations obtained by means of 'judicial or other proceedings'. The House of Lords considered that 'other proceedings' was not limited to a procedure akin to a judicial proceeding, but could apply to *talaq* divorces which were essentially religious ceremonies. Lord Scarman remarked:[9]

> 'If the legislative purpose of a statute is such that a statutory series should be read ejusdem generis, so be it; the rule is helpful. But, if it is not, the rule is more likely to defeat than to fulfil the purpose of the statute. The rule, like many other rules of statutory interpretation, is a useful servant but a bad master.'

The purpose of the legislation was to give recognition in Britain to divorces validly obtained abroad, and the methods adopted by a foreign country in granting divorces was not a concern of the English courts.

Although it has been said that a single species followed by general words cannot create a genus,[10] the speeches in *Quazi v Quazi* lend no support to this view and there are numerous examples to the contrary. For instance, in *Parkes v Secretary of State for the Environment*,[11] the Court of Appeal held that in the phrase 'building or other operations' in s 290 of the Town and Country Planning Act 1971 'other operations' must be read as akin to building.

There is no need for the genus to be of an obvious kind, and the courts are willing to limit general words by reference to a fairly heterogeneous set of words. Thus in *R v Staniforth, R v Jordan*,[12] s 4(1) of the Obscene Publications Act 1959 provided a defence to proceedings relating to the possession for gain of obscene articles 'if it is proved that publication of the article in question is justified as being for the

---

8. [1980] AC 744, [1979] 3 All ER 897.
9. Ibid, at 824.
10. Eg *Alexander v Tredegar Iron & Coal Co Ltd* [1944] KB 390 at 396 per Scott LJ.
11. [1979] 1 All ER 211.
12. [1977] AC 699, [1976] 3 All ER 775.

public good on the ground that it is in the interests of science, literature, art or learning, or of other objects of general concern'. Section 4(2) permitted expert evidence to be admitted on such questions. The trial judge ruled inadmissible expert evidence purporting to show the psychotherapeutic benefit of the pornographic material to its readers. The House of Lords upheld this decision on the ground that 'other objects of general concern' were limited to matters of a kind similar to science, literature, art or learning and this was not the case here. Lord Wilberforce stated:[13]

> 'even if this is not strictly a case for applying a rule of *ejusdem generis* (the genus being one of intellectual or aesthetic values), the structure of the section makes it clear that the other objects, or, which is the same argument, the nature of the general concern, fall within the same area, and cannot fall in the totally different area of effect on sexual behaviour and attitudes. . . .'

This statement shows that the rule of *ejusdem generis* should not be too narrowly interpreted and that the notion of a 'genus' simply indicates a reasonably identifiable category of items or values.

The cases show that the application of the *ejusdem generis* rule is limited by the basic duty of the courts to have regard to the purpose of the statutory provisions under consideration. The *Quazi* case shows that the purpose of legislation may require general words to be construed in their most general sense in spite of the fact that they are preceded by specific words. In that case, the purpose was established by reference to an international convention to which the Act gave effect. However, even if a wide meaning does have to be given, the purpose will still restrict the scope. As Bowen LJ said:[14]

> 'But there is an exception to that rule (if it be a rule and not a maxim of common sense) which is that although the words immediately around and before the general words are words which are *prima facie* confined, yet if you can see from a wider inspection of the scope of the legislation that the general words, notwithstanding that they follow particular words, are nevertheless to be construed generally, you must give effect to the intention of the legislature as gathered from the entire section.'

2. Noscitur a sociis ('A thing is known by its associates')

The *ejusdem generis* rule is an example of a broader linguistic rule

---

13. Ibid, at 719.
14. *Skinner v Shew* [1893] 1 Ch 413 at 424.

or practice to which reference is made by the Latin tag *noscitur a sociis*. Words, even if they are not general words like 'or any other' preceded by specific words, are liable to be affected by other words with which they are associated. To quote Stamp J:[15]

'English words derive colour from those which surround them. Sentences are not mere collections of words to be taken out of the sentence, defined separately by reference to the dictionary or decided cases, and then put back into the sentence with the meaning which you have assigned to them as separate words. . . .'

Two illustrations show that the meaning of a word may be coloured by the context of the words used either in the same sentence or within the same Act read as a whole. An example of the former is *Westminster City Council v Ray Alan (Manshops) Ltd.*[16] Section 14(1) of the Trade Descriptions Act 1968 penalises the making of a false statement as to the nature of 'any services, accommodation or facilities provided'. A company announced a 'Closing Down Sale' at one of its shops, but continued trading normally and did not intend to close the shop. The Divisional Court held that the word 'facilities' was limited by the preceding words to things made available for use by customers and so did not include the broader notion of shopping facilities.

The second situation is illustrated by *Bromley London Borough Council v Greater London Council.*[17] Section 1(1) of the Transport (London) Act 1969 required the Greater London Council to develop policies and to encourage measures for 'the provision of integrated, efficient and *economic* transport facilities and services for Greater London'. In discussing the sense to be given to the word 'economic', Lord Scarman observed:[18]

'As a matter of English usage, the term "economic" . . . has several meanings. They include both that for which the appellants contend and that for which Bromley contends. It is a very useful word, chameleon-like, taking its colour from its surroundings.'

In the context, and especially in the light of s 7(3) which imposed a duty on the London Transport Executive 'as far as practicable' to make up any deficit emerging at the end of an accounting period, the word 'economic' meant 'being run on business principles'.

---

15. *Bourne v Norwich Crematorium Ltd* [1967] 2 All ER 576 at 578; supra, p 71.
16. [1982] 1 All ER 771.
17. Supra, p 70.
18. [1983] 1 AC at 841.

No useful purpose would be served by multiplying examples. It is sufficient to stress that, as in the case of the construction of a genus, the context may prevent words from being coloured by their associates. Words of inclusion had this effect in *Letang v Cooper*[19] where an action for damages for trespass to the person was held to be an action for 'breach of duty' within the meaning of the Law Reform (Limitation of Actions) Act 1954. The relevant words were 'negligence, nuisance or breach of duty', and it was argued that, since actual damage was an essential prerequisite of an action for negligence or nuisance, 'breach of duty' should be similarly restricted. The argument was refuted by the fact that the word 'duty' was immediately followed by the parenthetic words 'whether the duty exists by virtue of a contract or . . . independently of any contract . . .'; a breach of contract is of course actionable without proof of actual damage.

3. The rule of rank

The rule of rank is the second of the rules for the construction of statutes mentioned by Blackstone at the end of the third section of his *Commentaries* where it is formulated as follows:[20]

> 'A statute, which treats of things or persons of an inferior rank, cannot by any *general words* be extended to those of a superior. So a statute, treating of 'deans, prebendaries, parsons, vicars, *and others having spiritual promotion*' is held not to extend to bishops, though they have spiritual promotion; deans being the highest persons named, and bishops being of a still higher order.'

The rule is treated with contempt by Bentham: 'and who can be sure in such an assemblage what is a superior and what inferior? Suppose deans had been omitted, and prebendaries had been the first word, would canons have been to stand included or excluded?'[1] Yet there are cases where, as a matter of ordinary language, an omission is so striking that one would pause to treat it as included in general words although there is no question of the specific words constituting a relevant genus to which the general words might be limited. Surely most people would hesitate before including the Thames in a prohibition on salmon fishing in 'the waters of the Humber, Ouse, Trent . . . and all other waters in the realm wherein salmon be taken'?[2] If this

---

19. [1965] 1 QB 232, [1964] 2 All ER 929.
20. *Commentaries on the Laws of England* (1st edn), vol 1, p 88.
1. *A Comment on the Commentaries* p 140.
2. Coke 2 Inst 478.

type of problem can be solved by a rule of language, the *expressio unius* maxim is at least a safer guide than the uncertain rule of rank; but can the *expressio unius* maxim be applied to exclude the literal sense of general words?

4. Expressio unius ('The mention of one thing is the exclusion of another')

The effect of the Latin maxim *expressio unius est exclusio alterius*, sometimes stated in the form *expressum facit cessare tacitum* (that which is expressed puts an end to that which is unspoken) is that mention of one or more things of a particular class may be regarded as by implication excluding all other members of the class. An example is provided by *Dimbleby & Sons Ltd v National Union of Journalists*.[3] Section 17(3) of the Employment Act 1980 conferred an immunity from suit for actions taken during a trade dispute against 'a party to the dispute'. Section 17(4) granted an immunity for a limited number of actions (not including those in the case) taken against an 'associated employer', defined as meaning an employing company controlled by the employer in the dispute or by a third person also having control of that employer. Here a newspaper publisher sought an injunction to prevent a union from instructing its members not to produce copy to be printed by TBF Printers Ltd. The union was in dispute with TB Forman Ltd, which was an associated company of TBF Printers Ltd having the same shareholders. The House of Lords refused to hold that the action was covered by the immunity under s 17(3), since TBF Printers was a separate legal person from the 'party to the dispute', TB Forman Ltd. While not excluding the possibility of lifting the corporate veil in an appropriate case should the purpose of the statute so require, the creation of a separate immunity for actions against 'associated employers' in s 17(4) precluded such a wide construction of 'a party to the dispute' in s 17(3). A similar approach has been seen in *Re DML*.[4] The same applies to a series of words. The word 'land' is usually apt to include all kinds of mine, but a reference to 'lands, houses and coalmines' may mean that no mines are included in the word 'lands'.[5]

Yet, although it would be possible to multiply the above examples considerably, it is doubtful whether the maxim does any more than

---

3. [1984] 1 All ER 751.
4. Supra, p 113.
5. *R v Sedgley Inhabitants* (1831) 2 B & Ad 65.

draw attention to a fairly obvious linguistic point, viz that in many contexts the mention of some matters warrants an inference that other cognate matters were intentionally excluded. Allowance must always be made for the fact that the *'exclusio'* may have been accidental, still more for the fact that there may have been good reason for it. This last point is well illustrated by *Dean v Wiesengrund.*[6] Section 14 of the Increase of Rent and Mortgage Interest (Restrictions) Act 1920 provided that excess rent should be recoverable by the tenant by whom it was paid from the landlord or his personal representative. It was held that the omission of any reference to the tenant's personal representative did not prevent him from suing. The excess rent was made recoverable retrospectively, and the intention may have been to ensure that the personal representatives of landlords who died before the Act came into force could be sued. Jenkins LJ said:[7]

> 'The argument for the landlord is summed up in the maxim *expressio unius est exclusio alterius* which, applied to the present case, is said to compel the conclusion that the express reference to the legal personal representative of one of the parties excludes any implied reference to the legal personal representative of the other. But this maxim is after all no more than an aid to construction and has little, if any, weight where it is possible, as I think it is in the present case, to account for the *inclusio unius* on grounds other than an intention to effect the *exclusio alterius.*'

6. [1955] 2 QB 120, [1955] 2 All ER 432.
7. Ibid, at 130.

Chapter 6
External aids to construction

To repeat a passage from one of Lord Denning's speeches:[1]

> 'In this country we do not refer to the legislative history of an enactment as they do in the United States of America. We do not look at the explanatory memoranda which preface the Bills before Parliament. We do not have recourse to the pages of Hansard. All that the courts can do is to take judicial notice of the previous state of the law and of other matters generally known to well-informed people.'

In the first section of this chapter a little is said about the process of taking judicial notice of matters generally known to 'well-informed people', a phrase for which 'learned lawyers' should perhaps be substituted, and the extent to which these matters, when judicially noticed, may be used as aids to statutory interpretation. The vexed question of legislative history is briefly tackled in section B. Nothing need be said about the process of taking judicial notice of the previous state of the law. It is simply a matter of consulting the relevant statutes, decisions and textbooks.

A. INFORMED INTERPRETATION

An informed interpretation involves the use, as aids to construction, of the historical setting of the statute, dictionaries and other literary sources, the practices of classes of the community to which the statute applies, contemporary exposition, and other statutes on the same

---

1. *Escoigne Properties Ltd v Inland Revenue Commrs* [1958] AC 549 at 566.

subject. The last three of these items come mainly within the cognisance of lawyers, and the aid to be derived from dictionaries tends to be subordinated to that to be gained from judicial statements concerning the meaning of words. It is for these reasons that it was suggested that 'learned lawyers' might be substituted for 'well-informed people' in the quotation from Lord Denning.

1. Historical setting

The historical setting of the statute has been invoked as an aid to its construction in several cases which have already been mentioned. The following remark was made by Lord Reid in *Chandler v Director of Public Prosecutions*[2] in support of the conclusion that members of the Committee of 100 who obstructed an airfield acted for a 'purpose prejudicial to the safety or interests of the State' within the meaning of s 1 of the Official Secrets Act 1911, although they believed that nuclear disarmament would be beneficial to this country:

> 'The 1911 Act was passed at a time of grave misgiving about the German menace, and it would be surprising and hardly credible that the Parliament of that date intended that a person who deliberately interfered with vital dispositions of the armed forces should be entitled to submit to a jury that government policy was wrong and that what he did was really in the best interests of the country, and then perhaps to escape conviction because a unanimous verdict on that question could not be obtained.'

The fact that, in 1870, many Englishmen sympathised with insurgents against continental governments contributed to the construction of the words 'an offence of a political character' in s 1 of the Extradition Act 1870 adopted by a majority of the House of Lords in *R v Governor of Pentonville Prison, ex p Cheng*.[3] The offence must be of a political character *vis-à-vis* the State requesting extradition, and not the assassination within the jurisdiction of that State of a public figure from another country.

The examination of the historical setting of a statutory provision sometimes produces a conflict between the literal meaning and a purposive reading of the text. For example, in *Johnson v Moreton*[4] the historical setting of the Agricultural Holdings Act 1948 showed that it had been passed to promote general agricultural efficiency in the national interest during the post-war period. The protection of agricul-

---

2. [1964] AC 763 at 791.
3. [1973] AC 931, [1973] 2 All ER 204; supra, pp 62–3.
4. Supra, p 18.

tural tenants was part of this policy, and this gave support to the view that the tenant's right to appeal against eviction to the Agricultural Lands Tribunal could not be excluded by agreement with the landlord. This interpretation was adopted despite the absence in s 24 of the formula 'this section shall have effect notwithstanding any agreement to the contrary'.

The historical setting is relevant even for very recent Acts. For instance, in *Nottinghamshire County Council v Secretary of State for the Environment*[5] s 59(11A) of the Local Government, Planning and Land Act 1980 required that expenditure guidance 'shall be framed by reference to principles applicable to all local authorities'. On a literal reading, this appeared to exclude the adoption of principles which discriminated between high-spending and low-spending authorities. However, Lord Bridge of Harwich noted that 'as is well known, it has been government policy since 1979 to reduce or restrain the level of public expenditure, which includes, of course, expenditure by local authorities'.[6] The Act formed part of this policy and, indeed, in its other dispositions it introduced mechanisms for discriminating between high-spending and low-spending authorities in the distribution of rate support grant. Against this setting, a literal reading would be manifestly contrary to the purpose of the Act, since it would have the consequence that expenditure guidance could not be adapted to take account of the past records of authorities in reducing their expenditure.

These cases demonstrate that the historical setting is often a matter of general knowledge and that this can be established without recourse to documents in the legislative history of the Act.

2. Dictionaries and other literary sources

Reference has already been made to the use of dictionaries and other literary sources in aid of interpretation.[7] The example given was the definition of the word 'ethnic' in *Mandla v Dowell Lee*[8] for which the 1972 Supplement to the Oxford English Dictionary was referred to. However, the value of such sources is limited. It has been pointed out that dictionaries must be used with caution in certain situations— when, for example, the court is concerned with the meaning of a word

---

5. Supra, pp 88–9.
6. [1986] AC at 252.
7. Supra, pp 60–1.
8. [1983] 2 AC 548, [1983] 1 All ER 1062.

at a particular date[9] or the construction of a two-word phrase like 'unfair competition'.[10]

On the whole, definitions offered in previous judicial opinions are more influential, even if they do not constitute binding precedents. Thus in *Mandla v Dowell Lee*, Lord Fraser of Tullybelton relied heavily on a New Zealand decision on a similar statutory phrase.[11] Likewise, in interpreting what constituted 'information' which a local authority was permitted to publish, Glidewell J relied more on a Scottish judicial pronouncement than on a dictionary definition.[12]

The opinions of writers such as Coke are, when relevant, treated with as much respect in relation to statutory interpretation as in other cases. Further frequently cited examples of the use of literary sources are the consultation of works by John Stuart Mill and Sir James Stephen on the meaning of the phrase 'political crime'[13] and the consultation of works on political economy in aid of the interpretation of the expression 'direct taxation' used in the British North America Act 1867.[14]

3. Practice

As long ago as 1744 Lord Hardwicke said: 'The uniform opinion and practice of eminent conveyancers has always had great regard paid to it by all courts of justice,'[15] and nothing has occurred during the intervening years to suggest a change of attitude on the part of the courts. The practice of conveyancers is of assistance in cases calling for the application of a technical meaning, and it may, presumably, be the subject either of evidence or of judicial notice. In *Jenkins v Inland Revenue Commrs* the meaning of the phrase 'irrevocable settlement', used in s 21(10) of the Finance Act 1936 was in issue. It was suggested that the phrase extended to a case in which, although the settlement itself was irrevocable, it would have been terminated in effect if the settlor had gone through a variety of processes such as putting various companies into liquidation. Lord Greene said: 'It seems to me quite illegitimate to take a word which has a technical and precise meaning in conveyancing and then to argue that it has some extended meaning. If the legislature

9. *Hardwick Game Farm v Suffolk Agricultural and Poultry Producers Association Ltd* [1966] 1 All ER 309 at 323 per Davies LJ.
10. *Lee v Showman's Guild of Great Britain* [1952] 2 QB 329 at 338 per Somervell LJ.
11. *King-Ansell v Police* [1979] 2 NZLR 531, cited at [1983] 2 AC 563–4.
12. *R v Inner London Education Authority, ex p Westminster City Council* [1986] 1 All ER 19 at 32–3.
13. *Re Castioni* [1891] 1 QB 149.
14. *Bank of Toronto v Lambe* (1887) 12 App Cas 575 at 581 per Lord Hobhouse.
15. *Bassett v Bassett* (1744) 3 Atk 203 at 208.

wished to give to the word "irrevocable" some unusual and extended meaning of this sort, I ask myself why in the world did it not do so.'[16]

The situations contemplated in the last paragraph are those in which a word used in a statute had acquired a technical meaning by virtue of the previous practice of conveyancers. These situations must be distinguished from those in which the post-enactment practice of an officially-concerned body with regard to a statute is drawn to the court's attention as a possible aid to its interpretation. The view taken by judges in the past, and by many judges today, is that the practices and statements of such bodies are not admissible to help interpret the statute.[17] However, while admissibility is a matter for the discretion of the court, some judges are now willing to treat this material as influential in interpretation. For example, in *Wicks v Firth (Inspector of Taxes)*,[18] the House of Lords considered the tax liability of higher-paid employees for the scholarships received by their children and provided by a fund created by their employer. The Revenue argued that such scholarships were not exempt from tax under s 375 of the Income and Corporation Taxes Act 1970. However, the Revenue had issued a press release stating that it would treat as exempt scholarships awarded from a fund open to all to scholars who happened to be children of employees of the firm by which the fund was financed, which was not the case here. Lord Bridge of Harwich noted that, if the Revenue's arguments on s 375 were correct, there would be a legal liability to tax even in the cases covered by the press release. He continued:[19]

'This is not a decisive consideration, but in choosing between competing constructions of a taxing provision it is right, I think, to incline against a construction which the Revenue are unwilling to apply in its full rigour, but feel they must mitigate by way of extra-statutory concession, recognising, presumably, that in some cases their construction would produce a result which Parliament can hardly have intended.'

Conveyancers are not of course the only class of specialists whose practice may, in appropriate cases, be an aid to statutory interpretation. Commercial usage is, and for a long time has been, at least as important. For example, in *United Dominions Trust Ltd v Kirkwood*, the

---

16. [1944] 2 All ER 491 at 495.
17. Eg Jenkins LJ, *London County Council v Central Land Board* [1958] 3 All ER 676 at 678.
18. [1983] 2 AC 214, [1983] 1 All ER 151.
19. Ibid, at 230–1; cf Lord Templeman at 236. See further F Bennion, *Statute Law*, p 223, and *Statutory Interpretation*, s 253.

Court of Appeal had to construe the phrase 'any person *bona fide* carrying on the business of banking' used in s 6(d) of the Money-lenders Act 1900. Lord Denning said: 'In such a matter as this, when Parliament has given no guidance, we cannot do better than look at the reputation of the concern amongst intelligent men of commerce'.[20]

4. Contemporary exposition (often referred to by its Latin name, 'contemporanea expositio')

The justification for using contemporary expositions of the meaning of a statute is given in the following extract from Maxwell,[1] cited in the judgment of the Court of Criminal Appeal in *R v Casement*:[2]

'It·is said that the best exposition of a statute or any other document is that which it has received from contemporary authority . . . where this has been given by enactment or judicial decision, it is of course to be accepted as conclusive. But, further, the meaning publicly given by contemporary or long professional usage is presumed to be the true one, even where the language has etymologically or popularly a different meaning. It is obvious that the language of a statute must be understood in the sense in which it was understood when it was passed, and those who lived at or near the time when it was passed may reasonably be supposed to be better acquainted than their descendants with the circumstances to which it had relation, as well as with the sense they attached to legislative expressions. Moreover, the long acquiescence of the legislature in the interpretation put upon its enactment by notorious practice may, perhaps, be regarded as some sanction and approval of it.'

It is necessary to distinguish two forms of the contemporary exposition of a statute. Contemporary exposition may refer, firstly, to the way a text was interpreted by courts, legal writers and others in the period following its enactment. This shows how the statute was understood by those to whom it was addressed. Contemporary exposition may refer, secondly, to statements or statutory instruments issued by the government contemporaneously with the Act. This shows how the Act was understood by those responsible for its enactment.

An example of the former is *Mark Rowlands Ltd v Berni Inns Ltd*.[3] Section 2 of the Life Assurance Act 1774 provides that an insurance

---

20. [1966] 2 QB 431 at 454.
1. This passage is now on p 264 of the 12th edition.
2. [1917] 1 KB 98 at 138–9.
3. [1986] QB 211, [1985] 3 All ER 473.

policy must name the person whose life is insured under it. The Court of Appeal held that this provision did not invalidate an indemnity insurance policy taken out by a landlord and covering, among other things, the risk of death or personal injury to any person using a building, even though the persons covered were not specifically named. The Act, originally without a short title, was long known as the Gambling Act 1774, and in 1854 a judge had acknowledged the settled understanding that it did not apply to indemnity insurance, being confined to contracts to pay money on the occurrence of a specific insured event, eg if the king died within the year. Even courts that are not bound by them tend to respect a series of decisions on the interpretation of a particular statute and, even if they may consider the decisions to have been questionable, they may follow them because of the undesirability of disturbing past transactions. In the absence of such a danger, decisions on the interpretation of a statute do not appear to be any more immune from the liability to be overruled than decisions on the common law.[4] Similarly, great respect is paid to the opinion of writers such as Coke and Hale with regard to the construction of a statute, but no more so than is the case with regard to their opinions concerning the common law. The House of Lords has made it plain that reliance can only be placed on this form of contemporary exposition as an aid to the interpretation of ambiguous language in very old statutes.[5]

As regards contemporary official statements and statutory instruments, the courts are willing to use this form of contemporary exposition as an aid to interpret even very recent statutes. For example, in *Nottinghamshire County Council v Secretary of State for the Environment*,[6] the House of Lords in 1985 used the Rate Support Grant Report for 1982–83, submitted to the House of Commons on 5 February 1982 and approved by resolution of the House, to interpret a subsection inserted by the Local Government Finance Act 1982, which received the Royal Assent on 13 July 1982. The Act was intended to give retrospective force to the guidance contained in that report and so could be construed in the light of the report. As Lord Bridge of Harwich explained:[7]

---

4. Despite the view of Lord Reid in *Jones v Secretary of State for Social Services* [1972] AC 944 at 966 'that it should only be in rare cases that we should reconsider questions of construction of statutes or other documents', the House of Lords has been less reluctant to do so in more recent years: see *R v Shivpuri* [1986] 2 All ER 334, *Vestey v Inland Revenue Commrs* [1980] AC 1148, infra, p 176. See also A Paterson, *The Law Lords* (London, 1982) pp 165–6.
5. *Campbell College, Belfast (Governors) v Valuation Commissioner for Northern Ireland* [1964] 2 All ER 705 at 727.
6. [1986] AC 240, [1986] 1 All ER 199; supra, pp 88–9.
7. Ibid at 264.

'The reality is that the Rate Support Grant Report for 1982–83, which contained the relevant guidance and secured the approval of the House of Commons, was submitted to the House by the Secretary of State whose department was concurrently promoting the money Bill which became the 1982 Act. Is there any principle which requires us to put on blinkers and ignore this reality? I know of none. If we can regard the reality, then it seems to me that, to the extent that the meaning of provisions given retrospective force is open to doubt, the nature of the guidance by reference to which those provisions will operate, having been set out in a report submitted to and approved by the House of Commons before the enactment of the statute, is available as a contemporanea expositio of the draftsman's purpose.'

A similar approach was adopted in *Hanlon v Law Society*,[8] where regulations made in 1976 and 1977 were used to interpret the reference in s 9(6) of the Legal Aid Act 1974 to 'property recovered or preserved' in proceedings involving legal aid. That subsection began 'Except insofar as regulations otherwise provide . . .' and this was considered by the House of Lords as justifying the use of the regulations to interpret the meaning of the parent Act. Lord Lowry suggested:[9]

'A study of the cases and of the leading textbooks . . . appears to me to warrant the formulation of the following propositions.
(1) Subordinate legislation may be used in order to construe the parent Act, but only where power is given to amend the Act by regulations or where the meaning of the Act is ambiguous.
(2) Regulations made under the Act provide a Parliamentary or administrative contemporanea expositio of the Act but do not decide or control its meaning: to allow this would be to substitute the rule-making authority for the judge as interpreter and would disregard the possibility that the regulation relied on was misconceived or ultra vires.
(3) Regulations which are consistent with a certain interpretation of the Act tend to confirm that interpretation.
(4) Where the Act provides a framework built on by contemporaneously prepared regulations, the latter may be a reliable guide to the meaning of the former.
(5) The regulations are a clear guide, and may be decisive, when

---

8. [1981] AC 124, [1980] 2 All ER 199.
9. Ibid at 193–4.

they are made in pursuance of a power to modify the Act, particularly if they come into operation on the same day as the Act which they modify.

(6) Clear guidance may also be obtained from regulations which are to have effect as if enacted in the parent Act.'

Important as contemporary exposition may be, this does not prevent the courts from adopting an 'updating' or 'ambulatory' interpretation where the wording or the purpose of an enactment so requires.[10]

5. Other statutes on the same subject

As we have seen,[11] the external context of a statute includes its place within the general scheme of statutory and common law rules and principles. In particular, this context includes statutes on the same subject (known as statutes *in pari materia*). A later statute may expressly provide that it is to be read (or construed) as one with earlier legislation. In that event the court must construe all the statutes directed to be read together as though they were one Act. The result can sometimes be a surprising one. In *Phillips v Parnaby*[12] a conviction under s 21 of the Weights and Measures Act 1889 for delivering less coal than that shown on the weight ticket had to be quashed because the defendant had not been served with notice of prosecution. No such notice was required by the Act, but notice of prosecution had to be given under s 12(6) of the Sale of Food (Weights and Measures) Act 1926, s 15 of which provided that it was to be construed as one with former Weights and Measures Acts, including that of 1889. Judges and commentators frequently allude to the difficulties caused by referential legislation but the subject is beyond the scope of this book.

In *R v Loxdale*[13] Lord Mansfield said: 'Where there are different statutes in *pari materia* though made at different times, or even expired, and not referring to each other, they shall be taken and construed together, as one system, and as explanatory of each other'. Lord Mansfield was construing one of the poor law statutes of Elizabeth I and he treated later statutes as *in pari materia* with it.

It is unlikely that Lord Mansfield meant by 'taking and construing statutes together as one system' the same thing as 'reading them as one' with the possibility of consequences like those of *Philips v Parnaby*. However that may be, it seems that the present position is that, when an earlier statute is *in pari materia* with a later one, it is simply part of

---

10. Supra, pp 49–52.
11. Supra, p 48.
12. [1934] 2 KB 299.
13. (1758) 1 Burr 445 at 448.

its context to be considered by the judge in deciding whether the meaning of a provision in the later statute is plain.[14] Like the preamble and long title, it may not be allowed to raise an ambiguity, although it may help to resolve an ambiguity raised by other considerations. Earlier statutes are *in pari materia* with later statutes consolidating them, but there is no authoritative definition of the expression. It is said to be not enough that they should deal with the same subject matter, but a lot depends on how narrowly the latter term is defined. It is not very helpful to say that the statutes must form part of a 'system', and, with respect, it is difficult to believe that any greater assistance is to be derived from the oft quoted statement of an American judge, made as long ago as 1829, that statutes are *in pari materia* if they relate to the same person or thing, or to the same class of persons or things.[15]

However much an earlier and later statute may be *in pari materia*, the later one cannot be treated as part of the context of the earlier; but it may be used as an aid to the construction of the earlier statute if the two of them can be described as 'laws on the same subject' and if the part of the earlier Act which it is sought to construe may be 'fairly and equally open to different meanings'.[16] The mere fact that a particular construction of the earlier provision would mean that the later one is surplusage may be of no great significance, for it might have been enacted out of an abundance of caution. However, the courts are loath to regard a subsequent Act as unnecessary, since 'Parliamentary time is sufficiently precious for Parliament not to pass unnecessary Acts of Parliament'.[17] That remark was made by Forbes J in a case concerning the refusal by a Chief Constable to grant a pedlar's certificate under the Pedlars Act 1871 to a sales representative for goods made by the disabled on the ground, among others, that his hawking of goods from house to house would constitute an offence under the House to House Collections Act 1939. The court's attention was drawn to the Trading Representatives (Disabled Persons) Act 1958, which makes it an offence for an unregistered person, in selling or soliciting orders for goods, to represent that disabled persons are employed in their production. Had the Chief Constable's interpretation been correct, the 1958 Act would have been unnecessary to regulate an activity already prohibited by the 1939 Act. The court preferred to give the 1939 Act an interpretation that left room for a useful interpretation of the later Act. Equally, if a later Act has proceeded on the assumption that an

---

14. Viscount Simonds referred to statutes *in pari materia* in this way in *A-G v Prince Ernest Augustus of Hanover* [1957] AC 436 at 461.
15. Hosmer J, *United Society v Eagle Bank*, 7 Conn 457 at 469.
16. *Re MacManaway* [1951] AC 161 at 177.
17. Forbes J, *Murphy v Duke* [1985] 2 All ER 274 at 280.

earlier statute has a certain effect, the courts will prefer a construction which accords with Parliament's understanding.[18]

The foregoing discussion of statutes *in pari materia* as aids to interpretation has of course been solely concerned with the assistance to be derived in the construction of one statutory provision from the terms of another. Guidance by contrast or analogy may sometimes be derived from a provision of a statute other than that under consideration although there is no question of the two of them being *in pari materia*, but there is no obligation on the judge to consider such statutes as there is in the case of those *in pari materia*.[19] So far as judicial decisions are concerned, although those with regard to the meaning of words of one statute are not binding so far as words of another statute are concerned (unless it consolidates the other statute), they often have great persuasive force.

B. LEGISLATIVE HISTORY

'Legislative history' means (i) the legislative antecedents of the statutory provision under consideration, ie corresponding provisions in previous enactments since repealed and re-enacted with or without modification;[20] (ii) pre-Parliamentary materials relating to the provision or the statute in which it is contained, eg reports of committees and commissions reviewing the existing law and recommending changes; and (iii) Parliamentary materials, ie the text of a Bill as first published and successively amended in its passage through Parliament, explanatory memoranda, proceedings in committees and Parliamentary debates. All three of these items have claims to be regarded as part of the context of a statute but special rules, which are none too easy to state with confidence, apply to the use which a judge may make of them when giving reasons for his decision. In the first place, reference to legislative history is only permissible when he is in doubt about the meaning of the provision under consideration after considering it in its general context as defined by Viscount Simonds in *A-G v Prince Ernest Augustus of Hanover*;[1] secondly it is questionable

---

18. Browne-Wilkinson LJ, *Re Billson's Settlement Trusts* [1984] 2 All ER 401 at 406.
19. See supra, Chapter 2, section E.
20. This is not the same thing as statutes *in pari materia*. Those are considered as forming part of the legislative scheme, whereas legislative history is considered in order to see how a particular provision reached its present position on the statute book.
1. [1957] AC 436 at 461, supra p 54.

whether it is strictly correct for him to cite Parliamentary materials in any circumstances; thirdly, reference may only be made to the pre-Parliamentary materials listed under head (ii) above in order to ascertain the mischief which the statute, or the relevant part of it, was designed to remedy as distinct from the meaning of the particular provisions by which it was proposed to remedy that mischief. The practice in the United States and Western Europe differs from the English practice in all three respects.

The language of the last paragraph was chosen with care. It is often said, not without some justification provided by incautious judicial remarks, that the effect of the English rules is that the judge may not 'look at' Parliamentary and pre-Parliamentary materials, subject to the distinction between the mischief and the remedy in the case of the latter. Bad jokes are then made about the fact that the judges often do gaze into the prohibited areas and say that they have come to their conclusion without being influenced by what they saw there. Of course the prohibition is not one against all references to certain materials, it is against the utilisation of such materials as a reason for a decision. This point is vividly illustrated by *Black-Clawson International Ltd v Papierwerke Waldhof-Aschaffenburg AG*,[2] a case which will be discussed shortly, in which a report of a committee with a draft Bill and commentary annexed was thoroughly discussed in the House of Lords although the majority took the view that no significance could be attached to the commentary on the Bill as an indication of the intention of Parliament, even though that body had adopted it without any material alteration. It is only fair to those who made the bad jokes to say that they did so before the *Black-Clawson* case and that, after that case, one is left with a nagging question concerning the extent to which it is possible to consider a report for the purpose of ascertaining the mischief to be remedied without being influenced by its recommendations concerning the remedy. As Lord Hailsham remarked in 1984:[3]

> 'I once sat in an appeal about the interpretation of a statute which was intended to give effect to the recommendations contained in a blue book. On the committee which published the report had sat both leading counsel in the appeal and, unless I am mistaken, at least two or three of my fellow Law Lords. To exclude from our minds the contents of the report and its policy basis would have involved a mental agility of which I would have been totally incapable.'

---

2. [1975] AC 591, [1975] 1 All ER 810; infra, pp 159–61.
3. 'Addressing the Statute Law' [1985] Stat LR 4 at 9.

The principle underlying the dominant contemporary judicial approach to the use of legislative history as an aid to interpretation was clearly stated by Lord Diplock in *Fothergill v Monarch Airlines Ltd*:[4]

'The constitutional function performed by courts of justice as interpreters of the written law laid down in Acts of Parliament is often described as ascertaining "the intention of Parliament"; but what this metaphor, though convenient, omits to take into account is that the court, when acting in its interpretative role, . . . is doing so as mediator between the state in the exercise of its legislative power and the private citizen for whom the law made by Parliament constitutes a rule binding upon him and enforceable by the executive power of the state. Elementary justice or, to use the concept often cited by the European Court, the need for legal certainty demands that the rules by which the citizen is to be bound should be ascertainable by him (or, more realistically, by a competent lawyer advising him) by reference to identifiable sources that are publicly accessible. The source to which Parliament must have intended the citizen to refer is the language of the Act itself. These are the words which Parliament has itself approved as accurately expressing its intentions. If the meaning of those words is clear and unambiguous and does not lead to a result that is manifestly absurd or unreasonable, it would be a confidence trick by Parliament and destructive of all legal certainty if the private citizen could not rely upon that meaning but was required to search through all that had happened before and in the course of the legislative process in order to see whether there was anything to be found from which it could be inferred that Parliament's real intention had not been accurately expressed by the actual words that Parliament had adopted to communicate it to those affected by the legislation.'

1. The plain meaning rule

It would be possible to place an extremely restrictive interpretation on Lord Diplock's ban on legislative history because it was in terms confined to cases where the words of the Act are 'clear and unambiguous', but it seems more in accordance with judicial practice to extend it to cases where the judge is satisfied that one of two or more possible meanings of statutory words, read in a context bereft of their legislative history, best fits the purpose of the legislation. Thus understood, the ban is redolent of the words of Tindal CJ in the *Sussex*

---

4. [1981] AC 251 at 279–80.

Peerage case;[5] 'if the words of the statute are in themselves precise and
unambiguous, then no more can be necessary than to expound those
words in that natural and ordinary sense. . . . But if any doubt arises
from the terms employed by the legislature, it has always been held a
safe means of collecting the intention, to call in aid the ground and
cause of the making of the statute. . . .' Nowadays we call in aid 'the
ground and cause of the making of the statute' before deciding whether
the statutory words are 'precise and unambiguous'. Why should we
shut our eyes to legislative history which may be useful evidence of the
purpose of a statute now that the purpose is regarded as part of the
statutory context?

It is this apparently arbitrary exclusion of part of the context which
distinguishes the practice of the English courts with regard to statutory
interpretation from that of the courts of the United States and Western
Europe. One of the landmark cases in the United States' Supreme
Court was *United States v American Trucking Association*, and the
following is an extract from the judgment of Reed J:[6]

> 'There is, of course, no more persuasive evidence of the purpose
> of a statute than the words by which the legislature undertook to
> give expression to its wishes. Often these words are sufficient in
> and of themselves to determine the purpose of the legislation. In
> such cases we have followed their plain meaning. When that
> meaning has led to absurd or futile results, however, this court
> has looked beyond the words to the purpose of the Act. Fre-
> quently, however, even when the plain meaning did not produce
> absurd results but merely an unreasonable one "plainly at
> variance with the policy of the legislation as a whole" this court
> has followed that purpose, rather than the literal words. When
> aid to construction of the meaning of words, as used in the
> statute, is available, there can certainly be no "rule of law" which
> forbids its use, however clear the words may be on superficial
> investigation.'

Reed J had legislative history in mind when speaking of 'aid to construction', and the last sentence of the above passage certainly reveals
a difference between the practice of the Supreme Court and the House
of Lords.

Speaking of the contrast between the approaches to the problem of
interpretation by the French, German and Scandinavian courts on the

---

5. Supra, p 14.
6. 310 US 534 at 543–4 (1940).

one hand, and the English courts on the other, N S Marsh has said[7] that the English judge:

> 'does not generally feel himself under the same obligation to search as deeply as possible for the most satisfactory meaning of the statute, if he has to hand an interpretation which accords with the normal usage of language as employed in the text of the statute, and of the more obvious and immediate contextual implications of the text.'

The reference to the normal usage of language gives the clue to the justification of the English practice. To quote Lord Diplock again:[8]

> 'The acceptance of the rule of law as a constitutional principle requires that a citizen, before committing himself to any course of action, should be able to know in advance what are the legal consequences that will flow from it. Where those consequences are regulated by a statute the source of that knowledge is what the statute says. In construing it the court must give effect to what the words of the statute would be reasonably understood to mean by those whose conduct it regulates.'

It is quite right that the courts should take such internal matters as the preamble and long title into account because they would be taken into account by the normal user of the English language, but there are limits to the extent to which he, or (and this is where we approach the realities of the situation) his legal adviser, can be expected to consider non-statutory materials. We have seen that the long title and preamble can only serve in the first instance as pointers to a plain meaning, they cannot be allowed to raise an ambiguity, although they may, at a later stage, resolve ambiguities in the enacting words. No greater force should be accorded to legislative history, hence it would be preposterous to expect those acting on the statute extrajudicially to refer to that history when they consider the meaning of the statutory words to be plain without its aid. This justification of the English practice is unanswerable provided the distinction between plain meaning and ambiguity is as clear cut and workable as the practice assumes it to be.

2. Parliamentary materials

Although the justifications offered for the rule are various and have

---

7. *Interpretation in a National and International Context*, p 75. It is to be regretted that these lectures, delivered at the Centre for European Studies in Luxembourg in 1973 and published by UGA in Belgium in 1974, are not better known in this country.
8. *Black-Clawson*, [1975] AC at 638.

been different at different epochs, it has been generally accepted for well over a century that Parliamentary debates are not admissible as an aid to interpreting a statute. The rule is that expressed by Lord Reid in *Beswick v Beswick*:[9]

> 'For purely practical reasons we do not permit debates in either House to be cited. It would add greatly to the time and expense involved in preparing cases involving the construction of a statute if counsel were expected to read all the debates in Hansard, and it would often be impracticable for counsel to get access to at least the older reports of debates in Select Committees of the House of Commons; moreover, in a very large proportion of cases such a search, even if practicable, would throw no light on the question before the court.'

This statement was approved unanimously by the House of Lords in *Davis v Johnson*[10] and in *Hadmor Productions Ltd v Hamilton*.[11] In all three cases, Lord Denning MR in the Court of Appeal had referred to extracts from Hansard to justify a particular interpretation of the statutes in question. His approach was declared illegitimate in all three cases. This position was supported by the Law Commissions[12] and the Renton Committee[13] in their reports, and was also supported by a large majority of those who spoke in the debates on Lord Scarman's Interpretation of Legislation Bills in 1980 and 1981.[14]

The principal argument used to justify this rule is that for the vast majority of those who have to apply and interpret the Act, be they solicitors in practice, or magistrates, or judges in Crown Courts, Hansard is not easily accessible.[15] To permit its use would violate Lord Diplock's principle that legal certainty requires that citizens should be able to ascertain what the Act requires by means of accessible information. Equally, as Lord Reid stated, the sheer volume of material would excessively increase the work of lawyers and prolong litigation. As Lord Diplock pointed out in *Davis v Johnson*,[16] Parliamentary committees, unlike continental legislatures, do not produce reasoned

---

9. [1968] AC 58 at 74.
10. [1979] AC 264, [1978] 1 All ER 1132.
11. [1983] 1 AC 191, [1982] 1 All ER 1042.
12. *The Interpretation of Statutes* (Law Com No 21; Scott Law Com No 11; 1969), paras 53–62.
13. *Report of the Committee on the Preparation of Legislation* (1975, Cmnd 6053), paras 19.20 and 19.26.
14. See 405 HL Deb, cols 276–306 (13 February 1980); 418 HL Deb, cols 64–83 (9 March 1981) and 1341–7 (26 March 1981).
15. See Law Commissions, paras 60–2; Viscount Dilhorne, 405 HL Deb, col 297.
16. [1979] AC at 329.

reports which might explain the adoption or rejection of amendments. The successive versions of a Bill would be of little value without an indication of the Parliamentary reasons for the changes in them, and the explanatory memorandum in its present form would be of no value to the courts.[17]

In addition, there are problems of the reliability and utility of Parliamentary materials. It is by no means clear that a particular statement can be said to represent a general understanding in Parliament of what that Act was intended to do. In *Hadmor Productions Ltd v Hamilton*, Lord Denning MR justified his interpretation of s 17 of the Employment Act 1980 by reference to a speech of Lord Wedderburn in the House of Lords. On appeal, counsel noted that, had this research of Lord Denning MR been put to him before the opinion was delivered, he would have adduced a number of other quotations to the contrary.[18] In many cases, researches in Hansard will be fruitless because the questions which have arisen never occurred to the promoters of the Bill or to members of Parliament.[19]

Most of these practical arguments relate ultimately to the constitutional value of the rule of law. Arguments have been adduced equally from the constitutional value of the separation of powers. The first is that the interpretation of statutes is the constitutional function of the courts, and that this should not be ceded to another agency. Lord Wilberforce made this point in relation to committee reports,[20] but it is equally applicable here. The second argument advanced by Lord Hailsham is less strong. He suggests[1] that comity between the different branches of the state requires that they should not criticise each other and that the courts would be led inevitably to criticise erroneous interpretations of the Act made in Parliament, if Hansard were to be admissible.

On the other hand, there is the argument put succinctly by V Sacks:[2]

'If the judicial role is to apply the intention of Parliament, it

---

17. It is too brief and it is only published with the Bill on its initial appearance in each House. Notes on clauses for the use of the Minister responsible for the Bill are not generally published.

18. See [1983] 1 AC 191 at 204, 232–3.

19. See Lord Reid, *Black-Clawson* [1975] AC at 614–5.

20. Infra, p 161; also D Miers, 'Citing Hansard as an Aid to Interpretation' [1983] Stat LR 98.

1. *Hamlyn Revisited* (London, 1983) p 69. The other argument from comity that Hansard may not be cited in court proceedings without the approval of Parliament (see Lord Scarman, *Davis v Johnson* [1979] AC at 350) is no longer valid since this rule was rescinded by a resolution of the House of Commons on 31 October 1980: see D Miers, op cit.

2. 'Towards Discovering Parliamentary Intent' [1982] Stat LR 143.

appears perverse that the judges refuse to seek the legislative intent in the very place where it might be found—that is, the background materials to the statute . . .'

There are a number of cases studied in this book where the problem posed to the court has been raised in Parliament and answered by the Minister, who considered the Bill clear enough not to require further elaboration on the point. Thus, the phrase 'a section of the public' in the Race Relations Act 1968 had been explicitly stated by Lord Gardiner LC not to apply to clubs.[3] Again, that Sikhs were protected by the phrase 'ethnic' was expressly agreed by the Minister at the time when the Bill was in Parliament.[4] The results in *Charter, Dockers' Labour Club* and *Mandla*[5] were in accord with what the Minister had considered implicit, even though the courts did not refer to Parliamentary debates. By contrast, there was divergence between the House of Lords and the reply of the Minister on the question of whether the Transport (London) Act 1969 permitted the subsidy of fares by the Greater London Council. As has been shown by J Dignan,[6] the decision in *Bromley London Borough Council v Greater London Council* on the interpretation of the Act was expressly contrary to a ministerial statement during the passage of the Bill. As V Sacks has shown,[7] Parliamentary debates may only rarely be helpful in resolving problems of statutory interpretation; but some judges, like Lord Simon of Glaisdale, have argued that it is wrong to ignore them when they do provide clear answers to the questions before the court.[8] Since practitioners are likely to have access to textbooks and commentaries on a statute, which may well digest the relevant elements of the Parliamentary and other materials on difficult points, the problem of accessibility need not be overwhelming. However, this remains clearly a minority opinion.

There are some cases in which judges have expressly referred to Hansard in their opinions as supporting justifications for the conclusions that they have reached.[9] Even those who, like Lord Hailsham,

---

3. 295 HL Deb, cols 98 and 156 (15 July 1968).
4. See St John A Robilliard, [1983] *Public Law* 348.
5. Supra, pp 81–2, 82–3 and 57–8 respectively.
6. 'Policy-making, Local Authorities and the Courts: the "GLC Fares" Case' (1983) 99 LQR 605, 622–4: see supra, pp 70–1.
7. Op cit, supra, note 2.
8. *Ealing v Race Relations Board* [1972] AC 342 at 361; also Lord Kilbrandon, ibid, at 367–8; Lord Reid, *Warner v Metropolitan Police Commissioner* [1969] 2 AC 256 at 279.
9. Eg Lord Upjohn in *Beswick v Beswick*, [1968] AC at 105; Lord Denning MR, *Sagnata Investments Ltd v Norwich Corporation* [1971] 2 QB at 624. For a full list see *Bennion*, pp 533–4.

'would forbid the use of *Hansard* almost over my dead body',[10] admit to a private reading of such material.[11] But, of course, it does not constitute an admissible legal justification for a decision. As he put it,[12]

> 'A judge who is impressed by a point picked up in private reading should of course put it before counsel to enable them to deal with it, and counsel must argue any such point of which he desires to make use without referring to the source.'

There is force in the argument that the issue might be better resolved by giving due weight to Parliamentary debates as guides to interpretation coupled with the sanction of costs for unnecessary citation, rather than by a blanket prohibition.

It should be noted that strong arguments have been advanced in recent years in the United States for refusing to admit legislative debates as guides to interpretation.[13] Although many of these arguments are transposable to the current position of English law, it is unlikely that English lawyers would accept the argument of some American authors that legislative debates may be consulted not for interpreting the meaning of statutory words, but to guide the creation of a legal rule where the statute provides none.[14]

3. Pre-Parliamentary materials

Although it would be possible to cite a fairly large number of instances in which judges have taken account or refused to take account of reports of advisory committees and the like, the present law on the subject can be adequately stated by means of a reference to three cases, *Eastman Photographic Materials Co Ltd v Comptroller General of Patents*, *Assam Railways and Trading Co Ltd v Inland Revenue Commrs* and *Black-Clawson International Ltd v Papierwerke Waldhof-Aschaffenburg AG*.

In *Eastman Photographic Materials Co Ltd v Comptroller General of Patents*, the legality of registering the trademark 'Solio' was in issue. The statute under consideration had been passed in consequence of a report of a departmental commission on the use of geographical

---

10. 'Obstacles to Law Reform' [1981] *Current Legal Problems* 279 at 289.

11. *Hamlyn Revisited* p 69; also 418 HL Deb, col 1346 (26 March 1981).

12. Ibid.

13. See R Dickerson, *The Interpretation and Application of Statutes* (Boston 1975), Ch 10; id, 'Statutory Interpretation in America: Dipping into Legislative History' [1984] Stat LR 76, 141; J W Hurst, *Dealing with Statutes* (New York 1982) pp 54–5.

14. See R Dickerson, *The Interpretation and Application of Statutes* pp 168–9, 178; R M Dworkin, *A Matter of Principle* (Cambridge, Mass 1985) pp 320–1, 328; id, *Law's Empire* (London, 1986) pp 342–3.

names. When speaking of that report Lord Halsbury said 'I think no more accurate source of information as to what was the evil or defect which the Act of Parliament now under consideration was intended to remedy could be imagined than the report of that commission.'[15]

In *Assam Railways and Trading Co Ltd v Inland Revenue Commrs*[16] a section of the Finance Act 1920 fell to be construed. It dealt with relief from English income tax on income which had already been taxed in a Dominion, and was enacted in consequence of a Royal Commission's report. Counsel for the appellants argued that the report should be received as evidence of the intention of the legislature in passing the section. The House of Lords rejected this contention, Lord Wright saying:[17]

> 'But on principle no such evidence for the purpose of showing the intention, that is the purpose or object, of an Act is admissible; the intention of the Legislature must be ascertained from the words of the statute with such extraneous assistance as is legitimate. . . . It is clear that the language of a Minister of the Crown in proposing in Parliament a measure which eventually becomes law is inadmissible and the Report of Commissioners is even more removed from value as evidence of intention, because it does not follow that their recommendations were accepted.'

Speaking of Lord Halsbury's action in the *Eastman* case, Lord Wright said that he 'refers to the report not directly to ascertain the intention of the words used in the Act', but 'as extraneous matter to show what were the surrounding circumstances with reference to which the words were used'.

The distinction between the admissibility of pre-Parliamentary materials as evidence of surrounding circumstances and their inadmissibility as direct evidence of Parliamentary intent has survived the *Black-Clawson* case[18] but only just. The question was whether s 8(1) of the Foreign Judgments (Reciprocal Enforcement) Act 1933 applied in favour of the defendant to a claim for money due on bills of exchange brought in England against a German company in whose favour a judgment had been given by a German court on an identical claim because, by German, unlike English law, it was out of time. At common law a foreign judgment obtained in such circumstances is not

---

15. [1898] AC 571 at 575.
16. [1935] AC 445.
17. Ibid, at 458.
18. *Black-Clawson International Ltd v Papierwerke Waldhof-Aschaffenburg AG* [1975] AC 591, [1975] 1 All ER 810.

a bar to English proceedings,[19] but under s 8(1) of the 1933 Act a judgment to which Part I applies 'shall be recognised in any court in the United Kingdom as *conclusive* between the parties thereto in all proceedings founded on the same cause of action, and may be relied on by way of defence or counterclaim in any such proceedings'. By a majority of 4 to 1 the House of Lords held that s 8(1) had not altered the relevant common law. The Act was the outcome of a report of a committee presided over by Greer LJ. A draft Bill, identical in all material respects with the terms of the Act, was annexed to the report, and there was a difference of opinion among their lordships concerning the admissibility of that report together with the clause-by-clause commentary accompanying the draft Bill as evidence of the meaning attached by Parliament to s 8(1) in relation to the facts before the court.

Lord Reid held the report to be inadmissible for this purpose, though admissible as evidence of the mischief against which the Act was directed. Lords Wilberforce and Diplock agreed with Lord Reid, but Lord Diplock's speech was the dissentient one; he considered that the terms of s 8(1) were plain and unambiguous. Viscount Dilhorne considered that the report was admissible both as evidence of surrounding circumstances and as direct evidence of intention. He was disposed to question the validity of the distinction in general, and in particular when applied to the commentary on a draft Bill adopted by Parliament without material alteration. Lord Simon of Glaisdale would, 'as at present advised', have admitted the report as evidence of intent. Accordingly there was a majority of 3 to 2 in favour of maintaining the distinction drawn by Lord Wright in the *Assam Railways* case provided the observations in the dissenting speech are allowed to count; and, as they had nothing to do with the reasons underlying the dissent, there can presumably be no objection to counting them.

The distinction between admitting pre-Parliamentary materials as evidence of the mischief against which statutory words are aimed and admitting them as evidence of the meaning of the words in their application to the case before the court is, it is believed, unheard of in the law of the United States and Western Europe. Can it be justified? Lord Reid justified it on the ground that, if pre-Parliamentary materials were accepted as evidence of what Parliament intended in relation to the case before the court, it would be necessary to abandon the prohibition of the citation of Hansard: 'If we are to refrain from considering expressions of intention in Parliament it appears to me that *a fortiori* we should disregard expressions of intention by com-

---

19. *Harris v Quine* (1869) LR 4 QB 653.

mittees or royal commissions which reported before the Bill was introduced.'[20] This is similar to the earlier reasoning of Lord Wright according to which the report of commissioners is 'even more removed from value as evidence of intention' than the language of a Minister of the Crown. There is of course much force in this reasoning, but it loses some of its strength when it is remembered that one of the grounds for rejecting Parliamentary debates is their inaccessibility. This does not apply to pre-Parliamentary materials.

After making the point that, if a clause-by-clause commentary on a draft Bill subsequently enacted by Parliament were admitted as evidence on the meaning of a particular provision, there would be two documents to construe instead of one, Lord Wilberforce said in the *Black-Clawson* case:[1]

> 'Legislation in England is passed by Parliament, and put in the form of written words. This legislation is given legal effect upon subjects by virtue of judicial decisions, and it is the function of the courts to say what the application of the words used to particular cases or individuals is to be. This power which has been devolved on the judges from the earliest times is an essential part of the constitutional process by which subjects are brought under the rule of law—as distinct from the rule of the King or the rule of Parliament; and it would be a degradation of that process if the courts were to be merely a reflecting mirror of what some other interpretation agency might say.'

It would indeed. But, if a judge who is *ex hypothesi* in doubt about the meaning of a statutory provision takes note of what its author thought it meant, it is a little tendentious to describe him as a 'reflecting mirror'. He is not obliged to act on the author's meaning and there are famous instances in which French courts have not acted on the intentions revealed in the *travaux préparatoires* which they have consulted. It is difficult not to have some sympathy with the point made by Lord Simon of Glaisdale (with acknowledgment to Aneurin Bevan) that rejecting the commentary as evidence of the intended meaning of a particular clause was like gazing in the crystal ball when you can read the book.[2]

The admissibility of pre-Parliamentary reports was strongly opposed by representatives of the legal profession during the debates on Lord Scarman's Interpretation of Legislation Bill in 1981. The

---

20. [1975] AC at 614.
1. Ibid, at 629–30.
2. Ibid, at 652, better reported in [1975] 1 All ER at 847.

principal argument was the inaccessibility of these documents to the ordinary practitioner and the increased cost of litigation which admissibility would cause.[3] This argument would call into question even the limited admissibility permitted by the *Black-Clawson* decision. However, there is little evidence that great inconvenience is caused to practitioners by the present rule.

The distinction between using pre-Parliamentary materials as a means of ascertaining the general purpose of a statute and using them as evidence of the intended meaning of a particular provision in its application to the case before the court is not so difficult to draw as is sometimes suggested; but, although it is occasionally necessary, any rule according to which evidence is admissible for one purpose but not for another requires to be justified, and, in spite of the undoubted strength of the reasons urged in favour of this particular rule, it is submitted that they do not justify it.

4. Treaties and international conventions

Treaties and international conventions are a frequent impetus for domestic legislation. The problems posed by Acts implementing them are different from those faced in purely domestic legislation, since the courts must strive not only to carry out the intentions of Parliament, but also to ensure that their interpretation will not be out of line with that of other signatory states. In particular, the questions arising are whether the treaty, even if not expressly enacted, can be used to interpret the statute, and whether the *travaux préparatoires* of the treaty are also admissible, as is laid down in article 32 of the Vienna Convention on the Law of Treaties and as is the practice in many countries.

On the first question, the Act frequently resolves the problem by including the text of the treaty in a schedule, as in the Carriage by Air Act 1961, which enacts the Warsaw Convention on the subject. In other cases, the Act seeks to give effect to the treaty by a more specific adaptation of English law. Here, there is no doubt, since the decision of the House of Lords in *James Buchanan & Co Ltd v Babco Forwarding and Shipping (UK) Ltd*,[4] that the treaty may be consulted to clarify the meaning of the statute. As Lord Diplock put it in *Quazi v Quazi*:[5]

'Where Parliament passes an Act amending the domestic law of the United Kingdom in order to enable this country to ratify an international treaty and thereby assume towards other states that

---

3. See especially Viscount Bledisloe, 418 HL Deb, cols 69–70 (9 March 1981) and 1341–4 (26 March 1981).
4. [1978] AC 141, [1977] 3 All ER 1048.
5. [1980] AC 744 at 808.

are parties to the treaty an obligation in international law to observe its terms, it is a legitimate aid to the construction of any provisions of the Act that are ambiguous or vague to have recourse to the terms of the treaty in order to see what was the obligation in international law that Parliament intended that this country should be enabled to assume. The ambiguity or obscurity is to be resolved in favour of that meaning that is consistent with the provisions of the treaty.'

This passage and other dicta make it clear that materials not contained in the Act, be they the unenacted treaty, versions of an enacted treaty in other languages, or the *travaux préparatoires* may only be consulted when the provisions of the Act are themselves ambiguous.[6]

Sometimes the question arises whether the Act or the English text of the treaty is a correct translation of a convention drafted in another language. In such a case, reference to other official versions is permitted and, in the case of conflict, reference may also be made to the *travaux préparatoires*. Such was the case in *Fothergill v Monarch Airlines Ltd*.[7] Article 18(1) of the Convention on Carriage by Air, enacted by the Carriage by Air Act 1961, made the carrier liable for 'damage sustained in the event of destruction or loss of, or of damage to, any registered baggage', but Article 26(2) required that, in the case of 'damage', the owner had to notify the carrier within seven days. In the present case, part of the contents of a registered suitcase was found to be missing after transit, but this was not notified to the carrier until four weeks later. It was held that for the partial loss of contents, notification to the carrier was required. Both the English and French texts of the Convention were contained in the Schedule to the Act and s 1(2) provided that, in the event of any inconsistency, the French text was to prevail. It was thus legitimate to compare the scope of the English word 'damage' with that of its French equivalent '*avarie*'. The House of Lords, like the majority of the Court of Appeal, considered that any doubts could be resolved by looking at French textbooks and judicial opinions on the subject, both as to the meaning of the word and as to the purpose of the Convention. Having consulted such material, the House of Lords did not consider it necessary to refer to the *travaux préparatoires* of the Convention. However, since Lord

---

6. Lords Salmon and Edmund-Davies in *Buchanan* [1978] AC at 161 and 167, but cf Lord Wilberforce at 152 (a case involving consultation of the French version of an enacted treaty); also Lord Brandon delivering the unamimous opinion of the House of Lords in *The Antonis P Lemos* [1985] AC 711 at 725–6, 731 (a case involving consulting an unenacted treaty).

7. [1981] AC 251, [1980] 2 All ER 696.

Denning MR had relied on them in the Court of Appeal, the House took the opportunity to give some guidance on when they might be consulted. Lord Wilberforce thought that they should be admissible only on two conditions: first, that the material involved was public and accessible, and second, that it 'clearly and indisputably' pointed to a definite legislative intention.[8] In this case, the minutes of the relevant meetings had been published by HMSO. Lord Fraser of Tullybelton alone dissented from this view, considering that the *travaux prépara-toires* could only be consulted if they had been published to the same extent as the Act.[9] Lord Roskill, while sympathising with this viewpoint, did not consider that the majority position would cause problems here, because disputes would only arise between bodies such as cargo underwriters, airlines and the like, who would be fully equipped with the necessary information.[10] The majority view has been repeated more recently in *Gatoil International Inc v Arkwright-Boston Manufacturers Insurance Co*[11] and must now be taken to represent current practice.

In order to resolve doubts, a statute may expressly permit the use of specified extrinsic material in its interpretation. Thus s 3(3) of the Civil Jurisdiction and Judgments Act 1982 provides that three reports forming part of the *travaux préparatoires* of the enacted Conventions may be used 'to ascertain their meaning and effect', and requires the reports to 'be given such weight as is appropriate in the circumstances'.

The difference in the judicial approach to *travaux préparatoires* in the case of treaties as compared with domestic legislation was justified by Lord Diplock on the ground that delegates to the conference giving rise to the treaty would have voted on the understanding that certain materials would be consulted, and that therefore no further clarification of the treaty's wording on a particular point was necessary. To consult the *travaux préparatoires* best ensures the comity of nations and uniformity of interpretation among signatories, and it also conforms to the conventions of draftsmanship of international treaties.[12] The same cannot be said of Parliamentary debates during the passage of domestic legislation.

5. Summary

It may not be out of place to conclude this account of the use made by

---

8. Ibid, at 278.
9. Ibid, at 288.
10. Ibid, at 302.
11. [1985] AC 255, [1985] 1 All ER 129, HL.
12. *Fothergill*, [1981] AC at 283.

the courts of legislative history with a concise statement of the author's views concerning the need for a change of practice: (i) the existing rule that there can be no reference to legislative history when the meaning of the statutue is plain without recourse to it should be retained; (ii) the existing ban on the citation of Parliamentary materials should be retained unless and until some means of presenting them in a short and simple form is evolved; (iii) the judge's existing power to refer to pre-Parliamentary materials when he has real doubt about the meaning of a statutory provision should be extended so as to enable him to rely on those materials, not merely as evidence of the mischief against which the statute was directed (being part of the circumstances in which it was passed), but also as a pointer to the meaning which he should attach to the particular provision under consideration. It must be recognised, however, that there is much to be said for two other views, namely (*a*) that no change of any kind in the existing practice is called for and, at the other extreme, (*b*) that the judge should have an unrestricted power to cite legislative history for any purpose whenever he considers it to be relevant, and whether or not he has any doubt about the meaning of the statute without recourse to such history.

Chapter 7
Presumptions

A. PRESUMPTIONS GENERALLY

Although the word 'presumption' is used with different shades of meaning in different branches of the law, its use always relates in some way to the burden of proof. The implication is that a particular conclusion is likely to be drawn by the court in the absence of good reason for reaching a different one. In the law of statutory interpretation there are two kinds of presumption which merge into each other, and the sovereignty of Parliament gives the clue to the nature of the first kind.

For the purpose of the present discussion let it be assumed that the courts will give effect to any law Parliament sees fit to pass provided it is expressed in clear terms. Allowance must be made for the fact that statutes are not enacted in a vacuum. A great deal inevitably remains unsaid. It is assumed that the courts will continue to act in accordance with well recognised rules:

> 'The mental element of most crimes is marked by one of the words "maliciously", "fraudulently", "negligently" or "knowingly", but it is the general—I might, I think, say, the invariable—practice of the legislature to leave unexpressed some of the mental elements of crime. In all cases whatever, competent age, sanity and some degree of freedom from some kinds of coercion are assumed to be essential to criminality, but I do not believe they are ever introduced into any statute by which any particular crime is defined.'[1]

Long-standing principles of constitutional and administrative law are likewise taken for granted, or assumed by the courts to have been

---

1. Stephen J, *R v Tolson* (1889) 23 QBD 168 at 187.

taken for granted, by Parliament. Examples are the principles that discretionary powers conferred in apparently absolute terms will be exercised reasonably, and that administrative tribunals and other such bodies will act in accordance with the principles of natural justice. One function of the word 'presumption' in the context of statutory interpretation is to state the result of this legislative reliance (real or assumed) on firmly established legal principles. There is a 'presumption' that *mens rea* is required in the case of statutory crimes, and a 'presumption' that statutory powers must be exercised reasonably. These presumptions apply although there is no question of linguistic ambiguity in the statutory wording under construction, and they may be described as 'presumptions of general application'. At the level of interpretation, their function is the promotion of brevity on the part of the draftsman. Statutes make dreary enough reading as it is, and it would be ridiculous to insist in each instance upon an enumeration of the general principles taken for granted.

These presumptions of general application not only supplement the text, they also operate at a higher level as expressions of fundamental principles governing both civil liberties and the relations between Parliament, the executive and the courts. They operate here as constitutional principles which are not easily displaced by a statutory text. Although the point lacks clear authority, it is probably true to say that some of them can only be rebutted by express words; nothing in the nature of implication, even necessary implication, will suffice. On the other hand, it is tolerably clear that some presumptions of general application are rebuttable by implication, which need not always be particularly necessary. The requirement of *mens rea* in the sense of guilty knowledge may be excluded by implication from the purpose and background of criminal statutes; more may well be required to exclude defences such as insanity or duress. The principle that no one shall be allowed to gain an advantage from his own wrong is of general application for it undoubtedly applies so as to qualify the effects of statutory words which are wholly unambiguous.[2] But it is somewhat easily rebutted by the statutory context.[3]

To be contrasted with presumptions of general application are 'presumptions for use in doubtful cases'. An example is the presumption

---

2. Eg *R v Chief National Insurance Commissioner, ex p Connor* [1981] QB 758, [1981] 1 All ER 769 (a woman convicted of the manslaughter of her husband was not entitled to a widow's allowance under s 24(1) of the Social Security Act 1975 notwithstanding its mandatory wording that 'A woman who has been widowed shall be entitled to a widow's allowance . . .').
3. Eg *Hipperson v Electoral Registration Officer for the District of Newbury* supra, p 78; *Workington Harbour and Dock Board v SS Towerfield (Owners)* [1951] AC 112 at 160.

that Parliament does not intend to act in breach of international law.[4] This applies where one of the meanings which can reasonably be attributed to the legislation is consonant with treaty obligations and the other is not. This example is on the borderline between the two kinds of presumption, for there are those who would say that the presumption in favour of a construction complying with international law can only be excluded by clear words and is not one which is merely brought into play in cases of ambiguity; but judicial dicta seem to be against this view.[5] The rules of language mentioned at the end of Chapter 5 are sometimes stated in the form of presumptions, and other linguistic presumptions, such as that the same word bears the same meaning throughout the same statute, have also been mentioned elsewhere in this book. We have seen how the purpose of a statute, in addition to forming part of its context which may assist the judge to the conclusion that the meaning is clear, may be taken into consideration at a later stage in order to assist in the resolution of an ambiguity. There is then a presumption that if, of two meanings reasonably attributable to the legislature, one would give effect to the purpose more than the other, that meaning is to be preferred. This presumption may conflict with others, notably that in favour of a strict construction of penal statutes. If, after applying the first two of the basic rules set out above on p 47 the judge is still in doubt concerning the interpretation of a statutory provision, rule 2 may come into play again, but this time as a presumption for use in doubtful cases. If, of two meanings which might reasonably be attributed to the legislature, one would and the other would not lead to a result which is contrary to the purpose of the statute, the latter meaning is to be preferred. Here too conflicts with other presumptions are conceivable; but, if we exclude the presumption concerning penal statutes, it is open to question whether the possibility of conflicting presumptions for use in doubtful cases presents great practical difficulties. At any rate it is certain that they could not be arranged in any kind of hierarchy, because their strength is so largely dependent on the particular facts. They are pointers to a certain conclusion, not rules obliging the judge to reach it.

Presumptions are often said to express 'policies of clear statement'. Whether this is the right way to regard presumptions whose operation is limited to particular branches of the law or to doubtful cases is open to question, but it is certainly an excellent way of describing the constitutional principles to be discussed in the next section. They can all be looked upon as warnings to the draftsman: 'If you do not express

---

4. See Lord Diplock cited at pp 162–3 above.
5. See supra, p 163 and note 6.

yourself clearly, there is a risk that the courts will hold that your words have not effected the changes in the law intended by those instructing you.' They are all presumptions for use by the courts in cases in which there is an ambiguity in the draftsman's words.

B. PRESUMPTIONS AGAINST UNCLEAR CHANGES IN THE LAW

1. The presumption generally

The main presumption against unclear changes in the law goes back to the days when by far the greater proportion of law was common law, and statutes were, for the most part, thought of as minor emendations of that law. In modern times it is possible to make a travesty of the presumption by stating it in some such form as that 'it is to be presumed that a statute alters the common law as little as possible'. So stated the presumption is of course ridiculous when applied to such matters as social welfare legislation concerning subjects on which there is not and never has been any common law. Sensibly stated, the presumption can be of undoubted assistance in resolving ambiguities. To quote Lord Reid in *Black-Clawson International Ltd v Papierwerke Waldhof-Aschaffenburg AG*:[6]

> 'There is a presumption which can be stated in various ways. One is that in the absence of any clear indication to the contrary Parliament can be presumed not to have altered the common law further than was necessary to remedy the "mischief". Of course it may and quite often does go further. But the principle is that if the enactment is ambiguous, that meaning which relates the scope of the Act to the mischief should be taken rather than a different or wider meaning which the contemporary situation did not call for.'

The presumption was one of Lord Reid's grounds for holding, contrary to the view of some other members of the House, in the *Black-Clawson* case that s 8 of the Foreign Judgments (Reciprocal Enforcement) Act 1933 did not apply to judgments given in favour of a defendant simply dismissing a claim made by the plaintiff. In the earlier case of *Maunsell v Olins*[7] Lord Reid had relied on this presumption in support of his conclusion that the word 'premises' in s 18(5) of the Rent Act 1968 did not extend to farm land. The provision under consideration being, in

---

6. [1975] AC 591 at 614.
7. [1975] AC 373, [1975] 1 All ER 16, supra, p 74.

his opinion, ambiguous, he was entitled to consider how it came to be where it was, and he traced it back to s 41 of the Housing Repairs and Rents Act 1954 the purpose of which was to get rid of the decision in *Cow v Casey*[8] which was not concerned with agricultural leases. The restriction of the scope of a statute to the immediate mischief it was designed to remedy was described by Lord Simon of Glaisdale in his dissenting speech as a misuse of the mischief rule, but Lord Reid was after all only speaking of a presumption to be called in aid in a case of ambiguity. The real difference between the majority and the dissentients in *Maunsell v Olins* was over the question whether there was an ambiguity.

An earlier instance of the presumption against unclear changes in the law in the form stated by Lord Reid is *Leach v R*.[9] Section 4(1) of the Criminal Evidence Act 1898 provides that the spouse of a person charged with an offence under any enactment mentioned in the Schedule *may* be called as a witness either for the prosecution or for the defence. Subject to irrelevant exceptions, a wife could not be called to give evidence against her husband at common law, and it was held by the House of Lords that s 4(1) had only made her a competent witness for the prosecution in the scheduled cases; she was not compellable: 'The principle that a wife is not to be compelled to give evidence against her husband is deep seated in the common law of this country, and I think if it is to be overturned it must be overturned by a clear, definite and positive enactment, not by an ambiguous one such as the section relied upon in this case'.[10] No useful purpose would be served by multiplying examples, but it should be pointed out that the presumption applies to changes in statute law. Thus, in *Bennett v Chappell*,[11] it was held that a provision in one of the Schedules to the Local Government Act 1933 under which a poll might be demanded before the conclusion of a parish meeting 'on any question arising thereat' had not altered the law previously laid down in a Schedule to the Local Government Act 1894 which had provided for a poll on any 'resolution'. The 1933 wording was said not to be 'sufficiently plain to indicate an intention to depart entirely from the basic conception of the Act of 1894, that only resolutions were liable to a poll demand'.[12] A change of language on re-enactment will, however, fairly readily be held to indicate a change of law, although this is much less so when the re-enactment is a consolidating statute for there is a well recognised presumption that consolidating statutes do not change the law.

---

8. [1949] 1 KB 474, [1949] 1 All ER 197.
9. [1912] AC 305.
10. Ibid, at 311.
11. [1966] Ch 391, [1965] 3 All ER 130, CA.
12. Per Russell LJ at 399.

This presumption is qualified by the fact that statutes are interpreted first of all in their ordinary meaning and only secondarily in the light of their legislative antecedents. Thus, in *R v West Yorkshire Coroner, ex p Smith*,[13] the majority of the Court of Appeal interpreted s 3(1) of the Coroners Act 1887 (a straight consolidation Act) as requiring a coroner to hold an inquest where 'the dead body of a person is lying within his jurisdiction', even though the death occurred abroad and despite arguments that the subsection merely re-enacted a provision designed originally to resolve conflicts of jurisdiction between coroners of neighbouring counties. On the ordinary meaning of the subsection, a corpse brought from overseas 'is lying' now within the jurisdiction of the coroner and can be subject to an inquest.

Suggestions that Parliament, in re-enacting legislation, must necessarily be taken to have endorsed judicial interpretations of the re-enacted provision can no longer be treated as correct since the House of Lords decision in *R v Chard*.[14] Section 17(1)(a) of the Criminal Appeal Act 1968 provided that the Home Secretary could refer 'the whole case' to the Court of Appeal and that 'the case shall then be treated for all purposes as an appeal to the court by [the defendant]'. On such a reference, the Court of Appeal (Criminal Division) refused to entertain matters raised by the defendant which were unconnected with the reasons for the Home Secretary's reference. In doing so, it followed decisions of 1956 and 1968 on similar wording in s 19(a) of the Criminal Appeal Act 1907.[15] The House of Lords held that the words 'for all purposes' must empower the court to consider all matters relevant to conviction, whether or not they were connected with the reasons for the reference. Lord Scarman,[16] with the concurrence of Lords Roskill and Templeman, took the view that there is no inflexible rule that, where once words in an Act have received a judicial construction and the legislature has re-enacted them without alteration, it must be taken to have endorsed the judicial construction. At best a presumption of endorsement might arise in circumstances where the judicial interpretation was well settled and well recognised. Even then, the presumption could not override the grammatical and ordinary sense of the words. Certainly courts have been prepared to overrule long-standing interpretations. For instance, in *R v Bow Road Justices*,

---

13. [1983] QB 335, [1982] 3 All ER 1098.
14. [1984] AC 279, [1983] 3 All ER 637.
15. *R v Caborn-Waterfield* [1956] 2 QB 379, [1956] 2 All ER 636, CCA; *R v Stones (No 2)* (1968) 52 Cr App R 624.
16. [1984] AC at 294–5. Lord Diplock's view (at 292) was that a subsequent re-enactment of a judicially interpreted provision did not affect its meaning.

ex p Adedigba,[17] the Court of Appeal overruled a decision of 1849 on a statutory provision which was re-enacted in 1872 and again in 1957.

Whether it is correct to talk in terms of a 'presumption' that decisions on earlier, re-enacted provisions continue to apply is perhaps debatable, but it is common practice, and the language of presumptions is occasionally used in relation to cases of statutory interpretation when the fact that Parliament had the opportunity to reverse the effect of a decision but did not do so is urged as a reason for following it. No doubt the position is simply that the re-enactment of a provision which had been judicially interpreted provides a reason of limited force why the courts should be more than ordinarily cautious in overruling that interpretation.

2. Special applications

Special examples of the presumption against unclear alteration of the law are the presumption against ousting the jurisdiction of the courts, the presumption in favour of a strict construction of penal statutes, the presumption in favour of individual liberty, the presumption against interference with vested rights, the presumption against interference with property, and the presumption in favour of a strict construction of revenue statutes. They can all be subsumed under the notion of policies of clear statement.

(a) *Ouster of jurisdiction* The presumption against ousting the jurisdiction of the courts is well illustrated by *Anisminic Ltd v Foreign Compensation Commission*.[18] The case concerned a determination made by the Foreign Compensation Commission under the Foreign Compensation Act 1950 of compensation payable for property sequestrated by the Egyptian Government. The Foreign Compensation (Egypt) (Determination and Regulation of Claims) Order 1962 required the original owner of property and his successor in title to have been British nationals on 31 October 1956 and on 28 February 1959 if they were to qualify for compensation. In this case the applicant company (the original owner) was a British national on the qualifying dates, but its successor in title was not. The Commission held that, in these circumstances, the applicant's claim must fail. The applicant contended that the nationality of its successor in title was irrelevant to its own claim for compensation, and it sought a declaration that the determination of the Commission was erroneous in law and a nullity. Section 4(4) of the Act provided that a determination of the Commission 'shall not be called into question in any court of law'. By a

---

17. [1968] 2 QB 572, [1968] 2 All ER 89, CA.
18. [1969] 2 AC 147, [1969] 1 All ER 208.

majority, the House of Lords held that this provision did not prevent a court from investigating whether the Commmission had acted outside its jurisdiction. The House concluded that the Commission had wrongly interpreted the Order and had thus committed an error of law taking it outside its jurisdiction. Accordingly, it granted the declaration sought. The subsection was thus limited to preventing the questioning of matters which did not affect the jurisdiction of the Commission. To construe the subsection otherwise would be to permit the Commission uncontrolled power, whereas Parliament must have intended it to restrict itself to the jurisdiction laid down in the Act and in the Order. The interpretation adopted by the House of Lords preserved the jurisdiction of the courts to supervise inferior tribunals. Although the presumption against ouster of this jurisdiction can be displaced by express wording, it is difficult to conceive how Parliament could have been more explicit than it was in s 4(4) of the Foreign Compensation Act 1950, and it gave up the attempt to oust the jurisdiction of the courts in relation to the Commission soon afterwards.[19] Quite apart from their constitutional position as guardians of the rights of citizens and defenders of the rule of law, the courts take the view that they are the only tribunals really fitted for the task of settling disputes about points of law,[20] and who is to say them nay?

(b) *Strict construction of penal statutes*   The phrase 'penal statute' is used to cover both statutes creating criminal offences and those providing for the recovery of penalties in civil proceedings. In either case the present position is that if, to use the words of Lord Reid in *Director of Public Prosecutions v Ottewell*,[1] 'after full inquiry and consideration, one is left in real doubt', the accused or person from whom the penalty is claimed must be given the benefit of that doubt. Lord Reid proceeded to stress the point that it is not enough for the provision under construction to be ambiguous in the sense that it is capable of having two meanings, and the same point is embodied in the following frequently quoted passage from one of Lord Esher's judgments:[2]

> 'If there is a reasonable interpretation which will avoid the penalty in any particular case, we must adopt that construction. If there are two reasonable constructions we must give the more lenient one. That is the settled rule for construction of penal sections.'

---

19. Section 3(2) of the Foreign Compensation Act 1969 permits an appeal on a point of law to the Court of Appeal from a determination of the Foreign Compensation Commission.
20. See Griffiths LJ, *R v Knightsbridge Crown Court, ex p International Sporting Club Ltd* [1982] QB 304 at 312–3.
1. [1970] AC 642 at 649.
2. *Tuck & Sons v Priester* (1887) 19 QBD 629 at 638.

So understood, the presumption in favour of a strict construction of penal statutes is simply an example of the presumption against unclear changes in the law. For example, in *R v Allen*,[3] the question arose whether a guest who left a hotel without paying his bill committed a criminal offence within s 3(1) of the Theft Act 1978. The subsection provided that:

> 'a person who, knowing that payment on the spot for any goods supplied or service done is required or expected from him, dishonestly makes off without having paid as required or expected and with intent to avoid payment of the amount due shall be guilty of an offence.'

The House of Lords held that these words clearly did not cover the case where a guest left the hotel intending to pay at a subsequent date. Lord Hailsham LC added that, even if the words 'with intent to avoid payment' were equivocal and might possibly be read as including an intention to delay or defer payment of the amount due, any ambiguity must be resolved in favour of the accused.[4] (He also mentioned that this reading restricted the scope of the subsection to the mischief identified in a report of the Criminal Law Revision Committee which had proposed this amendment to the law, namely that of persons expected to pay on the spot leaving 'without having paid *and intending never to pay*' for goods supplied or services provided.) Allowance must of course be made for the fact that the presumption operates against the Crown with the result that it requires a liberal interpretation of sections which provide the accused with a defence. This was the ground of the decision of the Court of Criminal Appeal in *R v Chapman*.[5] Section 2 of the Criminal Law Amendment Act 1922 deprived men charged with unlawful intercourse with a girl between the ages of 13 and 16 of the defence of reasonable cause to believe that she was over 16, but there was a proviso that 'in the case of a man of 23 years of age or under, the presence of reasonable cause to believe that the girl was over the age of 16 years shall be a valid defence on the first occasion on which he is charged'.[6] The defence was held to be available to a man over 23 but under 24.

In earlier times the presumption was a good deal more than an example of the presumption against unclear changes in the law. This was especially true in the case of criminal statutes. If they were capable of two meanings, however unreasonable one of those meanings might

3. [1985] AC 1029, [1985] 2 All ER 641.
4. Ibid, at 1034.
5. [1931] 2 KB 606.
6. See now Sexual Offences Act 1956, s 6(3).

be, it was applied if favourable to the accused. Examples are *R v Harris*,[7] in which case someone who bit off a joint of her victim's finger was held not guilty of 'wounding', and the case mentioned by Blackstone[8] in which a statute of Edward VI deprived a man of benefit of clergy if he stole *horses*, but the judges refused to apply this to the case of a man who stole a single horse. Decisions of this sort were amply justified on humanitarian grounds, but they have been rendered unnecessary by the mitigation of the rigours of the criminal law. It is surely correct that under the modern rule it is only necessary that persons liable to a penalty should have the benefit of a genuine doubt about meaning, but not of a spurious one created by excessive literalism.

Undoubtedly some modern cases, such as *Fisher v Bell*,[9] have been inspired by the spirit of the old humane decisions. However, it is clear that the courts nowadays generally adopt a purposive approach even to the construction of penal statutes.[10] Principally they seek the interpretation which makes sense of the statute and its purpose, and the presumption of strict construction is merely an ancillary aid for resolving difficult cases. Thus in *R v Bloxham*[11] the House of Lords decided that an innocent purchaser, who subsequently realised that the car he had purchased was stolen and then re-sold it, was not guilty of handling stolen goods contrary to s 22 of the Theft Act 1968. Although citing the presumption in favour of the strict construction of penal statutes, Lord Bridge of Harwich preferred to rely on arguments which showed that to find a criminal offence in this case would be inconsistent with the provisions of the Act and with the report of the Criminal Law Revision Committee which led to its passing. Similarly, in *R v Clarke*[12] a person lied to the police about his immigration status following an arrest for the unlawful possession of a motor vehicle. He was charged with making a false statement 'to an immigration officer or other person lawfully acting in the execution of [the Immigration Act 1971]'. The House of Lords decided that it would go too far to find an offence where the statement was made during inquiries outside the specific procedures of the Act, and that only the clearest wording would convince their Lordships of the existence of an offence in these

---

7. Supra, p 11.
8. *Commentaries*, 1st edition, vol 1, p 88. It was not until 1850 that Lord Brougham's Act (c 21) made statutory words in the singular include the plural, and vice versa, in the absence of provision to the contrary.
9. Supra, p 73.
10. Eg Lord Roskill, *Anderton v Ryan* [1985] AC 560 at 573 and 578.
11. [1983] 1 AC 109, [1982] 1 All ER 582.
12. [1985] AC 1037, [1985] 2 All ER 777.

circumstances.[13] On a reading of the Act, the prosecution's interpretation was implausible, the presumption of strict construction merely providing a supplementary reason for finding no criminal liability.

Professor Glanville Williams has suggested that the presumption is not necessarily a disincentive to broad judicial interpretation of statutes intended to criminalise social wrongs:[14]

> 'Nowadays the criminal courts rarely apply the rule of strict construction. They will still apply it if they are in genuine doubt as to the intention of the legislature and if there are no considerations indicating the desirability of a wide interpretation of the statute. But if the statute admits of alternative interpretations and public policy suggests that the wider interpretation should be preferred, the courts will usually apply the wider one.'

He cites *Smith v Hughes*[15] where a woman was convicted of 'soliciting in the street' for the purpose of prostitution, even though she was at a window, making signs to men as they passed in the street. The Divisional Court held that, since the solicitation was projected to and addressed to persons walking in the street, it was made in the street. Certainly, the presumption was not discussed when the House of Lords adopted an objective, rather than a subjective notion of recklessness in *Metropolitan Police Commissioner v Caldwell*.[16] Even more strikingly, in deciding that a person could not be convicted of an attempt contrary to s 1 of the Criminal Attempts Act 1981 where the act attempted was impossible of fulfilment (here, receiving goods believing them to be stolen when this was not in fact the case), Lord Bridge of Harwich obliquely invoked the presumption by arguing that 'I should find it surprising that Parliament, if intending to make this purely subjective guilt criminally punishable, should have done so by anything less than the clearest express language.'[17] The majority of the House of Lords agreed with him. Less than a year later, delivering the opinion of a unanimous House of Lords, Lord Bridge of Harwich overruled his previous view without reference to the presumption and found that attempting the impossible was criminal after all.[18] Such

---

13. Per Lord Bridge of Harwich at 1048.
14. 'Statutory interpretation, prostitution and the rule of law' in C F H Tapper (ed), *Crime, Proof and Punishment: Essays in Memory of Sir Rupert Cross* (London, 1981) 71 at 72; id, *A Textbook of Criminal Law* (2nd edn, London, 1983) p 12.
15. [1960] 1 WLR 830, [1960] 2 All ER 859; also *Behrendt v Burridge* [1976] 3 All ER 285.
16. [1982] AC 341, [1981] 1 All ER 961; also *R v Lawrence* [1982] AC 510, [1981] 1 All ER 974.
17. *Anderton v Ryan* [1985] AC 560 at 583.
18. *R v Shivpuri* [1986] 2 All ER 334.

cases which have adopted an expansive, rather than a restrictive, interpretation of criminal statutes show the limited role of the presumption in favour of strict construction in the modern law.

(c) *Individual liberty* The strict construction of penal statutes is closely related to the presumption in favour of individual liberty, especially where custodial sentences are involved. As McCullough J succinctly put it in *R v Hallstrom, ex p W (No 2)*:[19]

> 'There is . . . a canon of construction that Parliament is presumed not to enact legislation which interferes with the liberty of the subject without making it clear that this was its intention.'

In that case, a doctor was held to have no power to detain a patient in hospital overnight and then let her out on leave, nor to renew a patient's detention order, where all the doctor wished to achieve was that the person should continue to come as an out-patient for treatment. The powers under the Mental Health Act 1983 were limited to detention in hospital for treatment and did not expressly permit compulsion for out-patient treatment, however much this might be in the patient's interests.

This presumption is important in limiting the scope of the police and other officials. They have powers to interfere with a person or to come upon his property only insofar as they are specifically authorised to do so. For example, s 2 of the Street Offences Act 1959 empowers the police to caution prostitutes. However, in *Collins v Wilcock*[20] the Divisional Court held that this did not empower a police officer to detain a suspected prostitute for questioning by taking hold of her arm. There could be no restraint of a person without arrest. In *Morris v Beardmore*,[1] the House of Lords held that the power to administer a breathalyser test under s 8 of the Road Traffic Act 1972 did not enable the police to enter the driver's property in order to administer it. However, cases studied earlier in this book demonstrate an alternative concern among the judges not to circumscribe police powers so as to render them ineffective. Thus the majority in *Wills v Bowley*[2] overrode Lord Lowry's objections based on the liberty of the subject, preferring to give s 28 of the Town Police Clauses Act 1847 an interpretation that would not unduly narrow the police's powers of arrest. In other cases, too, the conditions for the exercise of police powers have been widely

---

19. [1986] QB 1090 at 1104.
20. [1984] 3 All ER 374, see also *Bennion*, s 290.
1. [1981] AC 446, [1980] 2 All ER 753.
2. *Supra*, pp 87–8.

interpreted so as not to render them ineffective.[3] The tension between the two approaches is well explained by Lord Wilberforce in *R v Inland Revenue Commrs, ex p Rossminster Ltd*,[4] which concerned powers of entry conferred on the Revenue:

> 'The courts have the duty to supervise, I would say critically, even jealously, the legality of any purported exercise of these powers. They are the guardians of the citizen's right to privacy. But they must do this in the context of the times, ie of increasing Parliamentary intervention, and of the modern power of judicial review . . . While courts may look critically at legislation which impairs the rights of citizens and should resolve any doubt in interpretation in their favour, it is no part of their duty, or power, to restrict or impede the working of legislation, even of unpopular legislation; to do so would be to weaken rather than to advance the democratic process.'

Once one accepts that state interference must be effective, especially in maintaining public order or other aspects of the public interest, then the presumption in favour of individual liberty is necessarily qualified.

(d) *Vested rights* 'The well established presumption is that the legislature does not intend to limit vested rights further than clearly appears from the enactment.'[5] One striking modern illustration will suffice. *Allen v Thorn Electrical Industries Ltd*[6] was concerned with the Prices and Incomes Act 1966 under which the Secretary of State was empowered to make orders imposing a 'wages freeze'. Section 29(4) provided that 'an employer shall not pay remuneration to which this section applies for work for any period while the order is in force at a rate which exceeds the *rate of remuneration paid* by him for the same kind of work before July 20 1966'. Did 'paid' mean actually paid or contracted to be paid? The Court of Appeal unanimously came to the latter conclusion with the result that, where immediately effective pay increases had been agreed but not paid before July 20, the increased rate was the rate of remuneration paid before that date. Lord Denning MR had no doubt but added:[7]

> 'If I were wrong in this view, I am clear that, at any rate, the requirement in the statute is ambiguous and uncertain, in which

3. Eg *Holgate-Mohammed v Duke* [1984] AC 437, [1984] 1 All ER 1054; *McKee v Chief Constable of Northern Ireland* [1985] 1 All ER 1.
4. [1980] AC 952 at 997–8; also Lord Diplock at 1008.
5. *Re Metropolitan Film Studios Ltd v Twickenham Film Studios Ltd (Intended Action)* [1962] 3 All ER 508 at 517 per Ungoed-Thomas J.
6. [1968] 1 QB 487, [1967] 2 All ER 1137.
7. Ibid, at 503. The statute penalised employers who did not comply with it.

case the rights under the contract must prevail. No man's con-
tractual rights are to be taken away on an ambiguity in a statute,
nor is an employer to be penalised on an ambiguity.'

Winn LJ used language which, though less common among modern
judges, is surely no less significant:[8]

> 'I must reject as quite untenable any submission . . . that if in any
> case one finds (a) that a statute is worded ambiguously in any
> particular respect, and (b) finds also clear indications *aliunde* that
> Parliament intended that they should have the strictest and most
> stringent meaning possible, the court is therefore compelled to
> construe the section in the sense in which Parliament would have
> desired it to take effect, by giving the words their most stringent
> possible meaning. On the contrary, I think the right view is, and
> as I understand it always has been, that in such a case of ambigu-
> ity, it is resolved in such a way as to make the statute less onerous
> for the general public and so as to cause less interference, than
> the more stringent sense would, with such rights and liabilities
> as existing contractual obligations.'

There is more to interpretation in general than the discovery of the
meaning attached by the author to his words. Even if, in a particular
case, that meaning is discoverable with a high degree of certitude from
external sources, the question whether it has been adequately
expressed remains. This question has to be raised in the interests of
those who have to act and advise on the words under consideration. In
the case of statutory interpretation, there is the further question of the
role of the courts when they have doubts about the meaning which the
ordinary, or, where appropriate, the specialist, reader would attach to
the provision with which they are concerned. When they have notice
aliunde (from another source) of Parliamentary intent, who is to have
the benefit of those doubts, Parliament or the holder of the right? The
orthodox answer is 'the holder of the right' although, as we shall see,
this may require some qualification in the case of certain taxing
statutes. The issue is primarily a constitutional one. From the point of
view of interpretation pure and simple, it could be argued that, on facts
such as those of *Allen v Thorn Electrical Industries Ltd*, those who have
to act or even advise on the statute would not be prejudiced if the
benefit of the doubt were given to Parliament, for Parliamentary intent
in such a case is a matter of common knowledge for which all those
concerned should make allowance. Against such an argument it could

---

8. Ibid, at 508.

very properly be urged that the descent of the Gadarene slope into confusion would indeed have started if those who are concerned extrajudicially with statutory interpretation had to assess Parliamentary intent by criteria other than those which have been dealt with in this book. It only remains to add that, although they undoubtedly represent current legal opinion, the observations of Lord Denning MR and Winn LJ in *Allen v Thorn Electrical Industries Ltd* were technically *obiter* because no member of the Court of Appeal thought there was any ambiguity in the wording of s 29(4) of the Prices and Incomes Act 1966.

(e) *Property rights*   There is a general presumption that Parliament does not intend to take away private property rights unless the contrary is clearly indicated. Lord Atkinson stated[9] that there is a canon of interpretation 'that an intention to take away the property of a subject without giving to him a legal right to compensation for the loss of it is not to be imputed to the legislature unless that intention is expressed in unequivocal terms.' After all, the protection of property is generally regarded as one of the fundamental values of a liberal society. However, the modern state has found it necessary to abolish or to qualify property rights in significant ways in order to achieve socially desirable ends, for instance in the field of town planning or in the relationship between landlord and tenant. In consequence, the presumption has a more limited application than in the past. As Lord Scarman put it in *Secretary of State for Defence v Guardian Newspapers Ltd*:[10]

> 'there certainly remains a place in the law for the principle of construction which the judge applied, namely, that the courts must be slow to impute to Parliament an intention to override property rights in the absence of plain words to that effect. But the principle is not an overriding rule of law: it is an aid, amongst many others, developed by the judges in their never ending task of interpreting statutes in such a way as to give effect to their true purpose.'

That case concerned s 10 of the Contempt of Court Act 1981 which provides generally that no court may require a person to disclose the source of information contained in a publication for which he is responsible, unless the court is satisfied that disclosure is necessary in the interests of justice or national security, or for the prevention of

---

9. *Central Control Board (Liquor Traffic) v Cannon Brewery Co Ltd* [1919] AC 744 at 752; also Lord Warrington, *Colonial Sugar Refining Co Ltd v Melbourne Harbour Trust Commissioners* [1927] AC 343 at 359.
10. [1985] AC 339 at 363.

disorder or crime. Unlike Scott J at first instance, the House of Lords held unanimously that the presumption could not be used to create an exception to this press immunity where a person was seeking the return of his own property held by a newspaper. The wording of s 10 was clear enough to grant an immunity where the return of a person's property would lead to the disclosure of the source. (The majority of the House nevertheless ordered disclosure in the interests of national security.)

The courts do not differentiate between statutes which deprive people of property rights and those which merely restrict their exercise, since the two can frequently have the same practical effect.[11] For instance, the Matrimonial Homes Act 1967 created a right of occupation in the matrimonial home for a spouse, even if he or she was not the owner or tenant of the property. In *Tarr v Tarr*[12] the question arose whether the court's power under s 1(2) of the Act to make an order 'regulating the exercise by either spouse of the right to occupy the dwelling-house' included power to order the spouse who was the owner or tenant to leave the property. The Court of Appeal ordered a husband, who was the sole tenant of a council house, to leave the property so that his wife and child could live there. The House of Lords unanimously held that the power to 'regulate' the exercise of the right of occupation did not include the power to prohibit its exercise altogether. Lord Pearson said that the Court of Appeal's interpretation would make 'a very drastic inroad into the common law rights of the property-owning spouse'.[13] However, where a sufficient countervailing value is at stake, the courts are prepared to interpret statutes so as to override property rights. Thus in *Davis v Johnson*,[14] the majority of the Court of Appeal and of the House of Lords saw no difficulty in interpreting s 1(1) of the Domestic Violence and Matrimonial Proceedings Act 1976 as permitting the exclusion of an unmarried partner from the 'matrimonial home' of which he was tenant. The subsection specifically permitted such exclusion in the case of married persons, and the Act expressly provided that the subsection applied to a man and woman living together as husband and wife as it applied to the parties to a marriage. In earlier Court of Appeal decisions on the subsection it had been argued that Parliament could not have intended such a result, since it had provided no rules for regulating the property rights of unmarried partners comparable to those which existed for matrimonial breakdown.[15] However, the majorities in *Davis* con-

---

11. *Westminster Bank Ltd v Beverley BC* [1971] AC 508 at 529 per Lord Reid.
12. [1973] AC 254, [1972] 2 All ER 295.
13. Ibid, at 264.
14. [1979] AC 264, [1978] 1 All ER 1132.
15. See *B v B* [1978] Fam 26 and *Cantliff v Jenkins* [1978] Fam 47 at 51 per Stamp LJ.

sidered this argument to be of limited consequence where the purpose of the legislation was to prevent violence to the other spouse or to a child of the family.

Even if the presumption has some value, 'in the end', as Lord Pearson said in *Tarr v Tarr*,[16] 'one has to read the enactment in its context and come to a conclusion as to what it means'.

(f) *Revenue statutes* The presumption applicable to revenue statutes has much in common with the presumptions on penal statutes and against interference with property rights. If clearly worded, revenue statutes must be applied even though they operate against the subject in a manner that may appear to have been unintended by Parliament, but '. . . if the provision is reasonably capable of two alternative meanings, the courts will prefer the meaning more favourable to the subject'.[17] The unwillingness of the courts to tax the subject on unclear wording is illustrated by *Vestey v Inland Revenue Commrs*.[18] Section 412 of the Income Tax Act 1952 provided that a person ordinarily resident in the United Kingdom was chargeable to income tax on income resulting from rights to income or capital sums acquired by him 'by means of transfers of assets' to persons overseas. The taxpayers were beneficiaries of overseas discretionary settlements established by members of their families. The Revenue claimed that they were liable to tax on the money over which the various beneficiaries had rights in the hands of the overseas trustees of the settlements. Further, in the absence of statutory provisions apportioning the tax liability among a plurality of beneficiaries, the Revenue claimed the right to determine the tax liability of each of them at its discretion. Overruling a thirty-year-old precedent, the House of Lords held that the section only covered the tax liability of the transferor of the assets and not that of other beneficiaries. To make the latter liable, above all for amounts fixed at the discretion of the Revenue, would be, in Lord Wilberforce's words 'arbitrary, unjust and in my opinion unconstitutional'.[19] Since the wider interpretation proposed by the Revenue was beset by complexities and potential arbitrariness in determining the amounts due, the narrower interpretation in favour of the taxpayers was to be preferred.

There is, however, a complicating factor due to the legitimate state of war which exists between the subject and his advisers on the one hand and the Inland Revenue on the other hand. The former are bent

---

16. [1973] AC at 264.
17. Lord Thankerton, *Inland Revenue Commrs v Ross and Coulter* [1948] 1 All ER 616 at 625.
18. [1980] AC 1148, [1979] 3 All ER 976.
19. Ibid, at 1174.

on avoiding payments to the latter so far as they legally can, and the latter are bent on procuring statutory provisions which will, so far as possible, be foolproof. Nowadays the courts seek to strike a fair balance between the two sides and do not exclusively favour the tax-payer. In *W T Ramsay Ltd v Inland Revenue Commrs*[20] Lord Wilber-force restated the old presumption in a qualified form:

'A subject is only to be taxed upon clear words, not upon "intendment" or upon the "equity" of an Act. Any taxing Act of Parliament is to be construed in accordance with this principle. What are "clear words" is to be ascertained upon normal prin-ciples: these do not confine the courts to literal interpretation. There may, indeed should, be considered the context and scheme of the relevant Act as a whole, and its purpose may, indeed should, be regarded.'

In that and subsequent cases the courts have shown themselves more willing than in the past to examine the substance and not merely the form of tax-avoidance arrangements, and to consider the genuineness or otherwise of the transactions involved, in order to determine whether they are covered by a taxing Act.[1] The judges are more ready to co-operate in achieving the purpose of taxing legislation. As Lord Scarman put it in *Furniss v Dawson*:[2]

'What has been established with certainty by the House in *Ramsay*'s case is that the determination of what does, and what does not, constitute unacceptable tax evasion is a subject suitable to development by judicial process . . . Difficult though the task may be for judges, it is one which is beyond the power of the blunt instrument of legislation. Whatever a statute may provide, it has to be interpreted and applied by the courts: and ultimately it will prove to be in this area of judge-made law that our elusive journey's end will be found.'

While the courts are still not in the business of moulding taxing statutes to meet changing social needs, this approach does suggest that, in an era of purposive interpretation, the strict construction of revenue statutes has softened significantly.[3]

(g) *State benefits* The presumptions concerned with protecting the existing property or money of individuals have not been matched by

---

20. [1982] AC 300 at 323.
1. See, for example, *Inland Revenue Commrs v Burmah Oil Co Ltd* [1982] STC 30; *Furniss v Dawson* [1984] AC 474, [1984] 1 All ER 530.
2. [1984] AC 474 at 513–4.
3. See Mr Justice Vinelott, 'Interpretation of Fiscal Statutes' [1982] Stat LR 77.

any presumptions in favour of individuals claiming state benefits. Although the obtaining of grants, benefits and permissions from central or local government plays an important part in the life of the modern citizen, the courts have not considered it necessary to create any new presumptions. Instead, they content themselves with a purposive construction, even if this deprives the citizen of a welfare benefit. For example, in *Presho v Department of Health and Social Security*,[4] the plaintiff was laid off during a dispute between her employer and a union to which she did not belong. Section 19(1) of the Social Security Act 1975 provided that unemployment benefit was not to be paid to a person affected by a stoppage of work at his place of employment unless he could prove that 'he is not participating in . . . or directly interested in the trade dispute which caused the stoppage . . .' The insurance officer refused the plaintiff unemployment benefit on the ground that, if the union in dispute was successful, existing agreements would ensure that there would be a pay rise for all employees at the factory, including the plaintiff. The House of Lords upheld this view on the ground, among others, that 'if the expression "directly interested in the trade dispute" were to be given a narrower and more legalistic interpretation . . ., the way would be wide open for deliberate and calculated evasions of the basic provisions of s 19(1) of the Social Security Act 1975 as amended, with the result that the effectiveness of the subsection to achieve its manifest object would be much reduced'.[5]

Although the judicial approach to such statutes has been criticised, the absence of presumptions above all reflects a judicial belief in the sufficiency of purposive construction for resolving difficulties in the interpretation of statutes.

C. PRESUMPTION AGAINST RETROSPECTIVE OPERATION

The presumption against the retrospective operation of statutes concerned with the substantive law could perhaps be treated as a facet of the presumption against interference with vested rights, but it is more convenient to give a separate account of the subject. One of the best known judicial statements is that of R S Wright J in *Re Athlumney*:[6]

---

4. [1984] AC 310, [1984] 1 All ER 97.
5. Ibid at 319 per Lord Brandon.
6. [1898] 2 QB 547 at 551.

'Perhaps no rule of construction is more firmly established than this—that a retrospective operation is not to be given to a statute so as to impair an existing right or obligation, otherwise than as regards matter of procedure, unless that effect cannot be avoided without doing violence to the language of the enactment. If the enactment is expressed in language which is fairly capable of either interpretation, it ought to be construed as prospective only.'

In order that the presumption should apply, the statute must be genuinely retrospective in its operation. It is not enough that the circumstances on which the operation of the statute depends should have existed before it came into force. The statute must take away some vested right or impose a penalty for past acts which were not penalised when they were committed. For example, in *Commissioners of Customs and Excise v Thorn Electrical Industries Ltd*,[7] the Commissioners claimed value added tax on payments made to the company in and after April 1973 under an agreement for the hire of a television set entered into on 19 July 1972. The Finance Act 1972 received the royal assent on 27 July, and s 7, dealing with value added tax, together with regulations made under it, came into force on 1 April 1973. According to one of the regulations:

'. . . where goods are or have been supplied under an agreement to hire, they shall be treated as being successively supplied on hire for successive parts of the period of the agreement, and each of the successive supplies shall be treated as taking place when a payment under the agreement is received. . . .'

The House of Lords held that the supply of goods under a hire agreement was a continuing process, so that there was no question of the regulation operating retrospectively. Lord Morris of Borth-y-Gest said: 'The fact that as from a future date tax is charged on a source of income which has been arranged or provided for before the date of the imposition of the tax does not mean that a tax is retrospectively imposed'.[8] The case is also of some interest because both Lord Morris and Lord Fraser of Tullybelton[9] used language indicating agreement with the following remark in the judgment of the Divisional Court: 'If the meaning of words in an enactment is clear, there is no presumption against them having a retrospective effect if that is indeed the result they produce'.[10]

---

7. [1975] 3 All ER 881.
8. Ibid, at 890.
9. Ibid, at 896.
10. [1975] 1 All ER 439 at 447 per Thompson J.

In *Carson v Carson*[11] Scarman J had to construe s 3 of the Matrimonial Causes Act 1963 according to which 'adultery which has been condoned shall not be capable of being revived'. He held that this changed the substantive law according to which condoned adultery could be revived by subsequent desertion, and since Parliament had neither expressly, nor by necessary implication, made the provision retrospective, adultery was revived by a desertion which took place before the Act came into force. *Carson v Carson* may be contrasted with *Blyth v Blyth*[12] which turned on s 1 of the Matrimonial Causes Act 1963 under which a husband was for the first time permitted to give evidence in rebuttal of the presumption that adultery was condoned by subsequent matrimonial intercourse. It was held by the Court of Appeal, whose decision on this point was approved by the House of Lords, that s 1 operated retrospectively. The provision was treated as procedural and, to quote Lord Denning MR: 'the rule that an Act of Parliament is not to be given retrospective effect only applies to statutes which affect vested rights. It does not apply to statutes which only alter the form of procedure, or the admissibility of evidence, or the effect which the courts give to evidence.'[13]

Enough has been said in this brief account of the presumption against retrospective operation to show that the law on the subject is difficult because the distinction between statutes which operate retrospectively for the purpose of the presumption and those which do not is hard to draw. It also seems that there may be some inconsistency in judicial views concerning the nature of the presumption. Is it of general application in the sense that it applies unless rebutted by clear words or necessary implication, or is it a presumption which only comes into play when there is an ambiguity? The preponderance of authority undoubtedly favours the former view,[14] but the statement of R S Wright J quoted on page 185 above and the remark quoted from the judgment of the Court of Appeal in *Customs and Excise Commissioners v Thorn Electrical Industries Ltd* certainly suggest the contrary. Finally, the distinction between substantive law and procedure can be as difficult to draw in this context as elsewhere.

---

11. [1964] 1 All ER 681.
12. [1966] AC 643, [1966] 1 All ER 524.
13. Ibid, at 666.
14. The following sentence, now on p 215 of the 12th edition of Maxwell, *On the Interpretation of Statutes*, has frequently been cited with judicial approval: 'It is a fundamental rule of English law that no statute shall be construed to have retrospective operation unless such a construction appears very clearly in the terms of the Act, or arises by necessary and distinct implication.'

D. CONCLUSION

Now that courts adopt a purposive approach to the interpretation of statutes and admit a wider range of materials from which to ascertain that purpose, the role of presumptions in interpretation is necessarily less important than in the days of more literal interpretation. The use of a presumption might appear to be cutting short unnecessarily the search for the meaning of a provision in the context, above all, of its purpose. The justification for any particular presumption depends on its type. Presumptions of general application encourage a search beyond the ordinary and most readily apparent meaning of a provision in order to find the real legislative purpose. Other presumptions come into play only where a genuine doubt remains after all permissible methods of ascertaining the legislative purpose have been exhausted. In both cases, the purposive approach remains the principal method of interpreting the statute.

A further reason for the diminishing importance of presumptions is that the values they have traditionally embodied have declined in recent years, and the judges have not chosen to develop new presumptions embodying contemporary values. The purposive construction of legislative provisions, statute by statute, aided by the general principles of the branch of law in question, is preferred to the application of more general legal principles. Although Bennion's *Statutory Interpretation*[15] interestingly compares judicial approaches to statutory interpretation in this area with the provisions of the European Convention on Human Rights, the established presumptions of interpretation are of limited value as constitutional safeguards of individual rights. On the whole, in adopting the purposive approach to all statutes, the courts have preferred to co-operate in giving effect to legislative policies, rather than oppose them in the name of constitutional rights.

---

15. Part XIII, *Principle against Doubtful Penalization.*

Chapter 8
Concluding questions

By way of conclusion, it is appropriate to reflect critically on the rules of statutory interpretation as they have emerged from the preceding chapters. Much of what the Law Commissions recommended in 1969 and the Renton Committee in 1975 has been implemented by judicial pronouncements and by the enactment of an updated Interpretation Act in 1978. Even those thorough reviews did not suggest any revolutionary or comprehensive general legislative changes, but preferred to list a series of specific detailed changes. At the more exalted level of general principles, the subject does not lend itself to legislation. This fact enhances rather than diminishes the role of the academic writer. This chapter will consider how satisfactory are current judicial approaches and academic expositions of principles in producing appropriate rules of statutory interpretation. Finally, it will consider how far changes in drafting techniques could facilitate the interpretation of statutes.

A. THE COURTS

We have already considered the specific rules of statutory interpretation and improvements which could be made to them. More generally, it is appropriate to ask three questions about the current judicial approach to statutory interpretation:
1. Do the courts interpret statutes too narrowly without adequate regard to the social purpose of the legislation?
2. Is their approach to the interpretation of statutes designed to effect social change too conservative?
3. Are the courts too timorous when confronted with an obvious mistake or omission in a statute?

In each instance, the answer is 'at times yes, but not to such an extent as to merit wholesale condemnation, and there have often been important countervailing considerations'.

To begin with the first question, the Law Commissions' report concluded that:[1]

> 'There is a tendency in our systems, less evident in some recent decisions of the courts but still perceptible, to over-emphasise the literal meaning of a provision (ie the meaning in the light of its immediate and obvious context) at the expense of the meaning to be derived from other possible contexts; the latter include 'the mischief', or general legislative purpose, as well as any international obligation of the United Kingdom, which underlie the provision.'

Of course a literal approach need not be a particularly narrow one. An unrestrictive construction of general words may be excessively literal and insufficiently purposive, but the usual charge under this head is one of narrow literalism. The Law Commissions' report refers to cases which have been mentioned in this book: *Fisher v Bell* (flick-knife in a shop window not offered for sale),[2] and *Bourne v Norwich Crematorium Ltd* (cremation not 'subjection of goods or materials to any process').[3] The more difficult to defend is the construction adopted in the latter case. It was entirely non-purposive and, to say the least, highly debatable as an application of the ordinary meaning rule. The construction adopted in the former case was certainly not purposive, but it involved a penal statute. Even if it is accepted that there is no special presumption in favour of the strict construction of penal statutes, it is questionable whether the exposure of goods in a shop window should be treated as an offer for sale within the meaning of a statute addressed to shopkeepers. Many examples of what appears to be an excessively literal approach could be cited, but it would be wrong to treat them as typical of the current judiciary. In 1975 Lord Diplock noted 'a trend away from the purely literal towards the purposive construction of statutory provisions';[4] and in 1981 Lord Wilberforce described as 'a tired old myth . . . sedulously propagated by people who do not do their homework' the view that English judges are more literalist and narrow than continental courts.[5] Certainly the examples given in this book support the view that, at least nowadays, judges

---

1. *The Interpretation of Statutes* (Law Com No 21; Scott Law Com No 11), para 80(c).
2. Supra, p 73.
3. Supra, p 71–2.
4. *Carter v Bradbeer* [1975] 3 All ER 158 at 161.
5. 418 HL Deb, col 74 (9 March 1981).

adopt a purposive approach to statutory interpretation, rather than a narrow literal one.

As to the question whether the courts' approach to statutes designed to effect social change is too conservative, it is of course possible to cite numerous instances for and against such an hypothesis. The construction of housing legislation is an example cited by protagonists on both sides.[6] A body of case-law has come into being concerning the construction of the provision in successive enactments that, in the case of lettings of property of low value, the landlord impliedly undertakes to keep the premises reasonably fit for human habitation. It must be admitted that the Acts have not always been construed strictly in accordance with the view expressed by one writer:[7]

> 'Social legislation involves "the sacrifice of liability based on individual fault so as to place loss in accordance with social justice and economic expediency". The guilt of an individual landlord is quite irrelevant in this context.'

At the same time there are, as the same writer concedes, important instances of social legislation being construed in this way.[8] In any event, when statutory language has to be construed against the common-law background of the absence of liability on the part of a landlord to keep demised premises fit for human habitation, it would be completely wrong to ignore that background. If the intention of the legislature had been to eliminate all reference to the common law, the legislature should have used very different language. Furthermore the purpose of such legislation is often to strike a reasonable balance between competing interests. For example, Part VII of the Rent Act 1977 was primarily concerned with giving security of tenure to tenants,

---

6. See J F Reynolds, 'Statutory Covenants of Fitness and Repair: Social Legislation and the Judges' (1974) 37 MLR 377. M J Robinson in '"Social Legislation" and the Judges: A Note by way of Rejoinder' (1976) 39 MLR 43 suggests that the divination of social purpose is a challenge to the sovereignty of Parliament. See also M Partington, *Landlord and Tenant* (London, 1980) pp 29–35.

7. J F Reynolds, 37 MLR at 397, quoting J Unger, (1942) 5 MLR 266 at 269.

8. Eg *Summers v Salford Corporation* [1943] AC 283 (house not reasonably fit for human habitation when, owing to a broken sash cord, the bedroom window could not be opened without personal danger):

> 'The subsection must, I think, be construed with due regard to its apparent object, and to the character of the legislation to which it belongs. The provision was to reduce the evils of bad housing accommodation and to protect working people by a compulsory provision, out of which they cannot contract, against accepting improper conditions . . . It is a measure aimed at social amelioration, no doubt in a small and limited way. It must be construed so as to give proper effect to that object.' (Lord Wright at 293).

but provided an exception in that the owner of a dwelling-house could obtain possession of the property at the end of the lease where it was required as a residence for himself or a member of his family.[9] Where the interpretation of this exception is disputed, should a court give effect to the purpose of the Act as a whole by protecting tenants or to the purpose of the exception by protecting the interests of landlords? Could either of these possible interpretations be termed 'conservative' in the sense of unduly resisting the social change which Parliament had legislated to achieve?[10]

Another allegation of judicial conservatism often made in recent years is that judges fail to take adequate account of the fundamental rights of citizens when they interpret statutes. It is often said that judges have been unwilling to interpret immigration or race relations legislation so as to protect the interests of immigrants or ethnic minorities, and that they have been too willing to take a limited view of the purpose of such legislation.[11] Such criticism presupposes that the courts should go beyond the immediate purpose of the legislation and should define its purpose more broadly so as to accord with the moral rights of those affected by it. On the whole English judges refrain from such a widely creative role. They do not conceive their function to be that of rescuing individuals from any hardship or injustice which may result from what Parliament clearly intended to enact.

So far as each of the two questions which have just been discussed is concerned, if the choice is between the ordinary meaning, ascertained with due regard to the purpose of the statute, and something other than the ordinary meaning which appears to give greater effect to the statutory purpose, it is to be hoped that the courts will always opt in favour of the former. The fact that words do not always have an ordinary meaning, even after due allowance has been made for the context, and the fact that ordinary people, as well as lawyers, sometimes take different views about the ordinary meaning of words does not mean that there is no such thing. Most statutory provisions do have an ordinary meaning when fairly read in their context, and

---

9. See Schedule 15, Cases 9 and 11.
10. See *Pocock v Steel* [1985] 1 All ER 434, [1985] 1 WLR 229, where the Court of Appeal adopted a literal construction of Case 11 on the ground, among others, that it was an exception to the main policy of Part VII 'which evidently is to give security of tenure to tenants' (ibid, 438). Soon after, Case 11 was amended by the Rent (Amendment) Act 1985 so as to reverse this interpretation. (See also *Hewitt v Lewis* [1986] 1 All ER 927.)·
11. Eg R M Dworkin, 'Political Judges and the Rule of Law' (1978) 64 *Proceedings of the British Academy* 259 at 283–5 (reprinted in *A Matter of Principle* 9, 28–31); J M Evans, *Immigration Law* (2nd edn, London, 1983) pp 417–25; J A G Griffith, *The Politics of the Judiciary* (3rd edn, London, 1985) pp 95–112.

fair-minded readers will usually be in agreement with regard to that meaning.

But what about the case in which there is no ordinary meaning, or, if there is one, it produces absurd results? This raises the third question mentioned on page 188: Are the courts too timorous when confronted with an obvious mistake or omission? The answer would be a resounding 'yes' if they really were, in Lord Halsbury's words, 'bound to proceed upon the assumption that the legislature is an ideal person that does not make mistakes'.[12] But we have seen that there are cases decided both before[13] and after[14] those words were spoken in 1891 which show that they do not represent the typical attitude of the courts. It is easy to see why the courts act with greater caution when the apparent legislative error is one of omission, because the reading in of words which are not in a statute, even if it can be said that they are there by necessary implication, looks more like legislating than does the ignoring of statutory words; but the distinction is of doubtful validity. It might be thought to have gained some currency by the reference to the filling in of gaps in a statute as 'a naked usurpation of the legislative function under the thin disguise of interpretation'. These were the words of Lord Simonds in *Magor and St Mellons Rural District Council v Newport Corporation*,[15] and they are certainly not to be numbered among the most helpful of his observations on the subject of statutory interpretation. What was Lord Parker CJ doing but filling in a gap when, in *Adler v George*,[16] he read the words 'in the vicinity of' in s 3 of the Official Secrets Act 1920 as meaning 'in or in the vicinity of'? What was the Court of Appeal doing but filling in a gap when, in *Deria v General Council of British Shipping*, it added the words 'or is to do' to s 8(1) of the Race Relations Act 1976 in order to make good an obvious omission.[17] We saw in section E of Chapter 4 that Lord Parker could be said to have been merely stating expressly words which were already in the statute by necessary implication, but we also saw how thin is the line between that process and adding words in order to correct an obvious error. The course adopted by the Court of Appeal comes on the latter side of the line.

Surely it would be better for all judges to recognise that they possess a limited power to add to, alter or ignore statutory words in the circumstances mentioned by Lord Reid in his speech in *Federal Steam*

---

12. Supra, p 110.
13. See *Re Wainewright*, supra, p 99, and *Salmon v Duncombe* supra, pp 102–3.
14. *Western Bank Ltd v Schindler*, supra, pp 98–9.
15. [1952] AC 189 at 191.
16. Supra, pp 33–4.
17. Supra, p 34.

Navigation Co Ltd v Department of Trade and Industry.[18] The existence of such a power seems to be established by the authorities, and is
frankly recognised in more recent cases. For example, in *Western Bank
Ltd v Schindler*, Scarman LJ said:[19]

> '. . . our courts . . . have the duty of giving effect to the intention
> of Parliament, if it be possible, even though the process requires
> a strained construction of the language used or the insertion of
> words in order to do so. . . .'

As we have seen, such a view does not consider *all* fillings in of gaps
as naked usurpations of the legislative function, but concentrates on
developing rules concerning the limits of such a judicial power. All the
same, not all judges consider this power acceptable.[20]

The curious reluctance of some judges to recognise what amounts to
a power to rectify a statute when construing it, however limited that
power may be, is almost as great an obstruction to the development of
a jurisprudence of statutory interpretation as the equally curious reluctance of other judges and some writers to recognise that the ordinary
meaning of statutory words must yield to a secondary meaning when
the application of the ordinary meaning would lead to a result which
'cannot reasonably be supposed to have been the intention of the
legislature'.[1]

B. ACADEMIC LAWYERS

Why is it that, in the field of the general principles of statutory interpretation, the English academic lawyer has not, until recently, performed
his ordinary function of synthesising and criticising the case-law and,
where appropriate, making proposals for reform? The answer depends
partly on the nature of the rules of legal method and partly on the effect
of one landmark law review article.

Reference has already been made to the paucity of rules and confusion of principles which justify Lord Wilberforce's description of
statutory interpretation as a non-subject, at least so far as law reform is
concerned.[2] The point has also been made that a decision on the

---

18. Supra, pp 101–2.
19. Supra, p 99.
20. Supra, pp 100–1.
1. Lord Reid, *Pinner v Everett* [1969] 3 All ER 257 at 258, supra, pp 36–7.
2. Supra, p 36.

interpretation of one statute generally cannot constitute a binding precedent with regard to the interpretation of another statute, with the result that a general rule of interpretation, unlike other common law rules, can never be rendered more specific by the *rationes decidendi* of later cases.[3] The material to be analysed consists mainly of statements of position and of examples of judicial practice, rather than the rules and principles derived from decisions which academics customarily study. Even at the level of the meaning to be attached to particular words:[4]

> 'A question of statutory construction is one in which the strict doctrine of precedent can only be of narrow application. The *ratio decidendi* of a judgment as to the meaning of particular words or combinations of words used in a particular statutory provision can have no more than a persuasive influence on a court which is called on to interpret the same word or combination of words appearing in some other statutory provision.'

Since it is concerned with issues of legal method of this character, the study of statutory interpretation is different from that of ordinary legal subjects. All the same, the subject is amenable to an appreciable degree of systematisation. For a long time, it was dominated by an article entitled *Statutory Interpretation in a Nutshell* contributed by Professor J Willis to the *Canadian Bar Review* for 1938.[5] After warning his readers that it is a mistake to suppose that there is only one rule of statutory interpretation because there are three—the literal, golden and mischief rules—Professor Willis maintained that 'a court invokes whichever of the rules produces a result which satisfies its sense of justice in the case before it'.[6] No doubt the warning had its point in 1938 when practitioners' books tended to state the literal or plain meaning rule without any embellishments referring to the context, including the purpose, of the statute. The thesis was maintained so persuasively that English academic discussions long did little more than treat cases as illustrations of one or more of the three rules. Since the first edition of this book in 1976, there has been an upsurge of interest in the subject of statutes and statutory interpretation. Some authors have been concerned with philosophical questions about the nature of interpretation, drawing analogies from literary contexts.[7]

---

3. Supra, p 38.
4. Lord Diplock, *Carter v Bradbeer* [1975] 3 All ER 158 at 161.
5. 16 Canadian Bar Review 1.
6. Ibid at 16.
7. Eg R M Dworkin, *Law's Empire* (London, 1986) pp 49–62. For an analysis of different academic approaches to statutory interpretation see D Miers, 'Legal Theory and the Interpretation of Statutes' in W Twining (ed), *Legal Theory and the Common Law* (Oxford, 1986) Ch 7.

Others have looked at the sociology of the production and impact of legislation. Yet others, most notably Bennion,[8] have sought to provide a systematic and rational account of judicial practice in interpreting statutes. This book is situated in the last-mentioned tradition. In a common law system, judicial practice exercises a dominant influence over what is considered correct legal reasoning and thus merits the critical attention of any lawyer. This book represents a limited exposition of the general principles of statutory interpretation as they emerge from current judicial practice. Despite recent developments much remains to be done in this field if a full analysis of this aspect of legal reasoning is to be achieved.

C. LEGISLATIVE DRAFTING

If the difficulties of statutory interpretation have in part been ascribed to inappropriate judicial attitudes and to the failure of academic lawyers to provide a coherent exposition of contemporary judicial practice, the legislative draftsman is also a common target for criticism. We saw in Chapter 1 how drafting and interpretation are mutually dependent and how an excessively literal approach to interpretation can lead to excessively detailed drafting. In his evidence to the Renton Committee Lord Denning went so far as to say:[9]

> 'It is because the judges have not felt it right to fill in the gaps and have been giving a literal interpretation for many years that the draftsman has felt that he has to try and think of every conceivable thing and put it in as far as he can so that even the person unwilling to understand will follow it. I think the rules of interpretation which the judges have applied have been one of the primary causes why draftsmen have felt that they must have a system of over-detail, over-long sentences, and obscurity.'

Had this diagnosis been correct, the more purposive approach adopted by contemporary judges to interpretation should have made possible some reduction in statutory detail. Yet, ten years later, Lord Simon of Glaisdale argued that the recommendations of the Renton Committee 'have been completely disregarded; and statutes are still drafted in elaborate and incomprehensible detail to deal with every foreseeable combination of circumstances which might arise'.[10]

---

8. *Statutory Interpretation* (London, 1984).
9. *The Preparation of Legislation*, para 19.1.
10. 'The Renton Report—Ten Years On' [1985] Stat LR 133 at 135.

If changes in judicial attitudes have not had the desired effect, some have argued that the fault lies in the style of British legislative drafts-manship. Sir William Dale has claimed that other European countries adopt a less detailed and more principled style in their statutes, with less complicated wording and sentence structure.[11] He argues that there should be a change in the current style of legislation:[12]

'We need at least to reduce the verbal impedimenta; to be less fussy over detail, to be more general and concise; and to situate each rule where it belongs, in an orderly and logical development. On this level, the question is largely a matter of style and arrangement. A more profound change is also desirable: a deter-mination to seek the principle, to express it, and to follow up with such detail, illuminating and not obscuring the principle, as the circumstances require.'

Although this is not a book on legislative drafting, a few comments on these suggestions are appropriate.

The Renton Committee considered that the adoption of the 'general principle' approach to the drafting of our statutes would lead to greater simplicity and clarity. However, they accepted that this approach to a large extent sacrifices immediate certainty and recognised that this is unlikely to be acceptable at least in certain types of legislation, particu-larly fiscal and other public law statutes which define the rights and obligations of individuals in relation to the state. They also considered that it would be unreasonable to draft in principles so broad that the effect of the statute could not be assessed without incurring the expense of litigation.[13] As Lord Hailsham has observed:

'"Thou shalt not kill" sounds simple enough. But someone, sooner or later, must articulate this into murder, attempted murder, wounding with intent, manslaughter, causing death by reckless driving, professional negligence, the Fatal Accidents Acts, and very many other quite separate provisions.'[14]

In many cases the policy which a statute is designed to implement is far from simple; and the need to achieve a balance between competing

---

11. *Legislative Drafting: A New Approach* (London, 1977) compares the implemen-tation of an international copyright convention in the domestic laws of France, West Germany, Sweden and the United Kingdom.
12. Ibid, p 335. See also J A C Smith, 'Legislative Drafting: English and Continental' [1980] Stat LR 14; T Millett, 'A Comparison of British and French Legislative Drafting (with particular reference to their respective Nationality Laws)' [1986] Stat LR 130; Donaldson MR, *R v Northampton BC, ex p Quietlynn Ltd* (1986) 85 LGR 249 at 263.
13. *The Preparation of Legislation*, para 10.13.
14. 'Addressing the Statute Law' [1985] Stat LR 4, 5.

interests frequently leads to compromise solutions not capable of expression in terms of principles. Moreover Parliament is generally unwilling to pass legislation which leaves too much to be decided by the executive or the courts, as well as setting a high value on certainty of effect. Those who advocate the drafting of legislation in terms of principle argue that detailed legislation may fail to fit the circumstances of a particular case, thus leaving the citizen and the courts in doubt as to what Parliament intended; but it needs to be remembered that detailed legislation has the enormous advantage of dealing clearly with the great majority of cases likely to arise, unlike general statements of principle whose precise application may be difficult to determine, even in cases where they clearly apply. In the end, the test of good draftsmanship is whether a patient reading successfully conveys the intention of the legislature to the audience to which the statute is primarily directed.

The view that statutes ought, as far as possible, to be drafted in ordinary language was expressed as long ago as 1875 by Sir Henry (later Lord) Thring:[15]

'I have a very strong opinion indeed that you ought to use the best popular language, and never use technical language at all unless it be absolutely necessary.'

The difficulty of many modern statutes results not from the use of obscure terminology, but from the complexity of the subject-matter, coupled with the fact that most changes in the law have to be knitted into the complex fabric of existing statutory provisions; and Members of Parliament are not always receptive to 'the best popular language', sometimes preferring a more 'lawyerly' wording.[16]

The use of statements of principle or purpose is not alien to current drafting practice in Britain. They are sometimes used to introduce the whole or part of an Act. For example, s 1(1) of the Transport Act 1980 (not re-enacted in the consolidating Public Passenger Vehicle Licences Act 1981) stated:

'The purposes for which this Part is enacted include—
(a) redefining and reclassifying public service vehicles;

---

15. *Report of the Select Committee on Acts of Parliament (1875): Minutes of Evidence* p 121, para 1633. Thring gave evidence as the head of the Parliamentary Counsel Office, established in 1869.

16. For example, s 1(1)(b) of the Sexual Offences Act 1985 makes it an offence for a man to solicit a woman for the purpose of prostitution 'while in the immediate vicinity of a motor vehicle that *he has just got out of or off*'. Some MPs tried (unsuccessfully) to have the words 'just got out of or off' replaced by 'emerged from or alighted from in the immediate past': see amendment number 24 at the House of Commons Report Stage.

    (b) abolishing road service licences for express carriers as redefined;

    (c) making it easier for applicants to obtain road service licences, and restricting the power to attach thereto conditions as to fares;

    (d) providing for the designation of areas as trial areas in which road service licences are not required for stage carriage services;

    (e) making new provision for securing the fitness of public service vehicles;

    (f) substituting a system of public service vehicle operators' licences for the system of public service vehicle licences; and

    (g) providing an appeal against a refusal by the London Transport Executive to enter into an agreement with a person other than the Executive for the provision of a London bus service . . .'

Statements of purpose may also introduce sections[17] or schedules[18] within an Act. While they may aid understanding and on occasion assist in the interpretation of the provisions which they cover,[19] they have significant limits. Where the policy is complex and the provisions to be enacted are intended to achieve a variety of possibly conflicting purposes, it may be impossible to frame a comprehensive statement of purpose, or it may only be possible to do so in extremely general, and therefore unhelpful, terms.[20] Certainly, general statements of principle or purpose at the beginning of some continental or European Community legislation can be so vague as to be little more than a form of political propaganda, affording little or no guidance for the interpretation of what follows; and the same phenomenon is not unknown at Westminster.[1]

---

17. Eg s 5(1) of the Agriculture (Miscellaneous Provisions) Act 1976: 'This section shall have effect for the purpose of facilitating the production of seedless hops.'

18. Eg s 36 of the British Nationality Act 1981: 'The provisions of Schedule 2 shall have effect for the purpose of reducing statelessness.'

19. See eg *Fox v Lawson* [1974] AC 803, [1974] 1 All ER 783, in which the House of Lords was assisted in concluding that a provision of Part VI of the Transport Act 1968 extended to hours of work, driving and rest outside Great Britain by the statement in s 95(1) that 'This Part of this Act shall have effect with a view to securing the observance of proper hours of work by persons engaged in the carriage of passengers or goods by road and thereby protecting the public against the risks which arise in cases where the drivers of motor vehicles are suffering from fatigue.'

20. There is also the risk that any statement of purpose which appears in a Bill as presented to Parliament may be falsified beyond repair by amendments made during the Bill's passage.

1. See, for example, s 1 of the (now repealed) Industrial Relations Act 1971.

The view that British statutes should contain less detail has prompted two further suggestions. The first is that the state should engage in less rule-making. As the Renton Committee noted, though this may be approved in theory, modern governments faced with the complexities of contemporary society rarely consider it appropriate in practice.[2] The second and more common suggestion is that a larger proportion of the state's rule-making should be located elsewhere than in statutes. On this view, it is for Parliament to enact the general principles, and for the executive or the courts to produce the detailed rules necessary for their implementation, as need arises. Certainly in other European countries such as France, the provisions contained in primary legislation are supplemented by rules contained in subordinate legislation, expressed in judicial decisions, or contained in administrative circulars which guide administrative decisions and on which the citizen is entitled to rely. In practice, this merely has the effect of shifting much of the legislative material from primary legislation into decrees, judicial decisions, codes of practice and ministerial circulars. While the statute becomes easier to read, the citizen concerned to discover the law is sent on a paper-chase and has to collate the material found in all these different sources. This already happens to a significant extent in the British systems of law,[3] but to carry the process much further would be without obvious benefit to the citizen and his advisers. Furthermore, any such shift would have to be assessed in terms of democratic control. At present, statutes are subject to far greater scrutiny in Parliament than the provisions of subordinate legislation, codes of practice and departmental circulars, and, unlike them, can in general only be amended by the passing of another Act. Here again, what is at issue is the constitutional function of Parliament, and it is barking up the wrong tree to suppose that this could be altered by a mere change of drafting practice.

Britain's entry into Europe was expected by some to herald changes in drafting practice and statutory interpretation. In the event, these have not materialised. On closer scrutiny, continental drafting has not proved as flawless as Dale and others believed.[4] The many difficulties in the interpretation of European Community legislation have necessitated extensive use of reference to the European Court of Justice under article 177 of the Treaty of Rome. The interpretation of domestic

---

2. *The Preparation of Legislation*, para 7.3; cf A Samuels, 'The Interpretation of Statutes' [1980] Stat LR 86 at 86–7, 107–8.
3. See R Baldwin and J Houghton, 'Circular Arguments: The Status and Legitimacy of Administrative Rules' [1986] *Public Law* 239.
4. See Law Commission, *Report on the Proposed EEC Directive on the Law relating to Commercial Agents* (Law Com No 84; 1977), paras 38–41.

legislation has not been significantly affected, though the presumption of conformity to treaty obligations is applied in relation to Community law.

D.   CONCLUSION

Although these concluding reflections have been concerned principally to analyse some of the current criticisms of statutes and statutory interpretation and have discovered them to be less well founded than might be supposed, it must not be thought that the current situation is satisfactory. Improvements can undoubtedly be made by way of a more effective purposive interpretation by judges, a more systematic and coherent exposition of the general principles of judicial practice by academics, and the production of more readable statutes by draftsmen. The principal difficulties lie in the implementation of currently accepted ideals for these activities, rather than in the adoption of radically new ideals. We are concerned here with the attitudes and practices of legislators and lawyers and the methods they adopt. These cannot be transformed at a stroke, but can be expected to improve slowly in response to criticisms voiced by Members of Parliament, lawyers and other sections of the community.

Index